Heaven Is a Place on Earth

"This book could not have come at a better time. At a moment when it can seem as if this country will never put its pieces together, Adrian Shirk gives us so many instances, historical and present-day, of Americans finding ways to live in real community, to carve out places of freedom, to be brave enough to stare our unhappinesses in the face and ask What more could there be? In a voice electric with possibility, Shirk reminds us of the great risk and great possibility contained in the act of reimagining home."
—Alex Mar, author of *Witches of America*

"What kind of world will we create in the wake of a global pandemic and armed insurrection, in the midst of climate chaos, systemic racism, and inequity? In *Heaven Is a Place on Earth*, the brilliant Adrian Shirk is looking for an existence that is more than just mere existence, more than 'waged labor,' a life that is less extractive, capitalistic, and crushing. A life that is, instead, meaningful, creative, and beautiful. In these pages, I found myself believing such a thing might be possible, and you will too—a testament to Adrian's tremendous power as a writer, intellectual, and human. This is an important book for the moment we find ourselves in."
—Cameron Dezen Hammon, author of *This Is My Body: A Memoir of Religious and Romantic Obsession*

"As she physically travels all over our country and through some of life's roughest emotional terrain—grief, regret, inadequacy, betrayal, unrequited idealism—Adrian Shirk takes the reader on a rich, lyrical journey of what it feels and looks like to persist in hope. Whether those hopes are in the form of a utopian farm cooperative formed in the 1800s or earnest hipsters gathering in upstate New York, even if you don't share their same dreams Shirk's writing leaves you wanting to treat hope, as she puts it, as a vocation. *Heaven Is a Place on Earth* is not so much a study of utopianism as a meditation. Shirk has a skillful way of weaving together the scraps of seemingly unrelated snippets and insights into a gorgeous quilt of meaning. Utopian-ists want what we all want—fulfillment, happiness, community—but they don't give up when life refuses to deliver. This book is a raw examination of that combination of obsession and grit—and it's masterful."

—Kate Kelly, human rights lawyer and
author of *Ordinary Equality*

HEAVEN IS A PLACE ON EARTH

ALSO BY ADRIAN SHIRK

And Your Daughters Shall Prophesy:
Stories from the Byways of American Women and Religion

HEAVEN IS A PLACE ON EARTH

SEARCHING FOR AN AMERICAN UTOPIA

ADRIAN SHIRK

Counterpoint
Berkeley, California

HEAVEN IS A PLACE ON EARTH

Copyright © 2022 by Adrian Shirk
First hardcover edition: 2022

Library of Congress Cataloging-in-Publication Data
Names: Shirk, Adrian, author.
Title: Heaven is a place on Earth : searching for an American utopia / Adrian Shirk.
Description: First hardcover edition. | Berkeley, California : Counterpoint, 2022. | Includes bibliographical references.
Identifiers: LCCN 2021027708 | ISBN 9781640093300 (hardcover) | ISBN 9781640093317 (ebook)
Subjects: LCSH: Communitarianism—United States. | Belonging (Social psychology)—United States. | Utopias—United States.
Classification: LCC HM758 .S55 2022 | DDC 307.0973—dc23
LC record available at https://lccn.loc.gov/2021027708

Jacket design by Lexi Earle
Book design by Wah-Ming Chang

COUNTERPOINT
2560 Ninth Street, Suite 318
Berkeley, CA 94710
www.counterpointpress.com

Printed in the United States of America

1 3 5 7 9 10 8 6 4 2

For our friends

They say in heaven, love comes first
We'll make heaven a place on earth
BELINDA CARLISLE

Ascending a path that seems to lead nowhere, you come at
last to New Harmony, a disappointment.
MARGUERITE YOUNG, *Angel in the Forest*

It takes the crossing of continents, wars, an unexpected last
child for us to come into existence. Do not give up this extensive route of failures and impossible encounters too easily.
YANARA FRIEDLAND, *Uncountry*

And finally, [utopian literature's] most characteristic feature
is that it's very futuristic looking. I'm also future-oriented,
but it has to do with memory, with what I know is possible
because it already happened.
TONI CADE BAMBARA

CONTENTS

3: HEAVEN

4: THE GARDEN & THE CITY

1
GENRE

utopianotes
cruising

Amber, Laura, and I are driving through the back roads just outside of Nash-ville, away from Percy Priest Lake, singing along to Belinda Carlisle's 1987 bal-lad, "Heaven Is a Place on Earth." We're steaming in our damp swimsuits from the heat. Yellow poplars and crepe myrtles and sugar maples rush by the win-dows on the winding road to Amber's house. The chorus mounts to its third and final iteration through the car speakers. Laura, sitting shotgun, speaks back to the song: "I've always liked this part—where she goes, 'We'll make heaven a place on earth / Heaven *is* a place on earth,' like, that was FAST, Belinda!"

Laura and I have flown down from New York City for a weekend-length writing retreat in Amber's living room. All three of us are currently reading *Cruising Utopia* by José Esteban Muñoz, passing it back and forth as we leave it bookmarked on the coffee table. We are thinking along with him about how utopia is, or can be, any gesture that points to a better future, a gesture of fu-turity he finds repeated over and over again in the symbols and praxis of queer life, especially in the decades prior to the technocrat-takeover of things like New York's Pride March, which is a week away at that moment—and so cor-porate now as to be a figment of the outlaw queer imagination. Utopianism, for Muñoz, is something that's necessarily always in process, something that's simultaneously aspired to down the road and ushered into the present—the "now-future." I keep thinking of the way that 1960s and '70s gay liberationists named their organizations—the names always struck me as the kinds of ges-tures Muñoz talks about, names that point toward, but also make present, a world much larger, lovelier, and more fun than ours: Daughters of Bilitis, Gay Pagans, Alice B. Toklas Democratic Club, Council of Grand Dukes & Duch-esses of San Francisco, Order of Displaced Okies, Local Lesbian Association Kazoo Marching Band, Dykes on Bikes, Imperial Silver Fox Court, Lavender Menace, Lesbian Avengers, Free Beach Activists, Society of Janus, the Furies.

THE UTOPIANOTES

The pursuit of utopia is, at its heart, about our relationship with time. Utopians sit around dreaming about the beginning and the end, as a way to decide what to build in the present: What kind of human community will heal the scars of the past, and ensure a brighter future? Which systems or relationships do we wish would last forever, but will only ever be temporary? What will the end be like, and is there an end, and should we make it look like what we imagine the Edenic beginning looked like, if e'er there was one? There are other factors, of course—to each her own utopia, after all—but when the particulars are wiped away, the common questions are always temporal. Book writing is similar. When I started working on this book, I was twenty-nine years old, and by the time I finish I will be thirty-two, a three-year period where my own responses to these basically rhetorical questions would at once be fulfilled and rendered obsolete by the end of the process, which, like all books, and all utopias for that matter, has no real end.

Before I was conscious of this being a book, I had been dimly aware for some time that I was writing about American utopian communities. I had been reading, watching YouTube videos, visiting communes, staring at my smudgy laptop lost in my own personal utopian yearnings. I was writing a lot, reams of things I referred to even in the privacy of my own mind as "just notes," and I had finally amassed something like 120 individual Word files titled things like "Utopia_Nashville," "Utopia_Bruderhof," "Utopia_ Womanhouse," etc., etc. Each of these files contained floating narratives, orphaned thoughts, direct experiences, embarrassing disclosures, desperate prayers, voyeuristic observations, rants, passages from books, stolen photos, copy-and-pasted emails.

I watched as the files piled up. I kept thinking that any day now a shape would start to coalesce. I kept waiting for the notes to build toward the kind of legibility I so admired in other books about utopianism. But instead, I just kept on with the notes: "Utopia_Caliban and the Witch," "Utopia_North American Phalanx," "Utopia_Jenny Lewis," "Utopia_Soul City," on and on. A friend of mine, Anna, finally suggested that I just print out all the writing and look at it together, so I did, and that was when I was twenty-nine.

I was sitting at my desk over the hot stack of freshly printed writing, and suddenly I thought, *Oh, shit, this* is *my book*. All of this stuff, all of these little things that I kept thinking were the *precursor* or the thing that was eventually going to make way for the "real" book, in fact *was* the book. This was what I had to work with. This was what I'd had the whole time.

This was a powerful moment, for sure, but its power lasted only as long as I could stay out of its way—which wasn't very long at all. By that point, there were 150 pages of words which had been doing their own thing for years, creating a form, synthesizing information, telling a story without my own purpose or plan to guide the way. Yet, I failed to heed its inner logic, this interior intelligence of the writing, and instead, now that I had printed it out and had really "started working on the book," I thought, *Excellent— now I can discipline this writing into what it's supposed to be: a playful but straightforward social history of American utopian movements.*

There's a funny parallel between this moment of writing a book about utopian experimentation and the act of utopian experimentation itself. If I had listened closely to my own words, the ones I had already been writing, I might have known that sooner than later. A utopia is often only as good as its ability to be just out of reach, slightly beyond the understanding of its makers, eluding authorial intent. When a utopia becomes too self-conscious, too sure of itself and its aims, too top-down in its execution of a vision, it tends to teeter, eat itself like an ouroboros, collapse, terrorize, become the butt of its own joke. The utopianotes themselves had created a record of this arc, but they also offered an antidote or a response to this problem in their very form. If the history of utopian experimentation is largely a comitragic tale of the brief triumphs of collective innovation followed by (sometimes seismic) fracture and failure, followed by more collective innovation and then more failure, then whatever value there may be in engaging utopian thought must be about process, not progress; experiment, not end result; accumulation of notes, and acceptance of no final conclusion. Utopianotes build. Each new entry is a valuable contribution to an ever-growing body of knowledge, introducing new directions, possibilities, ideas, desires, needs, and detours.

All of that was already clear in the writing, but I pressed on anyway, for two years, determined to produce a clear, confident, highly readable pop-nonfiction book about the history of American utopias—a kind of writing which I imagined might be a perfectly rendered utopia itself. In retrospect, this had a lot to do with my assumptions that utopian experimentation was about progress—where now it seems like such experimentation is actually about fracture and layering and failure, which fortunately is the only way, it turns out, I know how to write. And maybe that is where the two things form meaning for me—the making of a utopia and the writing of a book about the making of utopia: it doesn't really matter if you do it right, or get out of its way, or wield power over its ultimate meaning—because I never did let go of the Platonic ideal of my utopia book. And the egomaniacs and boy kings and bad theologies never stopped trying to build their heavens on earth, either, but the quest for utopia persists anyway, still, and so did the book.

Is this where I have to talk about Thomas More? Here's the gist: More wrote a novel in the sixteenth century called *Utopia* about a traveler stumbling upon an uncharted nation by that same name, a socialist, crime-less, autonomous, peaceful, completely homogenous society ruled by benevolent King Utopus. The narrator takes great pains to walk us through the mechanisms of this well-oiled world, an extremely tedious trope of all utopian literature to follow. More's book does importantly introduce "utopia" into the English lexicon, from the Greek meaning "no place." This definition seems like a missed opportunity. And almost everything I have ever read, from any era, about utopianism takes More's *Utopia* as its interpretive moment and his "no place" as literal. I have nothing against More's novel as an artifact, as something to situate the history of utopian discourse within, but I also find it boring as a starting place. Was it sincere? Was it farce? Was he too much of a fascist to lend any of his ideas credence? Other people are working these questions out in other books about utopia.

Because of this etymology, as soon as I start relying on the word "utopia" it becomes a misnomer, in part because it is a word often used as a jab, to trivialize, to characterize a project that is too naïve, too implausible, too irresponsible, too "out-there" to work. We might think we know what we're talking about when we're talking about utopia, but it's never a one-note definition: its assertive "no place" immediately suggests that it's an imaginative term, or as Alex Zamalin defines it in *Black Utopia*, "a radical act of philosophical speculation" that has a long history, predating More's novel and extending forever into the future. For my purposes, I use utopia as an earnest critical term—never a pejorative—a term which I use again and again to refract my belief that a better world is in fact fucking possible, even if I'm not sure how. I only know that I have to take that seriously, even if it means I'll mess it up. "In order to even approach utopian thinking," says Avery F. Gordon in her amazing compendium of utopian conversations, *The Hawthorn Archive: Letters from the Utopian Margins*, "we have to stop associating the utopian with the impossibly idealistic . . . and using it as a weapon against others and ourselves." If we cast it as never worth thinking about, then we won't—we'll stay right where we are, taping up the crappy cardboard infrastructure of the current system because utopian dreaming is only for losers.

And utopia, to me, doesn't mean just any community that has ever formed out of its own need to practically survive, but specifically ones that have intentionally understood themselves as world-building a way out of a death-dealing system, in the service of making, if only briefly, some idea of heaven on earth—not just for themselves, but, however foolhardy, for all of humankind. That's the utopian scale. Eschatological. Zamalin says, "Utopia is like religion not because of dogmatic theology or secular truths it postulates, but because it conjures powerful, irrepressible, sometimes ecstatic feelings: of salvation, of being at home in the world, and of reconciliation with strife." There is something faith-based in this posture, and something action-oriented simultaneously.

In his study of American utopians, *Paradise Now*, Chris Jennings also distinguishes them from other kinds of civic reformers, saying, "Rather than trying to improve the world in any of the usual ways—through electoral politics, prayer, propaganda, civil disobedience, armed insurrection—[utopians] intended to catalyze a global revolution by building a working prototype of the ideal society." Utopia-making is a practice rather than a program; it's action and not theory, or it's the dissolution of that dichotomy. But it can take numerous forms. While intentional communities and communes are common forms, they are not utopia themselves. If the ever-broadening definition of utopia that this book continues to use compels you to ask, So, is *this* a utopian community? it probably is.

On the one hand, this book is telling the stories of both present-day and long-gone Americans trying to scrabble together utopia in a variety of ways, against a variety of odds. Within these stories is a practical and moral inquiry of my own: how can I live a life "in community" in the United States today, one which is not primarily organized around private property and the acquisition of personal wealth? Is it possible to resist atomization, the sociological term that describes our society's current trend toward living in small, isolated units? What is moving or replicable within the histories and ideas of utopia-making in this country? What about those histories is doomed or dangerous, or just dumb? This is not exactly a history, nor a neat theoretical argument. It's not a book about whether one particular utopian experiment is better than the other, or whether utopia as a project is good or bad. It is also not significantly about uncovering the doomed or dangerous things that have happened in the lives of different utopian communities or experiments, or those that have turned into cults or violent institutions— not least of which is this godforsaken country. Much has been written about these things, and they are facts that this book tries to take for granted as a real part of the whole.

To be clear, this country has no singular claim to utopianism, which is itself a global and ancient phenomenon—but it has been a ferocious and focused laboratory of utopian experimentation since the beginning. Thinking about utopia in an American context is important to me, above all, because this is my homeland, for eight problematic generations on both my mother's and my father's sides, hailing from a long line of white capitalists who built the major cities of the Pacific Northwest. The United States is a place I understand and a place I can actually say something about. But utopianism within an American context interests me, too, because the United States begs specific kinds of questions about utopianism from its outset: how do we

live together in a country founded on the idea (though not the practice)—
and was it even the idea, or is that revisionist, too?—of creating a society
of coexistence and unity, personal liberty and religious freedom, populism
and democracy, while profoundly and defensively violating those principles
from the get-go? The settlers wiped out the worlds that were already here
to make a new one. They enslaved people to bear out the labor of bringing
about that new world. They stood on plinths and declared it good and free.
And who is this "they" I keep referring to? White people? The founders,
and their henchmen, and the descendants of their henchmen, all the way
down? We have still not reckoned with or rectified these violent contra-
dictions and denials as a country in a meaningful way, and so the pursuit
of a life that might be actually good and free had to continue somehow, to
unfold in thousands of ungovernable ways, in this place where we said it
was supposed to happen. And so, every single tiny time a community in
the United States does or makes something utopian—something that was
supposed to be impossible under the current paradigm, that had all rational
forms of power stacked against it, but did the thing anyway—little fissures
form in the veneer of imperial control that reveal the current of real freedom
that runs hotly beneath it.

This book also happened to come to life at a moment of perennial American
utopian uptick. A recent *New York Times* article reports that the number of
communities listed in the Foundation for Intentional Community's direc-
tory (an eighty-year-old clearinghouse of U.S. utopian activity) nearly doubled between 2010 and 2016, to approximately 1,200, with a collective es-
timated population of somewhere around 100,000 known communitarians,
many of whom are my millennial peers. But how does such an uptick avoid
simply repeating the same tragicomedy of errors as their forebears, and the
people—like myself—who report their stories? And how narrowly have we,
as a culture, been defining what constitutes utopian activity and what does
not? In *The Hawthorn Archive*, Gordon agitates against a similar line I kept
finding myself up against when I began to read or talk about utopianism,
"a definitional world or discourse of utopia with a deeply racialized histo-

riography and a narrowly exclusive set of literary, aesthetic, philosophical, historical, and sociological references." Because, as Gordon says, still today "the libraries reflected the state of the field," the utopian has commonly come to mean for us a fixed set of references, at least in the United States— the Shakers, the Harmonists, the Oneida Community, Amana Colonies, the early Mormon settlements, and Robert Owen's New Harmony. Rogue white Protestants all variously awaiting the end of the world, or optimistic white secular moderns who've finally come up with a system to prevent all human suffering. As this book, which you are reading, came together I realized that I longed to think about utopianism as an ahistorical project, a moveable feast, a continuous tradition, and above all a necessary and never-ending mode of moral revision, though it took time to articulate that.

The writing of this book also gave form to a desire and an action, to actually start living a different way, though it's hard to say yet, and I really shouldn't, what that different way is. The posture of acting like, or even thinking, that one has arrived somewhere or triumphed is almost always the death knell of whatever was good in the thing itself, so I'll let that sit for now and work it out in the story. There are, to be clear, many contingencies in the story—in addition to where I happened to be at various times, there was also the issue of what kind of mood I was in and what I had access to, both personally and generationally, through being white and middle class, and also what year it was: the autobiographical story of this book begins in 2015 and ends in 2020; it occasionally drifts to the late aughts of my college years in Brooklyn, or my late-nineties childhood in Portland, Oregon. In terms of a historical timeline, there is no schema—I move between the eighteenth century and the twenty-first century and somewhere in between those two ports multiple times.

The book, finally, operates from a few very loose hypotheses, but ones which only occurred to me along the way, in the process of writing it, and not before:

1. that the atomization, segregation, and exploitation of American lives structured by capitalism is an evil, to which utopian experimentation in this country has been a consistent response,

2. that the experiments themselves are numberless and extremely varied, and each contains to different extents bits and pieces of replicable models, gestures, and thoughts,

3. that no such utopian alternative can or should last for too long lest it accrue power and money in all the same ways as the American system errs toward, and

4. that these movements and communities have often been or are aware of each other, and not infrequently collaborative with their utopian contemporaries, even when their theologies or politics differed, and that this is noteworthy in a world where we take sectarianism and partisanism for granted as forces that make groups intractably unable to contend with difference.

So I move through these histories and stories fairly rapidly, less as a historian or a reporter, and more as a traveler, each site or community or question functioning as a kind of prompt and interrupt for my ability to imagine a future, for myself and others. My hope is to invite you into the spirit of inquiry that led to some of the things I named above, hypotheses which themselves may very well have changed by the time you are reading these words.

utopianotes
white men

I am in Hudson, New York, staying for three days as the guest of a house sitter in the palatial nineteenth-century home of a pair of married architects. I've hung out with the house sitter, my new friend Claire, for only the length of a single lunch one week ago during which we both ended up stress-crying in front of each other over a shared salad entree before I decided to join her this weekend. It was a leap of faith into new friendship on both our parts. We know each other only as adjunct instructors at the same college, which also happens to be where I pursued my undergraduate degree. She is now doing pirouettes in the ballroom-like landing upstairs. I can hear her socked feet spinning. We are interlopers from the land of apartment life. The house includes a giant Maine Coon cat named Noodle, eleven-foot-high ceilings on both floors, and a long, low wall of adjoining bookshelves that stretch from the front door all the way to the back. As expected, the architects have an extensive poetry and critical theory collection, a lot of which addresses ideas of utopia.

I draw some books from the bookshelves: *Utopia* by Sir Thomas More; an issue of *Sites & Stations* from the mid-1990s themed "Provisional Utopias"; *America's Communal Utopias*, edited by Donald E. Pitzer; *Socialism: Utopian and Scientific* by Friedrich Engels; and *The Architecture of Happiness* by Alain de Botton. I begin to read and take notes, but, oh my God, did I end up with texts all and only by white men?

UTOPIA, THE BRONX

In the summer of 2015, I was twenty-six years old and had just moved to the border of the Bronx and Yonkers. My husband, Sweeney, was entering his second year of a PhD program in theology at Fordham University, and we had left Brooklyn so he could be closer to campus. I'd been reluctant to relocate, separated from work and friends so that my life had become a continuous march of arduous commuting, but we decided it would only be for a year, after which we could reassess. We were living on a combination of his graduate assistant stipend and my income from freelance writing and adjunct teaching. Our new apartment was the spacious garret of a two-family row house in Woodlawn Heights, a neighborhood made up of undocumented Irish nationals, separated by the Bronx River and its attendant parkway from the Caribbean neighborhood of Wakefield. My father-in-law, born in the Irish diaspora of Woodlawn, was running a small law office in North White Plains, and by December he would suffer several strokes in his frontal cortex, which would place him in a three-month coma that would change all of our lives forever.

At the time, I was in the habit of taking the 2 train back and forth between the Bronx and Brooklyn for work. It is the longest and slowest route of the whole MTA system, running so excruciatingly local through the Bronx that, on some late nights, headed toward the end of the line, it feels like the conductor is fucking with you: 176th Street . . . 180th . . . 184th . . . The upside is that from Wakefield–241st all the way to 149th–Grand Concourse, the train runs above ground. It's a beautiful ride during daylight, and especially at sunset: through Mott Haven and Morrisania, Tremont and the east side of the botanical gardens and the zoo, the Bronx, in all of its twenty-first-century action and architectural and geological variety, rolls out before you like an urban pastoral, like a sixteenth-century Bruegel painting, if Bruegel had ever had the honor to paint the Boogie Down. There is sweeping verdant Mosholu Parkway, filled with groups of teenagers and grandmas

on benches; big angular Dutch homes latticed on the front, next to hulk-
ing multifamily Victorians, next to huge Art Deco complexes and prewar
apartment buildings taking up one block, then the next; bundles of discount
franchises bunch up under the tracks (Rainbow, Family Dollar), but also
rows of barber shops, braiding salons, bodegas, and botanicas; big huge elms
bust up alongside and between buildings; a dense and wild ecosystem un-
furls up around the Bronx River; the bend at West Farms where the Bronx
River Art Center juts up from the single-story landscape like a spaceship,
bordering the edge of Hunts Point and the reclaimed Concrete Plant Park;
community organizations, a public hospital, and high schools face the train
windows, eye-to-eye, many of the buildings reconstructed cheaply in the
1990s; and then darkness, as the train hurtles underground.

The point is—it's beautiful. That Bronx stretch above ground made that
long ride feel like a luxury. Yet I often felt frustrated on these rides, fried
and worn out, but attaching to landscapes in this way is a habit of being I've
developed over years in the face of despair, when I feel helpless or trapped in
circumstance. And what I saw from those windows, and on the streets, was
not the Bronx I'd heard about—from movies, media outlets, other white
people. At the time, a single cursory Google image search of the Bronx still
shuffled up the same old algorithm: 1970s and '80s devastation, burnout,
empty lots full of trash, a ten-minute YouTube clip from a car window
surveying the burned-out blocks of Charlotte Street in 1980. The immediacy with which these images appeared froze the imaginary of the Bronx
in a distant past, while in the present none of this was true anymore, and
maybe—to appropriate the words of the late mayor Ed Koch, whose tenure
oversaw some of the Bronx's most profound civic neglect—"nothing ever
was the way you think it was."

What I could see was that the Bronx was *happening*. It was lively. It was
dignified. It had depth and beauty in a way that so much of the rest of the
city had been drained of, its social and cultural riches fleeced by gentrification. I sat on the train and looked out the window, and I saw a beautiful,
dynamic municipality, and I wondered—though I could have wagered a
guess—why I didn't know anything about how the Bronx rebuilt itself.

I siphoned this question into a piece of writing that I could use to help me figure it out. I researched the Mid-Bronx Desperadoes and the Banana Kelly Community Coalition, and all of these other local grassroots organizations which had single-handedly rebuilt the borough during the decades of fires and disinvestment, when the city had all but abandoned it. It took only a very gentle pressure, a casual perusal of reports and archived articles, paying attention to the repetition of organizers' names and affiliations, to suddenly have revealed before me a whole history intact, which had always been there, the story of a generation of direct action—cooperative squatting, homesteading, and sweat equity—from within the community which had made it so that the kinds of devastation of the neighborhoods in the 1970s and '80s is virtually invisible today. I ended up marshaling the research into a story about the community-controlled reconstruction of Charlotte Street—which, by 1984, through the of the work of organizations like the Mid-Bronx Desperadoes, had turned several lots of scorched earth into a small neighborhood of affordable free-standing houses.

By winter, my father-in-law, Dan, was in a coma.

And thus, in the last years of Dan's fifties, and the last years of our twenties, Sweeney and I became his de facto caretakers. In the immediate aftermath of the strokes, for three months, we spent nearly every night in the Westchester Medical Center, pressuring doctors for additional tests, awaiting surgery outcomes, crying and drinking bourbon in waiting rooms, arguing with neurologists, consulting palliative care specialists, and crowding around Dan in his semi-vegetative state while we gulped down sixteen-ounce cups of burnt coffee, telling him every single story he had ever told us, in a nearly psychotic bid of belief that he could hear and understand what we were saying.

There were many nights I spent alone at the hospital with Dan when Sweeney was teaching. I'd sit at his bedside, under the greenish glare of the hospital lamps, listening to the phlegmy hack of the patient who was sharing his room on the other side of the curtain. I'd read him books, bits of articles from a recent *New Yorker*, while he blinked his watery eyes at me. Sometimes he'd hold up his hand, indicating for me to stop. He'd drift in and out of sleep. I'd play songs he liked from my phone: Jethro Tull, the Hollies, the Grateful Dead, but eventually he'd squint and turn away. I'd tell him about what I'd been up to, and lots of stories about himself, about my early encounters with him. We'd known each other since I was nineteen, when Sweeney and I met. Sometimes he'd smile at appropriate moments in the stories, and other times he'd just fix on me with that blank, wet stare and I wouldn't be sure if he'd registered any of it.

Dan and Sweeney's mother had divorced several years earlier, so almost immediately, Sweeney—the eldest of the three siblings—became his father's legal healthcare proxy. He ultimately had to be put in charge of interpreting the vague advanced directive, making decisions about intubation, life support, and a heart valve transplant while Dan remained in physical and verbal apraxia—all of which the extended family was largely in disagreement about. Sweeney had to act decisively, keep his face drawn and mute and calm—everyone looked to him for assurance or authority, though he was, of course, making it up as he went and losing his shit every other night on the privacy of our balcony or his mom's back deck. Then, one day, Dan wrote his own name on a whiteboard we got from the dollar store. The neurologist asked him what his name was, and in quivering script with his left hand he wrote: Daniel Sweeney. Later that week, he started talking. He responded raspingly to word opposite prompts by the ICU speech pathologist when she covered the open valve in his throat with her index finger while four or five of us, who'd been haunting these hallways all winter, stood around listening—all this only days before we were going to take him off the feeding tube.

We had help from extended family, but Sweeney and I were the main agents of care and coordination for the years to come, and the labor and grieving and rehab and bureaucracy-fighting was relentless, on top of all the ordinary economic precarity of late-stage capitalism into which we had come of age: the housing bubble burst during my first year of college, and the fall after I graduated had seen the Occupy Wall Street uprising. Our cumulative debt-to-income ratio had relegated my peers and me into veritable serfdom by the time we were eighteen. We'd watched the expansion of the for-profit prison industrial complex. We'd, in fact, spent our entire sentient lives bearing witness to a global economy built so openly on speculation, extraction, exploitation, war, and waste that there was no single scales-falling-from-our-eyes moment. The so-called private sector had taken over the planet and turned it into a death-machine. It happened right in front of us.

I had, at the time, multiple low-wage or contract jobs all over the city; I was reporting and writing a book against deadline; I'd get home to Wood-lawn for a day or two, in between jobs, and drive to New Rochelle to hang out with Dan, who was by then trapped miserably and suffering in a nursing home he couldn't get out of while Sweeney fought for a year and a half, forty hours a week, to enroll him in Medicaid. Dan had severe aphasia, nerve damage, and muscle loss. He had great difficulty speaking, and could not walk. Between work, commuting, multiple jobs, Sweeney and I would trade off days to go visit him, by which time he was able to speak a little bit: about his commitment to Trump's bid for president, some verses from songs we'd listen to together, his thoughts on Whitey Bulger while we watched a movie, and his never-ending stream of despair and complaint about still being alive. "Get me outta here," he'd say, over and over again. "I want to die." I took him to weekly robotics physical therapy, where he walked with electronic prosthetics for one hundred feet down a hallway, attended by three hot young therapists who he'd flirt with, in spite of everything, while they stretched his calves. "Tell them about my bicycling," he'd say to me, grinning. "Tell them about Brazil." And I'd tell them about his wild journeys, biking across the country, facing off with pirates on the Amazon during a fishing trip. "Wow," they'd say, indulging him, rotating his ankle. "You're quite the adventurous person." In these moments at therapy, he seemed most like himself.

During this time, two of our grandmothers, whom Sweeney and I were close to, both died, suddenly, within three months of each other. But we couldn't pause.

A year went by, and I could feel life draining out of us—a life that was, itself, unsustainable, burned out, preserving a center that could not hold anyway. We sat on our roof one night, drinking beer. Sweeney asked, as he was regularly in the habit of, when I wanted to have a baby.

I took a deep swig. "What?"

"I'm ready whenever," he said.

"I'm exhausted," I said. "We're, like, barely getting by with all of your dad stuff. The sink is full of dishes—the house stinks. I can barely keep our life, like, taped together. A baby?"

"I could watch a baby," he said. "I'm home a lot. I could just write my dissertation, do the night shifts."

"But you're not thinking about my body. Or my quality of life. I don't want to just give birth and then get on the 2 train while you're home with a baby. Just the time it takes to—I don't want to be living like this, so stressed out, caring for your dad every day, with a baby, or pregnant."

"Nothing's ever going to be perfect, no perfect time—this is the thing. You always focus on the negative."

There were a thousand calls to make, hours more to wait on hold, gigs to scratch together. Eventually, my first book came out, and then I was touring that book all over the country, still teaching five or six classes a semester to make ends meet, still figuring out how to safely transfer Dan into the front seat of my now late grandmother's Honda Civic to take him to appointments, to the diner, to the bathroom. Alternatives seemed sealed off. Sweeney and I fought constantly, unable to negotiate a way forward.

In the summer of 2016—several months after Dan's strokes, and still caring for him every day—something else happened. Sweeney and I found ourselves at a small church in the northwest Bronx that gradually and permanently changed my perspective about utopia, God, and what is generally possible in relation to both of those things. During what Malcolm X famously called "the most segregated hour in American life," I sat in a row of stacking chairs in a radical multiracial congregation called New Day in a rented-out cafeteria of the oldest Catholic girls' school in New York State.

The sermon that morning was part of a "queer liberation" series for the month of June. The reading, from the book of John. And in the announcements, the pastor rallied for everyone to join the Northwest Bronx Community and Clergy Coalition in an upcoming march against an urban planning initiative that threatened to develop the dense, vibrant neighboring district of Jerome Avenue into commercial and luxury housing. There was going to be a town hall, followed by three weeks of marches. I wondered at that moment about the connection, held fast and translucent as fishing line, between the presence of my white body in the Bronx and these particular attempts at gentrification. I felt my tailbone shift on the cold, hard plastic of the stacking chair as the congregation moved into a time of praise. The freestanding projection screen filled suddenly with song lyrics drawn from the Old Testament prayer of Jabez. Then a gospel melody sounded from the keyboardist. "Enlarge my territory," everyone sang, in unison. "Enlarge my territory." People began to rise from their chairs. "Enlarge my territory." Some had their hands in the air. "Enlarge my territory." Everyone was standing now, Black, white, brown, queer, straight, trans, cis, documented and undocumented. I felt a deep, sharp shiver run through me to the floor, as I stood, too, already wondering whether I had the right to join in. Even though Jabez was using the metaphor of property, and even though I had previously associated this line of scripture with the prosperity gospel, I could feel us all, communally, in that moment, reinterpreting what it meant. No one in this room meant private ownership when they said, "Enlarge my territory." Rather, everyone was looking toward a much more expansive idea of the divine commonwealth.

Sweeney and I met in college as fresh-faced anarchists, each of us at different but equally unbidden spiritual crossroads. That fall, he stumbled out of the bathroom at a bar we were at underage, a cigarette tucked behind his ear, and stood jaunty and drunk in the doorjamb, wearing his shredded trousers and waistcoat, and said, as though it were a surprise to even himself, "This feels weird to say, but—I'm practically Catholic." By our early twenties, we were exploring hip nondenominational Christian churches, seeking a community that might temper a rigorous understanding of our own theologies. But my intense feeling of needing to belong to these faith communities had eventually been overtaken by a drawn-out confrontation with all of the ugly theology at the core of even the most cutting-edge congregations, gradually revealing their heinous ideas around gender and sexuality. I had eventually decided that I would never belong to a church again. But then, one night, several months into my father-in-law's slow recovery from his initial coma, Sweeney was at an old Irish bar near Fordham, and a young woman overheard a conversation he was having with a couple of friends about our sordid journey through twenty-first-century white Protestantism, and she interrupted to say that, in fact, just a couple of blocks from there was a church we should check out—that we might like—called New Day. Her face is hazy now; so much that he wonders if it ever happened at all. We went to New Day the following week, and we never saw the woman again.

In some ways, that first morning at New Day, the service looked a lot like those other church plants (small Protestant congregations that branch off from a larger organization to "plant" themselves in urban neighborhoods) I'd hung out in during my earlier twenties—the borrowed space, the DIY communion table, the contemporary music, the projection screen. But the variety of voices and people present at New Day was markedly different, not to mention the fierceness with which the gospel of John was drawn into the movement of queer liberation, not through qualifying nor skimming nor tossing out words, but as a radical act of taking back interpretive authority over a text that had previously been weaponized against the queer people who were now finding in it instead the story of their freedom. It was clear to me that the people gathered there had *made* this church, and not the other way around. And while it wasn't a commune, or even a known movement, the gathering there at New Day Church did seem connected to a continuous subterranean American tradition of building utopia—literally meaning "no place," one that, according to the laws of capital and conquest, should not even be able to exist.

Sweeney and I continued to show up every Sunday, and I learned, slowly, that seated in those stacking chairs were many of the people who were a direct part of the Bronx rebuilding legacy I had been writing about the year before, who were members of these grassroots organizations who had put sweat equity into their buildings and neighborhoods, who had done these extraordinary decades-long projects to stay and rebuild the Bronx through the seventies, eighties, and nineties, and more recently who'd been major organizers in Occupy Wall Street, and who were singing, among other things, in four-part harmony, "Enlarge my territory."

•

Though the particular history of the Bronx was just unfurling for me then, I had been long drawn into the geography and palimpsest of New York City in general, and the ways that it wears and survives its ravages. In college, while I was living in, and gentrifying, Bed-Stuy, I wrote a sprawling collection of ghost stories about the Brooklyn neighborhoods that were decimated by the mid-twentieth-century construction of the Brooklyn–Queens Expressway, under the forty-year reign of parks commissioner-cum-city planner Robert Moses—who had also, in his own words, "taken a meat axe to the Bronx," primarily by blasting multiple highways through its formerly tight-knit communities. Each of my short stories took place in a different decade, in Red Hook, Bay Ridge, Sunset Park, Bed-Stuy, the Navy Yard, Coney Island, Jones Beach. While I wrote those stories, Sweeney and I were living in an apartment building, or otherwise on the same block, with a bunch of our best friends. I was attending Pratt Institute and feeling very firmly within a family unit. Our rent was funded largely by student loans, and some part-time jobs, but over time the loans artificially inflated the economy of the neighborhood, and so as I fancied myself a historical chronicler, a time traveler through fiction, exploring the physical decimation of these neighborhoods, I was myself decimator.

I understood this to some extent, but the intensity of the irony was lost on me. Still, when I think about that project now I can see more clearly why I found those histories so compelling, in the way that looking back at a body of work reveals over and over again that you have always only been thinking about the same thing: the whole project of urban renewal, which is what the Brooklyn–Queens Expressway came out of, was a kind of fascist thought, a purified, sanitized vision of the future—masquerading as a sincerely hoped for utopian infrastructure where human life could be engineered into order by a strongman with a bird's-eye view.

Fascist visions of paradise erase texture, layer, history, so that we exist only in a simple unified present. Its method is to create fictions of purity and continuity which serve to exclude most people, to prevent criticism and complexity, so that those who "belong" or feel belonging will yield to becoming part of the machine, because it appears to benefit them. In her book *Re-enchanting the World*, Silvia Federici, paraphrasing the Native scholar Paula Gunn Allen, presses that "loss of memory is the root of oppression, for obliviousness to the past renders meaningless the world in which we move, strips the spaces in which we live of any significance, as we forget at what cost we tread the ground we walk upon and whose histories are inscribed in the stones, fields, and buildings that surround us."

The Bronx itself is built upon the lives and villages and "deep, ancient heaps of oyster shells" of the Pequot, Lenape, and Siwanoy nations, who Federici affectionately terms North America's "first commoners," which is to say the first stewards of the continental commons. A fragment of those commons, and the spirit of those commons, still exist in the Bronx, both expressed through the actions of the Bronx rebuilding movement, and through Co-op City, arguably the largest piece of cooperatively owned real estate in the world. In his essay "Utopia, The Bronx" (from which the title of this chapter is blithely lifted), the writer Ian Frazier chronicles the construction of the northeast Bronx's Co-op City, his narrative starting point not the 1960s when it was built, but in the fourteenth century when the Indigenous people—the Pequot—still peaceably populated the salty edges of the mainland, fishing from the granite outcropping that Co-op City was later built on. During the Dutch settlement of New Amsterdam, in the 1640s, the colonists massacred the Pequot as part of a targeted extermination that lasted for the better part of that decade, all but forgotten from public history, invisible, sanded away. For Frazier, it seems that the magnitude of Co-op City's meaning cannot be fully understood without first putting it in this larger context of both erasure and the Bronx's spirit of place: the twentieth-century leftists that the Bronx had helped incubate forged this community on top of a genocide.

As a photonegative to the loss of memory about the Bronx rebuilding movement, I think, too, for instance, of Woodlawn, the neighborhood Sweeney and I were still living in when we ended up at New Day. Woodlawn was chock-full of current and former IRA members and other people involved in the Irish freedom movement, who had been living in the multiracial Northwest Bronx for generations, and who had opened bars like the

Jolly Tinker where the angel-woman told Sweeney about New Day, many of whom eventually became racist cops.

Fascist dreams and utopian dreams are not infrequently indistinguishable at first, but their differences are much easier to catch when those dreams are playing out on the public stages of our cities. The spiritual fight against something like urban renewal or gentrification (or other forms of fascism masquerading as progress) is a fight against forgetting the difference.

These days New York City seems to be living out the dreams of the very rich and very powerful—like a gated community that you earn your way into, or struggle bitterly to survive on the margins of, as though it has always been this way, and only ever will be. And yet the city's sheer density and volume make it physically impossible to erase all traces of the past, such that, for instance, the Bronx remains a visible reminder that that fascist story, told by the politicos and powerbrokers, is not true.

In *Rebel Cities*, David Harvey writes, "The term 'city' has an iconic and symbolic history that is deeply embedded in the pursuit of political meanings. The city of God, the city on a hill, the relationship between city and citizenship—the city as an object of utopian desire, as a distinctive place of belonging within a perpetually shifting spatio-temporal order—all give it a political meaning that mobilizes a crucial political imaginary." The Bronx in particular, then, the place where my specific understanding of utopian possibility developed, is my city on a hill—which itself is just a metaphor for heaven.

Despite its prevalence in our spiritual and secular imaginations, there's very little about heaven at all in the Christian or Hebrew Bible—and if you omit the sentences that refer to "the heavens" (which almost always seems to be about the literal sky and weather), then you really have just a handful of verses that address heaven as an actual place. And in those verses, you have just a few repeated and incongruous details: heaven is a kingdom; heaven is a house with many rooms; heaven is a place where one can have citizenship; heaven is a city; it's a city to come; it's a city that will ultimately give way to "a new heaven and a new earth"; it's a city where you will find treasure so long as you give everything you own away in this lifetime. It's a city, loud and clear.

No single writer in the various texts that make up the Bible has more to say about heaven than John of Patmos, the "Revelator," to whom the book of Revelation is ascribed. He addresses heaven head-on in his apocalyptic visions, actually visits heaven and tells us what he sees: heaven is a city with streets paved in gold (or in some translations, just a city "made of gold")— but also other minerals and gemstones, too (jade, sapphire, jasper, agate, emerald, onyx, carnelian, chrysolite, beryl, topaz, jacinth, amethyst). It's in that description, by crazy John of Patmos, that the twelve gates guarding the heavenly city are cast as being made entirely of pearl. "But nothing unworthy will be allowed to enter," he repeats, using that gospels mash-up style he writes in, collaging together bits of Jesus's speech from earlier canonical books. "No one who does what is detestable or false will be there. Only those whose names are written in the Lamb's book of life will be in the city." Oh, that city—there it is again. John writes at length about heaven, notably that during his brief heavenly ascension, he saw "a great multitude that no one could number, from every nation, from all tribes and peoples and languages, standing before the throne and before the Lamb, clothed in white robes, with palm branches in their hands," a multiracial city.

The emphasis on heaven being a city is interesting given that the popular conception and creation of American utopias—those communities that wanted to be cities on a hill, heaven simulacrums—have been so thoroughly framed as pastoral, or as an escape from industrialization and modernity. But, overwhelmingly, in the Bible at least—heaven is big and pluralistic and urban. In fact, the whole idea of pastoral exit is antithetical to the Judeo-Christian eschatological story because, in that tradition, paradise begins in a garden and ends in a city.

We need our cities. We can barely afford to stay in our cities. And yet, perhaps obviously, the pastoral utopian escape *from* cities—whether in the nineteenth-century wilds of mystical socialisms or the twentieth-century hippie commune—did not yield final answers, either. The rural fantasy of escaping back-to-the-land has been so overwhelmingly white and often available only to those who had the privilege to leave town, and anyway it aids in the further disinvestment of our urban centers, the metric of our spiritual health. So, we need new ways of having utopian dreams, and the Bronx and New Day Church appeared to me in my late twenties as places that were articulating answers simply by the strategies of their continued existence.

•

A year and a half into caring for Dan, Sweeney—after forty hours a week of fighting phone lines, standing in queue, sitting by his bedside, running errands, filing and refiling papers, researching public assistance, bribing bankers and landlords, and more—finally won MAGI Medicaid, as well as a traumatic brain injury provision, which allowed us to move Dan into an apartment four blocks from us, with state-paid twenty-four-hour home health aides, all of whom were Black women from Wakefield or Mt. Vernon. Sweeney's hair started to go gray. He started to drink more. Regardless of the home health aides' continuous presence, our participation was still required daily: administering insulin and Dunkin' Donuts ice coffees, scheduling and shuttling to the doctors, the hospital, the pharmacy, various therapies and errands, wheelchair walks to the park or the pub, fielding suicidal ideation and stock market obsessions next to Dan's sixty-four-inch TV set while his stroke recovery regressed by the light of his preferred viewing of twenty-four-hour Fox News broadcasts.

Meanwhile, I finished my book tour, my slate of classes and tutoring, a semester of living out of my backpack or on the road. Then, on Christmas day a couple of months after settling Dan into his new place, I ended up in the emergency room with what turned out to be shingles.

The chicken pox virus from childhood hides out in the spinal column until you get stressed out enough that it travels like a phantom along a nerve path, showing up as painful pustule-like hives on your torso, back, or, in my case, on my face and neck and eyeball. I was laid up for a week with fevers. I watched all of *Mindhunter* in a sweaty pile on the couch. I watched a documentary about The Farm in Tennessee, and another about Rajneeshpuram in Oregon. I canceled flights. I felt rage and exhaustion. I made myself tea and soup, in regular rotation. I wondered about all the choices and circumstances that had led us away from where we'd wanted to be—with friends, making art and books, being neighbors or communards, having kids.

For most of the decade we'd been together, Sweeney and I had some idea in mind of what our lives might coalesce into: the open home, the loosely organized gathering space, a residency or low-cost misfit boarding house, the multi-structure commune, the low-overhead community life, something like this. But after ten years of talking, to each other and to various combinations of our friends, we were no closer to that idea—though the vision had, in a way, gotten clearer, so clear sometimes I could reach through the scrim, could sort of see the place and form we might be living in if only all of the conditions lined up just so. But when I looked at our immediate surroundings, I saw us unhappy and overworked in an apartment that already took so much time to just keep moderately clean, and scraping for writing time anywhere I could get it, and fatigue, and a kind of growing rigidity with which the future was imagined.

The plan now was much narrower: in a couple of years, Sweeney would be going on the thinning academic job market, and then I could teach a little less for a while, and we would stay in Woodlawn, caring for Dan, in this airless holding pattern of unrelenting emotional exhaustion, unmoored from any kind of community or vision larger than the acquisition of some fiscal security. The years dribbled out like a slow, gray trickle into a sewer grate. My despair was bloated and cartoonish. I stared out the window next to my kitchen sink at the dead trees lining my quiet street and thought, *This is hell.* The thought felt ridiculous, but also loud. All of my efforts having gone for so long to just making life work had made a powder keg of my rage. I rose up like a demon in a haunted carnival ride. I was covered in scabs. I looked terrifying. I felt a few things, irrevocably: *Life is not to die.* This cannot be what life is for—for being isolated and worn out, in a city full of people we know and love? For running ourselves ragged, to develop a career and make just enough money to keep the dumb life going, to maintain our atomized existence as a self-contained unit that touches no other meaningful edges of anyone else's lives, making plans every once in a while to go see someone—who is also ragged, isolated, and tired? To feel as ragged as the person we are supposed to be taking care of, and who we will need to figure out a way to take care of for a long time to come?

I left that night for Brooklyn. I sat in my friend Lina's apartment in Clinton Hill, a couple of blocks from where we'd all gone to college and where I now worked, curled up on her couch, during the largest snowstorm of the decade. She had spent half the year on porn sets in the San Fernando

Valley producing a podcast about the economic ripple effect from the rise of free streaming. That weekend, she murmured behind her bathroom door, on the phone with a long-awaited source who wanted to talk about the recent suicide of his wife, a popular porn actress. Afterward, we watched the drifts pile on the streets from her fourth-story apartment.

"What do you want to happen, when you go home?" she asked, refilling our coffee mugs in her kitchenette.

"I don't know." I was bundled on her couch. "I need to know this won't be life forever. I need him to stop being a martyr. I need him to stop drinking."

"But—what do *you* need?"

"I don't know. The answers feel so dumb—impossible—or repetitive."

"Like what?"

"Like—I want to be in the Catskills, start a residency, have more time to write, and sleep, and have kids, and actually get to enjoy that. But I've been saying that for years."

I trudged through the snow to the Walgreens on Myrtle Avenue to get my ghastly $200 eyeball ointment, while my health insurance was mysteriously terminated, and then, every few hours, I had to apply the gooey medicine directly to my eyeball from a tiny metal tube the size of my pinky finger. In a nuclear-option move, Lina paid for my friend Amber to fly up from Nashville, and then it was all of us in the apartment, figuring out what kind of vision or ask I needed to bring back to Sweeney, whenever I returned. All of my answers were about what Sweeney needed to do, how he needed to change, but all I touched was vapor when I tried to reach for those answers about myself.

"Let's change gears then," Amber said. "What are you working on right now?

"A new book—just an idea of a book. Notes. Lots of notes on American utopian movements."

"Alright," Amber said. "What kind of notes, though?"

I was fixated on the stories of communities that had formed alternative ways of living in or under or outside of capitalism, or which had blurred the lines of public and private, of family, of marriage, of labor. Sometimes it meant urban homesteaders, sometimes it meant survival armies, sometimes it meant those nineteenth-century celibate doom cults in Western New York, sometimes it just meant a home or a space I'd once visited that had somehow created a porous existence that was both public and private, sometimes it meant radical Christian communities.

The radical Christian communities I was interested in almost uniformly held various verses from the second chapter of the book of Acts as the cornerstone of their theology. The handful of verses all address, very briefly, the ways that the apostles lived communally following the resurrection—and the ones that come up the most are verses 42–47. The Catholic Workers, the Jesus People movements, Old Order Mennonites, the Amish, the Shakers, the Oneida Community, the Harmonists, ancient monastics, Father Divine's International Peace Mission Movement—they all pointed to Acts 2 as the bedrock of their beliefs about how to live, how to restore the "original church" as a communal, countercultural existence.

In Acts 2, we're coming off the day of Pentecost, in first-century Jerusalem. The city at that moment is full of Jews who've gathered from every nation for the annual Feast of Weeks, and also Roman pagans for the festival harvest, and a mix of hybrid-believers and gentile-converts. The political situation is in disarray from a major uprising that has just ended in the public execution, by decree of the ambivalent official Pontius Pilate, of a little-known wandering prophet and militant weirdo. The crucifixion and resurrection have just happened—a little more than a month earlier. The apostles have hidden out for a while because they thought, *Well, we're gonna die. The state is going to kill us, because we have made the state extremely afraid, so much so that they killed our leader.* But then—this is Acts 2—the holy spirit led the apostles into the streets, men and women, and especially women, and they preached, in a language so powerful, or in languages so numberless, that everyone in Jerusalem, that multiethnic city, could understand what they were saying: the resurrection has happened, the impossible has taken place, and so all of the other things Jesus was talking about when he was alive—that the meek are kings, and kings are clowns; that the poor are getting free and love has overcome death—must also be possible. That is the good news. Then, after the apostles convert a bunch of people in the streets, thousands it says, they and all the new followers go underground.

42 They devoted themselves to the apostles' teaching and to fellowship, to the breaking of bread and to prayer. 43 Everyone was filled
with awe at the many wonders and signs performed by the apostles.
44 All the believers were together and had everything in common.
45 They sold property and possessions to give to anyone who had
need. 46 Every day they continued to meet together in the temple
courts. They broke bread in their homes and ate together with glad
and sincere hearts, 47 praising God and enjoying the favor of all the
people. And the Lord added to their number daily those who were
being saved.

But let's think a bit about what it is these ancient converts actually do
together during this time, taking that almost random scrap of scripture as our
object of inquiry: They devote themselves to the teachings of Jesus, they practice fellowship, break bread together—which could mean observing communion, but it could also just mean having meals together. Above all, they are in
each other's presence *daily*, and living in each other's homes. They renounce
private ownership. They give their assets away to the poor. They're made up
of every nationality present at that time in Jerusalem. They live communally,
they kind of drop out of society. I'm not sure if they work. It seems like they
don't, because it isn't mentioned once, it doesn't say, "And then they went
about their waged labor as per usual." It seems, rather, like they are *hanging out*
and that they are relaxed and full of joy. They are holding all things in common, including things like—alongside work and struggle—pleasure, loafing,
eating, drinking, dancing. These are also things of the spirit. *The Lord added to
their number daily those* who were getting free. And the movement grew.

Of course, some of the American movements that take this scripture
up as their cornerstone through which to innovate a new existence, away
from materialism and authoritarianism, were born out of their own deformed aims: separatism, sexism, racism, xenophobia, notions of purity. So,
while I found myself interested in the various communities of refusal they'd
created, they were not sites of utopian inspiration I could hang out in permanently, or for very long at all. Instead, it seemed like a real American
utopia is the accidental creation of something mixed, of something entirely

new and therefore ungovernable, that creates cracks though which an alternative future—and present—can eke through. It is communities born of experimentation, of new combinations, that seem especially utopian to me. The dream of the "restoration" of something believed to be old or original (which is always just a fantasy anyway) is suspect, and often rooted in concerns fundamentally about staving off death: death of tradition, death of the self. And death, in the words of the late public theologian Rachel Held Evans, "is something empires worry about, not something gardeners worry about. It's certainly not something resurrection people worry about."

There had always been peasant uprisings, uprisings of the underclasses, and crucifixions of radical leaders, long before Jesus' time—but the resurrection, or at least a belief in the story of it and the story of what the apostles did in its wake, seemed to say something different about this history. Another way of reading that moment in Acts 2 is not that it's describing a community formation to be literally adhered to by all true believers going forward, but that it's highlighting the thought-to-be impossible things that the event of the resurrection radically reframed: these uprisings, which have always happened and will continue to happen, these impossible communities that will form against all odds and always have, which will live out a spirit of abundance and solidarity in a world that swears the law is scarcity and rift, are themselves the eternal and ongoing heirs to the true reality, and they shall live, and live abundantly.

It's hard to explain without sounding like a zealot. Maybe I am a zealot.

What I'm saying is, the resurrection, if thought about this way, served as much as an atonement as it did a reminder: do not believe the lies—do not believe the lies that empire tells about what is possible and what is not. Do not give way to evil.

Which, it turns out, is the literal motto of the Bronx.

The motto was established long ago by the Bronck family, those rich white nineteenth-century land barons who "settled" the mainland. They put it on their flag. What did they think it meant at the time, emblazoned in pretentious Latin? What did they think they were protecting themselves from? Was it a reminder of what lay within them? Did they already know who they were? It appeared on crests and signs for the Bronx throughout the nineteenth and twentieth centuries, but it wasn't until 1970 that New York officially ratified the motto into city administrative code. It is amazing poetic justice: 1970, the year that would kick off what documentarian Vivian Vázquez Irizarry calls the "decade of fire," orchestrated for profit through a conspiracy of racism, exploitation, slumlords, and real estate insurance companies, fires that were not the fault of the residents, though the residents were, through every effort, made to feel like it was their fault.

Do not give way to evil. Surely this means something different than what the Bronck family first intended. What is evil? People from the Bronx know: the powers that exist to erase and condemn entire peoples and histories; all of the forces that frame the Bronx as a nexus of scarcity and decay, when it is actually a unique multiracial model of urban abundance and dignity; all the forces that separate us from our understanding of the divine, forms of separation that invariably issue from empire—capitalism, racism, sexism, classism, greed, and power; the false stories told about what is possible and what is not. And it is this kind of knowledge that positions the Bronx to be a teacher of utopian strategy, just as much as the usual suspects of American utopian history.

Is an American utopia possible, then—is it even worthy of consideration? When we think about what kinds of shit we're commonly told *are* possible, the question becomes less absurd: For instance, that which supports the status quo is always possible. There's always money to build a wall, but forgiving student loans is somehow impossible. There's money to bail out banks, but not mortgages. There's money to fund wars, but not universal healthcare. There are endless ways to expand the prison system, but the question of abolition is ridiculous. There's always time and energy to engage in long, drawn-out evictions of families from their homes on Jerome Avenue to make room for luxury units, but scarce resources to make sure that housing is available to everyone.

In fact, when we think about what *is* treated as possible under capitalism, it seems that, invariably, evil is possible. If that is our option under the current paradigm, then why not become utopian dreamers? Why not insist on the dream? Be like the Bronx. Do not give way to evil.

utopianotes
Robert Moses's grave

I wander to Robert Moses's memorial at Woodlawn Cemetery. That is some *Heart of Darkness* shit. His headstone sits at the furthest point away from either of the cemetery's street entrances, a two-mile hike on foot across ancient bumpy pathways. His stone is encased in the only brutalist-style mausoleum on site: a spare, stone structure which oddly mirrors Moses's dystopian modernist aesthetic of rational order. The crypt keeper (let's call him that) leads me to the pink granite square behind which lie Moses's ashes. He gestures to the high gate just beyond the mausoleum wall, separating us from the rushing traffic of Jerome Avenue, which turns into I-87 at this intersection, a major artery that eventually jams clear through the Catskill Mountain region. "This *used* to be an entrance into the cemetery," he says. "But then Robert Moses built the Major Deegan running right through, so they had to close it."

A BRIEF HISTORY OF
AMERICAN UTOPIANISM

If I were to follow my own moral logic, a brief history of American utopianism would start with a fieldtrip somewhere fresh. It would start for
instance in Weeksville, among the first free Black American intentional
communities. Weeksville sits in the Venn of the neighborhoods of Crown
Heights, Bed-Stuy, and Brownsville, in Brooklyn, and has been in continuous existence since the early nineteenth century and is now partially
enshrined as a living museum. Or it would start in the 1980s, at Short
Mountain Sanctuary in Middle Tennessee, where Radical Faeries created
a communal life close to the land with a low carbon footprint, away from
the homophobic violence of society. Or it would start in Harlan County,
Kentucky, in the twenty-first century, where a multiracial, multi-sexual-
orientation coalition of coal miners and coal country lifers blocked the railroad tracks from coal transport when their company laid them off without
pay. They camped on the tracks—made homes, beds, had meals together,
played games, choreographed dances to "Old Town Road," and for six
months created a provisional utopia out of thin air, before they finally got
paid, packed up, and went home.

But I'm not going to start somewhere fresh, because, as I mentioned before, the moral logic of my own writing wouldn't penetrate for a while yet.

I finished cycling through the shingles virus in Lina's apartment, wondering if or how I would ever return to my own. Snow fell upon all the
living and the dead. Then, without going back to Woodlawn, I retreated to
Rochester to be with two other friends, and to visit the site of a lost utopian
community, though I had not yet decided which one. And so it is that the
first fieldtrip in this story begins where most stories about American utopia leave off—in Western New York, where a whole generation of utopian
fervor famously took place from the late eighteenth to the mid-nineteenth
centuries: the divine socialism of the Shakers, the "free-love" Perfection-
ism of the Oneida Community, the sci-fi pragmatism of the Fourierists,

33

the stirrings of Mormon Zionism, and the Harmonists' Millenarian vision of Harmony, just over the Pennsylvania border. It is this region, time period, and these communities and movements that are often representatives of what academe is commonly talking about when they talk about American utopianism, as though utopianism is a distinct historical phenomenon locked in the past.

Kelly and her new husband picked me up at the remodeled Amtrak station. I passed through a halogen-lit underground tube tunnel to get to the parking lot. Kelly howled at me from her warm car. It snowed eighteen inches that night. We pulled a couple of tarot cards on my behalf: Temperance and the World. In the morning, Kelly and our friend Sofi sat around drinking coffee in her kitchen while I finalized which particular utopian site I'd be taking us to, and I chose more or less at random: the site of the Sodus Bay Phalanx, a long-gone secular utopian community based off of the writings of French author and wacky theorist Charles Fourier. It wasn't an obvious choice, nor very thought out. Because, of course, in and near Rochester, there are so many communities to choose from, not just in terms of ghostly historical presence, but ones which are currently marked by an interpretive center: the Oneida Mansion House, the Ebenezer Colonies, the remaining buildings of the Skaneateles Community, the birthplace of the Megiddo steamship ministry, Joseph Smith's childhood home where he first saw the angel Moroni.

But the former site of the Sodus Bay Phalanx seemed like a good place to start. It was now part of a land trust dubbed "Alasa Farms" and open to the public year-round, having been used for a variety of utopian purposes over the last hundred and fifty years. Most recently it had become host to an animal sanctuary. Anyway, the other options would have taken more planning, more driving, more interviewing, and self-disclosure to well-meaning docents and archivists, and I was so tired.

Perhaps the spiritual and physical fatigue was why, partly at least, I'd been so drawn to the histories of American utopian communities in the interim, the peace they seemed to believe in, their communisms that surpasseth program and blood ties, but which were rarely, if ever, able to sustain for more than a few years or months. It's hard to feel comforted by the idea of these movements for very long, though, especially in America, itself a sort of utopian project, misguided and gone wrong from the outset like all the rest. How can I take seriously the idea of utopia in an American context, where the spirit of world-building and the clarion call of "more perfect" immediately made known its imperial aims by expelling and exploiting a whole universe of peoples who were already there, or who were forced from somewhere else to bring that vision into being? It's difficult to prevent immediate foreclosure on the subject of utopia in America—the name itself already bedecked in shimmery colonial piping, perhaps offensive to be using at all—with all its attendant optimism and escapism, and often whiteness, at least as far as the history-keeping goes.

But I kept coming back to the histories of these particular communities, the ones in Western New York that historians agree are "utopian," as subjects and as sites of inspiration. There was something important there, and also their projects pointed to others, in multiple directions. But my research was increasingly fueled by other, more personal, yearnings: there was my nostalgic sense, for sure, my sincerely primal and mystical feeling that there is some better hereafter or long-before, always just out of reach. Then, similarly, there was my search for home, at a moment in my adulthood by which I thought I'd have resolved the feeling of statelessness carried over from my own fractured family, caught between houses and coasts, silences and erasures, with no resting place, no place that is constant and marked by my presence.

Disappointment and fracture are perhaps necessary to utopian thinking, though. It seems that utopia, or a utopian idea, needs to be ephemeral, needs to be allowed to fail, in order to be an agent of any good. It needs to be a mere stake in the ground, a marker or memory that says (as a friend of mine once described) "something good tried to happen here once" more than it needs to be a permanent solution. A thin reading of utopia as "no place" implies a place too perfect to actually exist, which is to say a place that definitively does not. It seems more like a utopia is something that, according to the laws of capital and conquest, was never supposed to be able to exist, but somehow did, for a blip in time, and if any longer than a blip, the utopia became a dystopia.

•

My friends and I drove out of the flat snowy expanse of Rochester, across the Genesee River, through the dead hardwood and hemlock forests and gnarled apple orchards. Kelly had been trying to get pregnant for a year. Sofi was mourning a lover who'd just left her for Israel. I had to put medicated eyedrops on my shingles-wrecked eyeball every two hours, and mid-application I looked out the window as we drove past the NY-31 exit to Palmyra.

Palmyra, New York, is the hometown of Joseph Smith; the woods outside of which is where he found those golden tablets that begat the Mormon church. The landscape in that area is not exactly inspiring—it's a bit tubercular, flat, a pewter-colored "Rust Belt" midwestern sheen. But that's where it happened: The spirit of the prophet Moroni met Smith in the trees when he was fourteen years old, and a few more times over the next decade. Then Smith married. And when he was ready, Moroni brought in the big guns: Heavenly Father and Jesus himself presided over the digging up of those golden tablets in the tract of forest behind his parents' house, which contained the true history of lost tribes' exile to North America, and their witness to the resurrection.

Smith and his new wife, Emma, retreated to her father's land in Harmony, Pennsylvania, and Smith spent three years translating the tablets in that drafty farmhouse. Just a decade or so earlier, that very town, Harmony, marked the utopian settlement of the pietist Christian prophet George Rapp, who'd dragged a bunch of followers from Germany to live out a life of all things in common on the western frontier, purifying themselves for the coming of the Lord. (The Harmonists were also early purveyors of steam-engine technology, and supported themselves with cooperative textile production and agriculture.) While the Harmonists had, by the time Smith arrived, relocated onto another settlement (also named Harmony, further west in Indiana), I have to believe that Smith knew well the recent history of this place, that there were even some hangers-on or defectors with whom he conferred during those long cold nights of translating the tablets. Maybe he learned a bit about the inner workings of their communal self-governance, the principle of the "shared purse," or about Rapp's ideas of the nearing Millennium. Maybe he examined the few remaining distinctive brick abodes, with their unique central heating systems. But I don't know. I can't find any evidence that Smith knew anything about their movement. Either way, he donned his gemstone glasses and transcribed the mish-mash of the "ancient Egyptian" language in which prophecy was scratched out. And what emerges from this? A movement! A whole new way of living, and of understanding life: prophets are among us, listen! And I am one of them, and I say: Jesus came to America, and uniquely blessed this place where his earliest descendant heirs had absconded to. The garden of Eden is in Jackson County, Missouri! Jesus has a father, and his father has a father, and the family unit is the most sacred of all the bonds, so sacred that it is the state we shall remain in and return to in the Celestial Kingdom. And so we must architect on earth a way to get going on that, and to live against the grain of atomization and in community—which kind of looked like how the Harmonists had been living.

And true communal living was what separated the wheat from the chaff, when it came down to the early Mormons. Smith preached and proselytized in Harmony, building his flock, eventually moving his burgeoning community of Latter-day Saints to Kirtland, Ohio, where Smith's itinerant missionaries were having a lot of success converting people. In Kirtland, the new larger consolidated LDS community began building their first temple, the town and the movement flourishing around it—but when Smith inaugurated an "anti-bank," a communal trust wherein all community members invested their assets, people freaked out, and many members left, and the non-Mormons of Kirtland rose up to tar and feather him out of town. But those who remained committed LDS believers moved west to Missouri, then to Illinois with that shared purse, and they went on to build encampments in Nauvoo, and then splintered into a variety of distinct sects on their ways further West, almost all of which (say, the FLDS) are still communal (and extremely repressive). Many things happened after this. The largest band of Latter-day Saints ended up in the Utah desert creating one of the more elaborate communitarian societies in American history around that filmy, sulphur lake, later amassing capital and commerce in all the usual ways—family by family, man by man—eventually becoming a world power.

•

Sofi, Kelly, and I finally arrived at a plot of land, a farm perched above the south shore of Sodus Bay, Lake Ontario: Alasa Farms.

Alasa Farms is a public land trust and the current home of Cracker Box Palace, a nonprofit organization that leases the 627 acres to run a sanctuary for abused and neglected farm animals.

We squeaked tire tracks up to the gatehouse through the bone-dry snow in Kelly's bright red Vibe. Then we pulled up in front of a barn and got out of the car, facing the gentle white slopes that terminated just beyond the trees at the lake's edge. It was a beautiful, freezing blue day. The snow was deep and muffled all sound except for the distant thrum of an ATV. White blanketed as far as the eye could see, except where it had been trotted through by the farm's community of ungulates. A truck was parked near us, belonging to one of the regular volunteers who feeds and cares for the horses in the barn. He waved to us from the open barn door but didn't say a word.

As my friends wandered toward one of the horse paddocks, I had to reorient myself: What was it about this piece of land that had intrigued me?

Here is the story of this place, as best I understand it: There's evidence of permanent dwellings on this parcel going back to the end of the Ice Age. The Seneca Indians were here then and are here now. Before settler colonialism and broken treaties, they'd rest in a stand of sycamores alongside the lake during their summer fishing trips, then migrate back to their more temperate homes due south. Then the European colonists came in the mid-eighteenth century and, for the first time in human history, privatized this piece of property for agriculture. But those crops failed. And in the early nineteenth century, the Shakers moved onto this land, followers of Mother Ann, who was believed to be the incarnation of Christ's second coming. The Shakers raised a barn, lived communally, made beautiful wood furniture, and performed ecstatic prayer under a doctrine of total celibacy. Later, when the Erie Canal was being developed, New York State usurped the property by eminent domain, but the Canal lost traction before they could build, and so they let it go fallow. The land remained unmolested. Then, in the 1840s, the Fourierists moved in, a French utopian socialist movement

grounded in the creation of thousands of self-sufficient, egalitarian cooperatives, called phalanxes, worldwide: the ideal phalanx would look something
like a modern-day college campus, housing no more than 1,623 residents
each and containing its own cottage industries, schools, and daycare, to ensure total equality of the sexes. (Fourierists managed to develop about thirty
phalanxes in the United States alone, including the famous Brook Farm,
but most of them fell apart exceptionally fast.) It was through their history
that I'd tracked down this site. The Sodus Bay Phalanx fell apart within a
year and a half, everyone tired and hungry and out of money and fighting
about vegetarianism. After the Fourierists, the property was a stop on the
underground railroad, in the guise of—my best guess, according to the real
estate notes of the era—a wealthy lawyer's private residence. Later still, after
the Great Crash of 1929, the land was bought up by the grandson of Henry
Strong, president of Eastman Kodak who had made his fortune—get this—
as a buggy whip manufacturer. Said grandson, Alvah, used the inheritance
from his grandfather to turn the property into a Model Farm, where he em-
ployed the out-of-work and displayed the wonders of twentieth-century agricultural innovations to the devastated Depression-era United States. I don't
know he long he stayed, or what happened after. Now, the property belongs
to New York State, and is leased, as I mentioned, to Cracker Box Palace.

We padded through the snow to a group of woolly sheep of all colors
and sizes huddled near a broken shed. In the middle of the sheep squad was
a single perm-white llama, who stood a full foot and a half taller than them,
staring at us accusingly, a bright green halter strapped around his snout. The
sheep backed away sweetly, dumbly, hiding behind the fence, or standing
sideways so they could see us from one eye. The llama stood guard.

They were the happiest sheep in the world. I recalled listening to photographer Isa Leshko talk about her series *Elderly Animals* while we were
both in residency at the Millay Colony a while back, and how farm animals
very rarely get to live out their natural lives, even close to it, which is central to the magic of her photographs—and so there is something miraculous
about this moment as we, these old animals and I, look at each other over the
fence. Utopian, even, a world where all the animals will be in their thirties,
fat off the land.

And standing on Alasa Farms, I can feel the buoyant, utopian joy the place is marinated in. Despite its history of so-called failure, it seems to continue producing endless utopian innovation, among which I count the survival of happy animals that were only ever intended to be bred for profit, capital, and conquest, but are here still, producing no profit whatsoever. My friends and I leap around in the snow, laughing, moving from pasture to pasture. I forget everything for a while: the shingles, the lost time, the old wounds, the fractured family, my father-in-law, Sweeney's heels dug in, the feeling of never arriving but only ever being *on my way* home, though a long way off.

This physical layering of utopian life on particular plots of land is not so un-usual in the United States. Once an eighteenth- or nineteenth-century uto-pian community had cultivated a tract for communal living, unsurprisingly, the land was primed for the next generation's version. The weird thing is you don't have to do that much digging before you hit another stratum. You'll often find that, for instance, a permaculture intentional community in rural Oregon bought the land from the Jesus People Shiloh Youth Re-vival, and that they bought it from some descendants of the Aurora Colony, and so forth. There have, to be clear, been a lot of experiments, especially in the mid-nineteenth century. Ralph Waldo Emerson famously wrote a letter to Thomas Carlyle in 1840, saying, "We are all a little wild here with numberless projects of social reform . . . Not a reading man but has a draft of a new community in his waistcoat pocket." He wrote this letter while he himself was experimenting at Brook Farm in Western Massachusetts, and while the country was entering into what writer Amanda Kolson Hurley calls "Peak Commune." There is a lot of layering in the story of utopianism in America, and the general thrust of that unfolding sounds a little like this:

It's 1681 or 1763 or 1830. So-and-so Jansson or Van Wort of somewhere-or-other, Sweden or Germany or England, decides the Lutherans, or the Anglicans, were sent by the devil. There should be no mediation between man and God, no tyrant king bequeathing spiritual access. So he promptly breaks away to create the Community of True Inspiration or God's Real

People or We are the Realest Ones, etc. He and his small band of follow-
ers, who by then have adopted some kind of dress and mode of worship
to distinguish themselves, promptly have a mass burning of Lutheran (or
Anglican) hymnals and literature. Simple enough. They hang out in northern Europe. They live in a shared shack, or a final vestige of the commons.
But then that guy (Jansson, Van Wort, etc.) runs into so-and-so Bartlett or
Godrich or Randolf who, himself, is in the middle of trying to reform the
Dutch Reformed Church, but having no luck reforming the reformed, they
join forces. They bestow prophecies. The blending of their two groups produces a new name, and a new theology: the Zoar Community or the Harmony Society or the Most Divine of the Most Divine. They believe in adult
baptism or ecstatic dancing or that the end is nigh or that no one should
speak in church, but often, above all, they believe in communal living, of a
life where "all things are held in common" as modeled in the book of Acts
after the crucifixion when Christ's followers give up everything they own
and go underground for forty years or so, living in symbiotic communitarianism out of sight of the Roman Empire.

So, it's the early nineteenth century now and the new group—Zoar or
Harmony or what-have-you—embarks to scope out land for a settlement
in the New World, and for no reason I can figure out they dock in New
York, but often or sometimes go all the way to central Pennsylvania or
Illinois. There, they claim a tract of land in a snowy, muddy lowland near
a Swedish Methodist church that they already think is heretical, and they
build semi-underground log cabins, and everyone comes out from Switzerland or Sweden or Germany, tons of people dying on the way on the ship,
and tons of people dying in those freezing cabins, trying to live out their
imagined reconstruction of first-century "biblical" communism. But then
there are schools! Tanneries! Businesses of all stripes, operating in a sort of
small-scale divine socialism, for a little while at least—but then something
goes wrong (something always goes wrong): cholera or smallpox or they
don't make enough money or a violent husband or theological/ideological
disagreements or (usually) the commune leader says that God says that he
can have sex with whoever he wants, or that everyone has to stop having
sex altogether. Some people die, others run off to join a different utopian

community, sometimes (and not infrequently) to the Shakers, who by then have colonies all over the northeast, though Mother Ann herself has died. Others run to cities, others stay in the falling-apart community because they don't know what else to do and eventually a town forms around them, and they cash in on that, they incorporate, and within a generation the utopian project is erased, assimilated. It's just Yellow Springs, Ohio, or New Harmony, Indiana, or Aurora, Oregon. Or it's just the Amana Corporation or Oneida Flatware & Silverware.

But at the early stages of the community's unravelling, before things have really fallen apart, so-and-so Splendorf or Gilbert arrives one day. He's an American, born and raised. He looks on at the tannery, the communal dinners, the women's clothing, and he says, *My, my, this seems like a really cool thing you've all got going on here*, or he says, *The Lord is telling me I must start my own community, a corrective to this one!* (while just off stage or behind him someone is puking from a horrible flu, or others are coming to blows about the doctrine of total depravity, or the tannery is burning down). But first he literally tours utopian communities for a decade (this happens a lot), joining them and dropping out, or sometimes just dropping in for a bit—Woman in the Wilderness, Bohemia Manor, Mill Creek—then breaks with them, or begins to revise their beliefs and leaves when he finds he can no longer conscionably carry on. He goes to the woods, defeated, starts anew: A slightly different take on prayer, on agricultural practices, on belief about the holy spirit or sex or which rules the leader of the group is exempt from. Living with all things in common remains a constant, but the rest is up for grabs. Then, just like that, unbidden, people kind of form around him, developing a sort of celibate utopia that lives and thrives (in a way) for five years or one year or eight years. And then another guy visits this new commune, and says, *My, my, this seems like a really cool thing you've got going on here* . . . But then it's the late nineteenth century, early twentieth century even, and before that new guy can get his utopian community up and running, his socialist Transcendentalist communitarian settlement of whatever type, the United States is flush, wealthy, and everyone's like, "Who needs communitarianism? We've got houses and bread now!"

Utopia-making emerges in force especially during times of economic and social precarity—after wars, depressions, natural disasters, sexual revolutions. And when a utopia issues from a Christian framework or tradition—whether during the Second Great Awakening, or today in liberationist or fundamentalist communities alike—it almost unilaterally grounds the understanding of that divinely pure or sanctified life as something that takes place only by a life lived in community. Almost always, Christian or not, the American utopia vanquishes the nuclear family, the blood tie, the marriage, often sex, so that we are only, all of us, strangers and pilgrims together on the same path.

But it is also often the case that when we are talking about American utopian communities—when we look at a shelf in the library dedicated to the topic, for instance—we're framing it as a historically specific phenomenon, something that happened in the nineteenth century, largely in Western New York and its outlying colonies, that took the form of several particular movements, many of which passed through this particular piece of property—Alasa Farms—at one point or another. And it is also often the case that, under that rubric, we're talking almost exclusively about white Protestants, or people who have at least gone rogue from a European Protestant theology. And it seems to me that the life those communities created, which we call American utopias, was more or less a paltry mimesis—consciously or not—of the kind of life that North American Indigenous people had been living on that land for centuries and were, at that time in the mid-1800s, defending with their blood and bodies.

For this reason, perhaps, these European-descendant American utopian communities are inherently tragic not only because they are always, every single time, doomed to failure—and often quick failure, sometimes disastrous failure. They are tragic because they rarely consider at whose expense they exist, or what kinds of privileges they've been afforded to position themselves as makers of a "perfect" place. Do the makers of these communities forget, and always imagine that this time, unlike the others, they'll last forever? Or are they like me, a little romantically obsessed by the will to create an ideally communal life that I know will ultimately perish, that is only here for a second, that will ultimately be proved in time to have been the totally wrong thing, and yet which I must strive after anyway?

Despite all my certainty of folly, I am also sincerely seeking models, skimming communities—both historical and contemporary—for what might be useful or replicable in my own life, or in the lives of my friends, or (however crazy this sounds) more generally for my country people in all of their variety. What are the constant forms, the possible architectures, of developing a happy or ethical life under late-stage capitalism? What do you have to give up, or reduce, or invent? What does a shared ideology provide, and what does it threaten when it becomes the bedrock upon which the project exists? Could the basis of a utopian community be purely material then—co-housing, school, organization, residency? Or just a shared car and washing machine? And what about the horror of people not cleaning up after themselves? It is a question that had been pressing at my friends and me since our early twenties, but had become painfully urgent as the rapid piling-on of adulthood had taken place, and as Sweeney and I became young caretakers of his still-young father in one of the most expensive cities in the world. Now past the two-year mark of caring for Dan, it had become extremely clear that, since I do not come from a multigenerational household, nor belong to a dense city block or other organic forms of interdependence, my and Sweeney's lives will otherwise be (and already are) shaped by all the forces in the United States that, if left to work uncontested, will ebb toward isolation.

But if I think about it for more than one minute, it's not clear that I'd ever be a very good communard. I especially balk at all of my dreams of utopia because I am actually not a very attentive family member. I rarely make it back to the West Coast. I take forever to return my friends' phone calls. I google my book all the time to see what people are saying (not much). I let my mother-in-law and sister-in-law do all the cooking on Thanksgiving. I can be extremely lazy, not leaving the house for days—just writing, eating, reading, watching TV. I have been in a more or less monogamous relationship since I was nineteen years old, which became my life's primary infrastructure—and while I think, at least, I've been a pretty decent partner for a decade, I am beginning to feel despair about the whole thing at a moment when Sweeney needs me most—though he claims to need me for nothing. How do you learn to be the kind of person who could make a communal arrangement, much more complex than a marriage or a family, work?

I mean, sometimes it does work out. The Model Farm business operated by the Strong grandson lasted for a while and helped, in some small way, the United States recoup a bit of profit and morale. And the fact that the property eventually, a generation later and from a totally different group of people, became a resting place for abused animals, having been seeded by money a century before from the profits of buggy whip manufacturing, paints a picture about the arc of time that is kind of hopeful.

At Cracker Box Palace, there were horses everywhere clopping along snowy paddocks, cattle, ponies, donkeys, goats, a "bunny emporium," a giant hen-house, all kinds of creatures, tottering around in large open pens through the snow, or which had retreated into their sheds or barns. During our visit, we ran into a couple of other volunteers, locals who come to Cracker Box Palace of their own volition on weekends or free weekdays to feed and groom the animals, hang out with them, empty the slop, in a symbiotic therapeutic act.

A fluffy gray-and-white farm cat approached us as we skirted the horse stalls, meowing, trouncing through the snow, following us, even into the cold, deep drifts around the Shetland ponies. Then the cat started to lead us around: out to the disturbed horses, the one with the crooked back, the crusty mules. The cat had little puff-pant legs, stopping in front of each of the pens as we arrived, confidently leading us forward, look-ing back sometimes to make sure we were still there. The mules hee-hawed desperately, hoarsely, expecting snacks, their coats grown wildly into their eyes.

We passed by the bachelor farmhand housing, the "bunk house," left from the 1930s Model Farm era.

We passed by the old Shaker barn which has been turned into a mu-seum, shut for the winter, built in the 1820s.

We passed by the little welcome office, a small manufactured hut, which was shut for the weekend. Next to the office was an illustrated sign, also buried in the snow, covered in line drawings of animal portraits—Cracker Box Palace: Farm Animal Haven.

Cracker Box Palace is a refuge and rehabilitation center for neglected or abused farm animals. Animals brought to the Palace are cared for by veterinarians, immunized, put on prescribed feed programs, and provided physical therapy. Rehabilitated animals are trained and available for adoption. Animals unable to be adopted are welcome to live out their natural lives on the farm.

The sign boldly proclaims that the farm fields "will remain undeveloped forever, protected by a conservation easement held by the Genesee Land Trust."

That one gives me pause.

Forever! What a claim, considering the folks who started here—the Seneca, of course, and then the Shakers, the Fourierists, the farm of tomorrow, etc., etc., etc.!

I am very interested in human grappling with notions of forever, human hopes of forever. The folly of it gives me a sort of pleasure and a sort of peace.

I suppose that is why I'm interested in layered histories on particular pieces of land, too, the way they defy notions of "forever" as far we understand—sites where various stories play out in spacetime, unbeknown to each other. Places where the historical layers are especially rhythmic or rhyming, in conversation or creative dynamic with each other, creating a gravitational pull, like ghosts who cannot see even each other, and yet affect each other's energy fields nonetheless. Because why? Because I think the patterns of use in a particular place can tell us something about the place, if we listen closely—and can tell us something about what was being carried out there, and even what's to come.

Maybe there's a sort of story of long-game reciprocity in the end (I think of all that buggy whip money being eventually converted into an endowment for these horses' retirements), or some other kind of circle of meaning, the justice arc of which is long.

But the story is not always cheerful. The stories can twist, turn back on themselves, or reveal endings that are less morally triumphant than they first appeared. Because here's another: when the Shakers left Sodus Bay, they moved up the road to Groveland and reestablished their community for another decade or so. Later, they sold that property to the state under the conditions that the property would be used for "good purposes." First it became a treatment center for epileptics, then later the land was sold to the prison system. Today, the old Shaker farm is now the Groveland Correctional Facility, medium security. The prison chapel is the original Shaker chapel, thus nightmarishly bringing together two of our country's most notorious innovations—utopian thought and the dystopian prison industrial complex.

What does it say about our country that the Shaker movement could be enfolded into the project of mass incarceration at the very moment when our prison system has become not only the largest in the world in terms of population, but the largest in the world per capita? To me, it suggests that the utopian is never far from its opposite, that our greatest strength is also our greatest weakness, that power will always accumulate in the same ways and marshal the same violence, and that growth, in this culture, works only in one direction. Ephemerality is a virtue. All movements that are truly pure of heart will die quickly and return to the compost heap, and show up later in the soil of society in some other form. The most successful communities will not even leave a trace, and you will never hear of them nor read about them in books, and you will walk on the land where "something good tried to happen once" and you will not know that anything happened there at all.

utopianotes
North American Phalanx

Lina and I go to Asbury Park, New Jersey—she's been dreaming of going for a while, longing for some Art Deco oceanfront escapism. I myself have very recently rewatched Kevin Smith's 1999 theological masterwork *Dogma* and newly realized that it was indeed the Asbury Park arcade, not Atlantic City, where God liked to go for earthly "constitutionals," to play Skee-Ball in human form. It is deep, hot summer. We plunge in the cold, choppy waters and then lie in the sun on that classic Jersey spit of beach.

On our drive back toward the city, I ask if we can "stop at a site" in Colts Neck. I try to explain the site's significance, but the context is only interesting in my head: At a stretch of ten whole years, from 1844 to 1854, the North American Phalanx was the single longest of thirty attempts to build a Fourierist phalanx in the United States. The other phalanxes lasted for a year at most, and some only a couple of months.

Lina and I drive for a long time around the swampy rural marshland thickets, past old farmhouses and huge bright orange-and-pink McMansions with lion statues and half-moon driveways. Finally, out on the little county thoroughfare named Phalanx Road, as we are heading toward the parkway, we spot it nearly engulfed in the trees and with no pull-out, no way to safely sidle up and squint and say, "Honey, what *is* a 'phalanx'?" Lost in the grass is one of those little standard-issue blue-and-yellow New York State historical markers:

North American Phalanx. Site of the 1844 cooperative agricultural community; founded by Albert Brisbane and modeled after the philosophy of French Socialist Charles Fourier. This communal experiment was a success until it was destroyed by a fire in 1854.

Behind the sign the land dips toward a thin brook that feeds this tiny, scrubby strip of woods—itself somehow undisturbed by the particleboard planned community it buffers from the sound of the road.

FELLOW TRAVELERS ON THE ROAD TO NOWHERE

For as many generations as there have been utopian communities in the United States, there has also been a long and parallel history of utopian groupies—the people who so deeply desire to drop out and make the world anew, but who lack the specific convictions or staying power that might allow them to cleave to one community or another. The groupies are messier and more disorganized in their longings than the decisive utopians, who themselves have finished worrying or wondering and are already committed to their daily labors in bringing about paradise. The groupies, on the other hand, are unclear about what they firmly believe, if not entirely lacking a comprehensive ethical system themselves. But their hopes are just as, if not more, utopian than the communities to whom they attach their curiosity, even if they—the groupies—are hard-pressed to commit to a program. Hope is their vocation. Their hoping, however shifting and sketchy, is endless.

They possess that defining feature of all proper groupies of any variety, an uncritical, ruthlessly naïve devotion, and it is from that depth at which this kind of endless hope can be felt at all. Like a crush, nourished in the shadows of your heart, the devotion does not necessarily seek completion or results. Utopian groupies are lovers of hope. It's ideally an unselfish love, an erotic exchange that happens only to ensure that the utopian project continues to grow and flourish and inspire other people through this act of creative love. For utopian groupies, it's not about eventually starting a community themselves, or even joining one, but about being a kind of accompaniment to what is already happening, which they did not start and which does not require their intervention. It's an exchange that results in books, magazines, movies, many road trips. Utopian groupies, like music groupies, are often road-bound, eventually road-weary. They are tied to no single place. They float from community to community, either in real life or as subjects of historical inquiry. They travel as a way to get by, as a coping mechanism, as a way to learn how other people are doing it or have done it, how others have created modes of collectivity, how others have fashioned a life outside of capitalism or have simply figured out creative ways to keep the overhead low together. They travel in order to figure out what they believe and how to live. I suppose I have joined these ranks.

Dreaming of some distant moment when I would no longer be a caretaker for my father-in-law, nor an itinerant adjunct, nor always longing for an elusive home, I'd started reading from a stack of books by some of these utopian groupies, about which I took lots of notes in no particular direction.

Paradise Now by Chris Jennings
In Utopia by J. C. Hallman
Cruising Utopia by José Esteban Muñoz
How We Get Free by the Combahee River Collective
Searching for Zion by Emily Raboteau
Utopia by Bernadette Mayer
The Hawthorn Archive: Letters from the Utopian Margins by Avery
    Gordon
The Cloister Walk by Kathleen Norris
The Modern Utopian, edited by Richard Fairfield
Utopia Drive by Erik Reece

Utopia owes a lot to its groupies, but what personal future was there in groupie-dom? Does being a groupie augur a kind of dreaming that eventually transmutes into something more, something of your own? The hopes for my own future lived largely in my mind, a kind of mainframe processing endless different calculations while I drove home from work on dark parkways piping New York City in my car, recently given to us by Sweeney's grandmother before she'd passed way, thus replacing my 2 train commute. Every new idea could hold for about two or three mental moves, and then I'd hit a wall: Where would we work? Who else would be there? Where would Dan live? Where was the money? I could fantasize, get drunk, sit out late with an old friend on a porch and describe new ideas, sometimes get flurries of excitement that would hold over the course of an evening before petering out by morning.

I did other kinds of dreaming, though, in my sleep. For as long as I could remember, my dreams had often been set in big communal environments, populated by no fewer than a dozen or more familiar faces, as central characters to the story and action of the dream; friends and family members, somewhere on an ambiguous compound, a summer camp or a vaguely post-apocalyptic battle camp, a school building or hotel, some kind of large festive event like a wedding, a party, an abbey or a castle fortress with many different buildings and corridors, houses I had lived in blown up to fantastical size. My dreams, during this time, continued in this vein and started to host visitations from my three recently departed grandmothers.

I dreamt of each grandmother, one month after their respective deaths: in the dreams, they were *almost* dead, but not quite, and always each of them in a different living room of a different house, while other people rushed around busied with various tasks. I'd round the corner and then—"Oh my God, I thought you were dead!" No, they'd say, no, no. Almost laughing. Their eyes had sunken and purpled, like Fred Gwynne in *Pet Sematary*. They had messages: a confession for my mother to be transmitted via landline; a worry about my husband's health; a dirty joke they'd wanted to tell me for years.

Before my first grandmother died, she sent Sweeney a letter. In it, she consoled him about his father who was in a coma at the time.

Six months later she died.

After her funeral, Sweeney's grandmother sent *me* a letter. In it, she consoled me about my other grandmother who had just died.

One month later *she* died.

The third grandmother—my father-in-law's mother—died without speaking or writing. She knew she was worried about Dan, but she couldn't remember why.

Then, as I've said before, when Dan woke up from his coma, he could not speak or walk.

By all accounts he is still a young man. I walk him in his wheelchair down by the Bronx River. He points to his forehead in agony when he cannot begin or finish a sentence. A clause. A compound word. "Medical," he says. "Scummy," he says. "I'm fucked," he says. He points to his forehead to indicate a physical blockage, a dam. The words are there, but no ladder, and the words beat against the dam until they go limp and die.

Before this, he was a defense lawyer, a storyteller, red-faced and laughing in the middle of a group of people. He told stories about the time when he beat the shit out of his ex-wife's lover! The time he bicycled through the vampire town in Nevada! The time he caught a shark in Brazil! The time, during the great flood of 1972, he and his friends sailed down the Bronx River on an innertube! He told stories, and the room reorganized itself around him.

He'd often tell me, when I first met him, "I used to be a Republican, but now I'm an anarchist," and he'd laugh, enjoying the shocking sound of it. His identity at that time was changing, though, as a newly divorced man. Money, security, and work had always been a huge source of stress and anxiety in his life, and he was beginning to toy with the idea of letting some of that go, not unlike the gray beard he had shaved off, revealing his very youthful face. Around this time, he began talking about this fantasy, quietly, of moving into a small rural trailer park community and living out his retirement there, dramatically different from the vision of retirement formed under the dual pressures of white Westchester upward mobility and doing right by his peasant Irish grandparents who'd gotten all the way here.

I often dream of him at night, rising from his wheelchair. Or tottering up a staircase. Or moving along a half-moon kitchen counter like a rookie at an ice-skating rink.

In the dreams, I feel joy, though not surprise. Because in the dreams I knew he could do it all along, that it had only been a matter of him just standing up. In this soft dream light he looks at me, across the room. He opens his mouth. I hear it before it happens. Speech bubbles out of him in slow, clear streams.

I don't know what he imagines, or dreams, is coming next now. In order to imagine a new world, you have to be kind of primed for it. You have to be dreaming of it already, so that you can recognize what you're looking at when it comes. That's where the groupie and the utopian distinction perhaps falls apart. One must, it seems, be a groupie first. One must be a lover of hope, a dreamer, a fool.

•

Erik Reece, author of *Utopia Drive*, is a twenty-first-century groupie who goes on a road trip that spans Kentucky, Ohio, Indiana, Virginia, New York, visiting the sites of various utopian communities, mostly those that are dead and gone, like a Shaker colony museum in Ohio and New Harmony, Indiana, where the followers of Robert Owen and the Harmonists once, respectively, set up shop. He does visit some living communities, too, none of which would consider their history nor their present "utopian" (a pejorative in this case), like Gethsemani Monastery where Thomas Merton lived and the Twin Oaks intentional community in central Virginia, which has been in continuous existence since 1967—but I suppose that is why a groupie's perspective is useful, in this case: they can call a community "utopian" and mean it as term of distinction rather than folly. Near the beginning of his book, Reece refers frequently to the writings of a man named A. J. Macdonald, himself a nineteenth-century chronicler of American utopias who has left us with one of the most robust nonprofessional records of utopian life of the period. Reece identifies with Macdonald, and through Reece's identification, so I begin to, and now I think of A. J. Macdonald all the time.

Off and on for thirteen years, from about 1841 to his untimely death during a cholera epidemic in Albany in 1854, A. J. Macdonald traveled from community to community, documenting what he found, and occasionally staying for a while to assist in the communities' visions. He was a Scotsman, an immigrant, who over those years amassed 747 pages of materials including notes, essays, sketches, watercolor paintings, and wood engravings—all concerning the communities he stayed with, and the members of the communities at hand.

Try to imagine Macdonald with me. A white European in antebellum United States full of ordinary yearnings: He wanted more fulfilling work, a happier life, a more communal national politics. He traveled around his new countryside talking to people, visiting their utopian encampments: Shakers, Fourierists, Owenites, Inspirationists, Perfectionists, anarchists, socialists, all of them abolitionists. There he is now, riding the train or a horse-drawn carriage or walking on foot over newly established state territory borders.

What did he hope to find? I'm genuinely moved by Macdonald, this man, his hopes as fragile as lace, who really tried to chronicle what he saw going on in American community-building in the middle of the nineteenth century, before the Civil War. Was he aware of how tenuous and brief all these projects would ultimately be? Is it arrogant of me to think that his perspective is somehow more foolhardy than my own? Was he an activist outside of his travels, engaged in the struggle for Black freedom? He never joined any community as a member, nor did he seem interested in joining. Rather, to take him at his own word in his never-published introductory essay to his sprawling manuscript, Macdonald traveled and collected these materials "because I thought I was doing good" and ultimately hoped to "increase the charity" of his readers toward the idea of utopia-making in general once they understood, through his writings, that "it was for Humanity, in nearly all instances, that these things were done."

He spent his first eighteen months in the States, from 1841 to 1842, at New Harmony, Indiana, among what was the waning Owenite community, founded by proto-socialist and company town dreamer Robert Owen, a Great Britain immigrant himself. A generation earlier, Owen was a Welsh-born child labor activist who founded a revolutionary worker-owned cotton factory in Scotland called New Lanark, where his employees were supplied room, board, nurseries and schools for their children, and guaranteed an eight-hour workday (though he aspired to a three-hour one—never managed that). Somewhere in the hang of industrialism and humanism, Owen saw the possibility of a world governed by a perfect rationalism: if all the working humans are fed, watered, and educated equally, and not torn asunder by private property, religion, or sex, we could live in paradise. This vision of "progressive paternalism" has its immediately obvious limits (like who's doing the watering, the feeding, the regulating, etc., Robert, hm?), but such realizations were not available to the benevolent boy-king Owen. He became so certain of the merits of his social engineering project that he then spent a decade trying to convince British Parliament to adopt his system on a broader scale, during which he let his revolutionary New Lanark community, as well as his own growing family, flounder. When his attempt at broader national support failed, he decided that any expansion of his project would be up to him alone. Magically, around that time, a London-based real estate agent apprised him of a tract for sale in America: a ready-made utopian colony that the aging German mystic Father Rapp of the Harmony Society was trying to get off his hands in frontier Indiana, replete with a fully operational communal infrastructure: granary, distillery, wharf, houses. So Owen bought the land, and there he went in 1824. And fifteen years later A. J. Macdonald, that good-hearted utopian groupie, rolled into what had become Owen's second failed socialist utopian project. He stayed in Indiana for over a year, but by then Owen had all but left to pursue yet another expansion, and New Harmony was falling apart. So eventually, Macdonald left, too.

After that, Macdonald spent time at the Shaker colony Watervliet near Albany, helped found the Fourierist Clermont Phalanx in Cincinnati, stopped in at the Prairie Home Community (for Universal Thought and Inquiry) in Ohio, the South Union Shaker Village in Kentucky, the fully cooperative city Modern Times out on the Long Island isthmus, the Raritan Bay Community, the North American Phalanx, and many others. He'd catch these communities typically, it seems, near or at their ends, but that's mostly because these communities had shelf lives under five years (and sometimes as brief as five months). So Macdonald would do what he could to help out, scramble to record their existence, by pen or by wood engraving, and then he would move on to the next.

The scholarly notes appended to Macdonald's archive at Yale indicate that some of the writings "were extracted from his 'Travels in search of employment,' a manuscript not present in the collection, and one whose title suggests that his emigration from Great Britain may have been driven by economics, with his research on utopians a valuable but ancillary project." I love this detail. There's something bumbly and incidental, then, about his quest. He was perhaps fleeing the fallout of the Panic of 1837—a massive global recession—and drawn into this examination of utopias unconsciously. It reminds me of a much more famous utopian groupie, the author Nathaniel Hawthorne, who joined the Transcendentalist Brook Farm (inspired by Fourierism) in Western Massachusetts for a year, among other hopeful, anemic artists and their fledgling apple trees, in order to save up enough cash to propose to his girlfriend. Once Hawthorne had enough money, he promptly left Brook Farm's collectivist fold, though he did, of course, later write *The Blithedale Romance*, a bestseller based on his experiences there. For Macdonald, it was different. What began as something defined chiefly by practical need, where the research acted as a vessel for him to figure something out about how to live and make a livelihood, eventually became *the life*.

Macdonald's susceptibility to this quest reminds me that being a utopian groupie—being a utopian, really, of any degree—is also, always, sort of about looking for home: reaching back for a home dimly remembered, a home dreamed of in the future, a home you are hoping to construct in the present, but which you also accept may be an exercise in perpetual wandering. Nonetheless, it is a home where you and everyone else will finally be free.

The definitions of freedom vary, of course, depending on belief or background, but in the mid-nineteenth century and now, utopian freedom followed a few constant themes: freedom of bondage, of capitalism, of private ownership, of waged labor; freedom from government, from patriarchal marriage, and from the nuclear family unit. Freedom from sex or freedom to have as much sex as you want. Freedom from God or freedom *with* God.

I mean freedom here, though, more along the lines of how Annie Dillard describes freedom in regard to the act of writing, which she calls "life at its most free." But there's a caveat: "Your freedom as a writer is not freedom of expression in the sense of wild blurting; you may not let rip. It is life at its most free, if you are fortunate enough to be able to try it, because you select your materials, invent your task, and pace yourself . . . The obverse of this freedom, of course, is that your work is so meaningless, so fully for yourself alone, and so worthless to the world, that no one except you cares whether you do it well, or ever." Alternatively, I might mean freedom here more along the lines that D. H. Lawrence intones in his weird mystic essay "Spirit of Place": "Men are free when they are obeying some deep inward voice of religious belief . . . Not when they are escaping to some wild west. The most unfree souls go west and shout of freedom . . . The shout is a rattling of chains, always was." Reflecting on the work of poet Gwendolyn Brooks, critic Hanif Abdurraqib writes that she was "writing of [Black Chicagoans'] triumphs and failures, and understanding that whole and complete life sat at the intersection of both. And perhaps that is freedom, more than anything." Or maybe I mean freedom in the way Audre Lorde means "the erotic," which she describes as "a measure between the beginnings of our sense of self and the chaos of our strongest feelings. It"—again, the erotic, or what I'm substituting as freedom—"is an internal sense of satisfaction to which, once we have experienced it, we know we can aspire. For having experienced the fullness of this depth of feeling and recognizing its power, in honor and self-respect we can require no less of ourselves."

It does sometimes feel outrageous for me, a white American woman, to use the word "freedom" so blithely, or to work after a definition, when it is Black Americans who taught this country, this stupid country, everything it will ever know about freedom.

But freedom is also something that my white Irish in-laws talked about a lot, connected as they felt to the Irish liberation movement their ancestors fought in, the pride they felt as the descendants of Irish peasants, but who had now been upwardly mobile white people in the suburbs of New York City for three generations. I found this attachment to rebel-hood by white people suspect, and yet I'd sing along enthusiastically to "Grace" and "Danny Boy" with Dan on his back porch in the little cabin he was renting on Lake Waccabuc the year before his strokes. I loved those songs. But I felt ambivalent about the whole thing, about white ethnic people rooting themselves in a resistance tradition they had never added to, until years later I went to an old Irish bar in Riverdale, a neighborhood in the upper northwest corner of the Bronx. The bar was called An Beal Bocht. Sweeney had heard there was a woman "with a voice of an angel" who sang there every Friday at six o'clock. I pictured her young and blond and lithe. But blessedly, when we walked into the dim bar-side of the room, wheeling Dan in with us accompanied by his favorite aide, there she was, the singer: sixty-something years old and queer as the day she was born, with close-cropped gray hair, a navy blue t-shirt, jeans, and an Irish brogue. We ordered beers and listened to her sing. Dan requested that she play "Grace," and she did, which she accompanied with the story of her visit to Joseph Plunkett's gravesite. Then she sang such a beautiful, full-throated version of it. And later as she sang the "Ballad of Joe McDonnell," a song about the Irish prison hunger strikers in the 1980s, I was frozen:

And you dare to call me a terrorist
While you look down your gun
When I think of all the deeds that you have done,
You have plundered many nations
Divided many lands
You have terrorized their people
You ruled with an iron hand.
And you brought this reign of terror to my land.

She could have been singing a liberation song for any colonized country, for queer liberation, for Black liberation. The way the melody works is beautiful, it lilts up and down, it does not terminate, it keeps flowing over the mountains, and the rivers, never stops. And that, too, is a real claim to freedom-seeking.

Around the time A. J. Macdonald departed from his eighteen-month stay at New Harmony, in 1842, New Harmony, as I mentioned, was already falling apart. Robert Owen's vision relied too much on his own kingship (which he did not see as kingship), and did not effectively develop leadership or sustainable community-making within his socialist cooperative, and this lack of planning had drawn a mish-mash of people who also lacked a unified vision or sense of purpose, or who had conflicting visions about what cooperative living required. In fact, Owen's vision for New Harmony had begun to disintegrate long before Macdonald arrived for his stay, as early as 1827, just three years after Owen's arrival in Indiana. As Owen began to bloat once again with the beauty of his vision, as he had bloated from New Lanark's glory, he abandoned his American encampment (just as he'd abandoned New Lanark) to travel around his new continent appealing to his new government's participation in his perfect mode of governance, if only they would listen, if only they would just come and see! While Owen did that,

A. J. Macdonald hung around with the last of the residents, talking to those who remained and noting their discontent, and their plans for what was next.

A. J. Macdonald is like Forrest Gump, always on the heels of important historical moments, his presence in them forgotten by time, a mere shade in the background. The only reason we know of Macdonald, that fellow traveler, probably the only way he's been preserved, is because of John Humphrey Noyes, the charismatic godfather of the Oneida Community in upstate New York. Macdonald had met Noyes while visiting the Oneida Community—a group of Perfectionists who lived in a sprawling Federal-style mansion not far from Schenectady. The Perfectionist theology posed a direct challenge to the reigning Calvinism of the time by positing that in fact we exist not in a state of total depravity about which we can do nothing (only by God's grace), but in a state of total perfection (because of God) to respond to accordingly by living the good life. The Oneida Community practiced a kind of luxurious communal living, constant prayer, cooperative child-raising, weekly exhaustive "mutual criticism" sessions, equality of the sexes, and a form of free love called complex-marriage, where any adult community member could have sex with any other consenting adult, and which, among other things, privileged the female orgasm in a practice they termed "male continence." They also manufactured silverware.

In any event, after vulnerable, choleric Macdonald's untimely death in Albany, Noyes—still the leader of Oneida at the time—caught wind of his fate and quickly sought the rights to Macdonald's papers upon finding out that Macdonald's brother didn't want to hang onto his stuff any longer. Noyes then went on to adapt much of Macdonald's research and writings into his own contemporary history of utopian movements that he published in 1870, under his own name, called *The History of American Socialisms*, a big boastful work that positions Oneida as a unique and divine success. (That Noyes sounds like a real piece of work.) After getting whatever use he wanted out of them, Noyes eventually donated Macdonald's papers to Yale (a place where Noyes himself had sought a divinity degree in his youth), and the contents of those papers at Yale—those notes, essays, sketches, watercolors, wood engravings—filter into almost every book I have ever read, so far, on American utopianism, as well as smaller forums.

For instance, A. J. Macdonald came to my attention the other day on contemporary photographer Katherine Cunningham's website, which is showcasing her recent series, "Utopia Remains." The series documents the former sites of long-lost utopian communities all over Ohio: empty fields, dilapidated barns, a 1990s public school building erected where a Shaker house once stood, etc. Paired with each photograph is a little historical narrative entry, each one including a section titled "Reason for Demise." A. J. Macdonald's work is cited in "Reason for Demise" in the entries for the abolitionist Prairie Home, Highland Home, and Fruit Hills communities, as well as the Clermont Phalanx. About her own work, and why it is she decided to spend all this time capturing the utopian history of her home region of the Rust Belt, Cunningham says, "I want these places to be recorded, if only to say that at this place, at one time, desire became action, and alternatives were exercised."

The passive voice here is curious. *Alternatives were exercised.* By whom? By the spirit of place? By the pulsing utopian heart which belongs to no single man? And then there's the flat past tense: *were exercised.* Implying that the exercise was finite, finished, and ultimately walked away from. Alternatives were exercised and then things just came to an end—like Macdonald, who died poor, sick, and alone, far from the hearth of community. But A. J. Macdonald is a true utopian groupie *because* he is a failure. His "failure" to resolve one alternative or another produced a yield we rely on now, a body of knowledge that has no final destination. What sometimes looks like throwing in the towel at the time is actually a sowing of the seeds, though he may not know it. A utopian groupie must live a life that generally yields no admiration in their own time because their interests were considered too weird or unproductive. I suppose the same is true for utopian builders. A true utopian shuts his mouth and goes about eking out this experiment with others. If you have too much say over your utopian ideals in your own lifetime, you usually end up like the megalomaniac Noyes, hiding out for the rest of his life in Canada from statutory rape charges.

New Harmony, as I mentioned, was the first place A. J. Macdonald ended up, and just a decade before he arrived, the utopian inhabitants had been quite different: five hundred of George Rapp's followers, the Harmonists of the Harmony Society, came to North America from Germany and signed legally binding agreements: each member would hand over all their possessions and assets and hold everything in common such that no one required individual payment for their contributions; in exchange for that, everyone's basic needs would be met; everyone would honor elected community leaders and generally commit to working in pursuit of the good of the whole society; and finally, folks who might want to leave were free to do so, and would be returned their assets, though if they had come penniless they would receive, as writer Amanda Kolson Hurley phrased it for modern readers in *Radical Suburbs*, a "cash donation on departure." There's something quite rational about this arrangement, where I'm generally prone to think of the Harmonists as wackadoos, waiting and preparing themselves for the Christian millennium, which they were. The celibacy for which they are so famous came from their theology which is that Jesus was a "dual being, male and female at once," the state which all were to prepare themselves for in the second coming. Sexual interaction thus created or reinforced that perceived separation of male and female—so men and women in this society were equals: all did the same work, for the same due; all voted on community matters.

The writer Marguerite Young first finds her inner "utopian groupie" through a lively interest she takes in the Harmonists' history, while she herself was living in New Harmony, Indiana, in 1936—though it is just an ordinary midwestern river town by then. Young, an Indianapolis native who's been living in New York City the last few years, rolls into New Harmony, where her semi-estranged mother and stepfather, floundering vaudeville actors turned small-town theater owners, are currently living a gentle Hoosier life. Young and her sister had been seemingly abandoned by their parents as children, and had been raised by their maternal grandmother, also named Marguerite. Young is thirty-two at the time of her arrival in New Harmony, having completed a dual degree in French and English and a master's in Elizabethan and Jacobean literature. In a 1972 Clocktower Radio interview with Charles Ruas, Young says her parents called to say, "You'll love this new town! It's the scene of two lost utopias, and it has in it the footprints of the angel Gabriel, and it has cruciform shapes on the doors, and a maze, and all these other beautiful objects."

Upon arrival in New Harmony, she's drawn deeply into the history of the area after she starts wandering around the town each morning, aimlessly, on foot. She eventually encounters an encampment of Depression-dispossessed Ozark refugees, coal miners, gathered at the edge of a ragged parcel of state land. Not far from their camp, Young finds a WPA park keeper, who tells her about a once-great communal socialist project founded by Robert Owen that took place in that very spot and, before Owen, Father Rapp's Harmony Society, which left behind the footprints of an angel cast in stone.

In the interview with Ruas, Young says that "the WPA worker was chiseling in the footprints of the angel—*just restoring them*—at I think fifty cents an hour, and I used to talk to him, and he would say, 'Well, I have to buy the baby shoes,' he used to say as he would explain to me the beautiful business of chipping in the angel's footprints." The Rappites believed the angel gave them the keys to paradise, which would come if they stuck around long enough.

As she wanders by foot through the sidewalks and alleys of New Harmony in 1936, Young remarks on its landscape, saying that gradually "the present faded, became of a texture with the past, as if today were only the conglomerate of all our yesterdays. Every item implied, however, desolation, since nothing lingers so like the memory of failure, especially if it has sought the extreme perfection." She, in this case, has both the Harmony Society and the Owenites in mind. An epic begins to take shape in Young's imagination. She makes plans to stay in New Harmony longer and starts writing and researching *Angel in the Forest*, a nearly four-hundred-page book that would become perhaps one of the most idiosyncratic chronicles of utopia ever written, part novel, part history, part autobiography, part dream, part farce. She grasps from the get-go how endemic failure is to the utopian attempt, but how utterly inaccessible and disturbing that fact is to the utopians in the moment of their failure—and it is from within that tragic tension that she develops the comic perspective of her book.

In a tangle of short chapters, *Angel in the Forest* chronicles those two local utopias that "sought the extreme perfection." When Father Rapp brought his flock there in 1814, he called it Harmony. When Robert Owen arrived in 1824, he called it (wild!) New Harmony, and many important innovations happened during their respective tenures. In Young's estimation, included in the two utopias' collective output were "the burning of Rome, city planning, explosion of stars, a new calendar, anarchy, a New Jerusalem, repression, expansion, moneyless Eden, exaltation of pearls, a three-hour working day, exaltation of horses, infinite regress, the united nations of earth, the many, the few, Lucifer, lotus-eaters, the falling of autumn leaves, the myths of Narcissus, good dentistry, many fictions."

What I think she means here is that the output was various and hard to track—even hard to track whose idea was whose. It's true—a lot of modern urban planning concepts came from Owenite colonies, particularly things like "garden cities," and Owen's particular socialist philosophies helped form the politics of the British labor movement. Rapp thought he and his followers were building a New Jerusalem, the city at the end of the world, the city that would be knit back together again when Christ came. Owen created the model for the worker-owned American business, the co-op apartment, the labor-note system in use in the nineteenth-century Long Island town of Modern Times, but also used today in places like Massachusetts's Berkshires region where residents have put the "Berkshare" in use. There were, in both communities, expressions of retrenchment and liberation, control and free love. All moneyless, each thought himself an Eden.

Father Rapp's Harmonists were a Millenarian Christian movement that had emigrated from Germany at the turn of the nineteenth century. They were celibate and lived communally in shared brick dwellings segregated by gender. Spousal ties were renounced. Everyone lived as brother and sister as they awaited the Second Coming of Christ, who was to appear, any day now, and burn the whole thing down in order to start the earth anew, with the Harmonists and a few others who believed, and lead a one-thousand-year reign leading up to the final (final!) judgment.

From time to time, the Harmonists collaborated with nearby Shaker communities, who shared most of the Harmonists' foundational beliefs and practices. They'd loan each other members when projects needed additional labor in exchange for English language lessons. The Harmonists carried out their collective labor dutifully, producing, chiefly, textiles, wheat, and whis-key, and developed robust trade networks down the Mississippi River that ended up making them quite wealthy. They worked and worked (Young again), "as if God co-operated in building a world which, in short order, God intended to destroy. Not that they strained after paradoxes necessarily, but that these were inherent in their human situation."

She pokes fun where any human might deserve it, for their pride or straight-up goofiness, but she's never disparaging of her subjects' sincere beliefs. Though she is not value-neutral in her assessment, either: she, for instance, recognizes something more enduring in the theology of Mother Ann's Shakers: "Ann built several cities, merely by shaking like a poplar tree whose leaves are silvered in the wind. When she shook, her followers shook—all ceasing to consider the where, and why, and whither, and what of things. Among celibate communities, Ann's seems the least frost-bitten, the freest from secondary aims, the most truly enthusiastic, as if no reason at all was necessary—God shaking, Ann shaking, everybody shaking. By comparison, Father Rapp's project fails both in grandeur and mysticism, becomes the acme of prudence."

Things evolved. While the Harmonists may have believed that an angel of God had touched down there in the 1810s and left a mark with its foot on the very spot the Harmonists should live until the end times came, the end times didn't come. As we know, in hopes to export his model else-where, Owen eventually bought from the Harmonists their fully functional existing utopian compound after they decided to downsize (numbers were fast shrinking). Many of the Harmonists had died, or had already left their community, and at least one former member had started his own separate religious movement, and the rest joined the Shakers or were radicalized into polygamy (and other things) by the Mormons cropping up in the region around them (New York, Pennsylvania, Ohio, in particular).

But, as Young knows, the world did not end when they thought it would, and the Harmonists moved on to a different settlement, and Owen followed with his project soon after.

Young calls Robert Owen "the world's greatest spokesman of Uto-pia," and she means it, even winking. She actually has a lot of respect for

Owen-the-young-man, which is significant for a figure often framed the fool. She tells his early life story rather sympathetically, particularly the various stages of his radicalization. While Owen in his late teens and early twenties was working middle management in English textiles, passing as upper middle class or merchant class, wearing his hand-me-down wig, he would, Young speculates, watch "each day a bargeful of boys and girls pass up the Thames, and what was their picnic? They were going to certain death in a cotton town. They would be themselves the crumbs thrown out to fatty birds. Meanwhile many withered citizens, one foot already in the grave, argued on the body of Jesus Christ made bread." Exploitation sickened him. Sectarianism sickened him. The Man sickened him. (Did he ever wonder, did he ever worry, if he was The Man?)

What is the role of self-loathing in utopia making? An ill which you are responsible for in some direct or distant way is the very thing you are trying to resolve—and in the process of resolving it you end up reinforcing all of the same things, the same sorts of power relationships. That is largely Owen's story. Perhaps it is also part of mine.

Leaving is always a crucial part of the utopian story. Owen's New Harmony saw defection within just the first year, where groups of people left to start communities in other parts of the Midwest based on his principles: cooperatively owned labor and homes, communal dwellings and domestic duties, egalitarianism. For instance, in 1825, about one hundred Owenites moved to central Ohio, to a verdant and fertile area around the Wabash River where there was a famous healing spring, and they started the colony of Yellow Springs. That, too, remained Owenite-inspired for exactly one year before they disinvested and incorporated as a regular small town, with a railroad stop. It also became the site of one of the most radical liberal arts colleges in America, Antioch College, the alma mater of Coretta Scott King, as well as the place where the term "intentional community" first emerged in the 1940s when the Foundation for Intentional Community— still the single largest organization in the country working to "promote peaceful, cooperative living arrangements"—planted its headquarters.

As I read more of Young's work, I realize we are both awed by the same sorts of things: she understands the layering and paradox inherent in the histories of American utopianism(s), how the opposite of what is hoped for is always near to her, near to Rapp, to Lee, to Brigham Young (of whom she is a descendant). It's an inevitable condition, she seems to say: Anti-capitalist Christian doomsday cult becomes one of the highest property sales in all of the United States at the time, a twenty-thousand-acre fully operative frontier town with everything in it. The Harmony Society become unwitting capitalists. *Of course, they did. Don't you get it?* "The facts of the case are these, finally—that the country churchyard was converted over to the uses of the Bethlehem Steel Corporation, of which it thus provides the shadowy background, and that the nineteenth-century dream of a New Jerusalem resulted in the twentieth century's dream of organized death . . . [The Harmonists] perished, presumably, and in that fact lies their chief charm."

Young left Indiana after she was done with the book and spent most of the rest of her adult life in New York, in Greenwich Village, adjuncting mostly, mentoring young writers, and writing quite a lot herself, while hanging out with artists and amassing an enormous collection of dolls. (The dolls are a chief highlight of her *New York Times* obituary in 1995, which is insane and kind of offensive, in my opinion, but maybe she would have been amused by that.) She was adamantly disinterested in professionalization. She went on to publish lots of essays, reviews, short stories, but in her own style and mode, and then two behemoth titles following *Angel in the Forest*: *Miss MacIntosh, My Darling* (1,200 pages) and *Harp Song for a Radical* (2,400 pages, though published in an abbreviated form posthumously). Her magnum opus, *Harp Song*, is a lyrical and psychedelic portrait of both the United States as a young country and of Eugene V. Debs—the first person to run as a socialist for president—as a young man. Her argument, if you can call the fever dream prose of that book argumentative, is that contrary to popular belief the United States *was* a utopian communitarian project from its outset, not a nation formed by individual accumulation of capital; that Debs and utopian experimenters did not function as a corrective to a broken country, but as the representative heir to what had been going on all along.

In an interview for Dalkey Archive toward the end of her life, Marguerite

Young says, "All the books I have written have been one book, from the beginning. The first poem I ever wrote, about loss, when I was five years old, expressed the themes of everything I would ever write." When asked to discuss her own obsessions, she instead redirects the question toward her subjects, to those she is writing about: "Debs was obsessed. James Whitcomb Riley was obsessed. And my characters are obsessed. The personages in the Debs book are obsessed, including Emma Goldman and Margaret Anderson. I have hundreds of characters . . ." The interviewer presses on: Will you describe *your* obsession?

It's the final question of what reads up to that point as an irritated interviewer. Young, who I imagine chain-smoking through her awesome wrinkles, shifts in her seat and gives her interlocutor a dead-eyed look. Her deflections till now have had a point to them that has been lost on the interviewer—and lost on me, too: it's not about *my* obsession, it's about a collective obsession for a better world, of which we are all a part. There is no better world to come from "my" obsession, my special interest, or even "yours," so stop asking me to present it that way. She doesn't say this, but it's latent. She lets the silence hang. She clears her throat. "I believe that all my work explores the human desire or obsession for utopias, and the structure of all my works is the search for utopias lost and rediscovered . . . All my writing is about the recognition that there is no single reality. But the beauty of it is that you nevertheless go on, walking towards utopia, which may not exist, on a bridge which might end before you reach the other side."

It seems to me utopianism is almost always responding to the same things: capitalism, war, tyranny, inequality, persecution, the impending end of the world, or a belief that the world has already ended. There are surface differences in the response, generation to generation, group to group, but not foundational ones. The makers of utopias are responding to the dregs of a violent empire by dropping out and simplifying the means of production. Owen saw the terrors wrought by industrialization, how the machine of capitalism was, among other things, killing child laborers and natural ecosystems, sowing sexual oppression and robbing any possibility for a happy human life. The Harmonists, I think, saw something similar at the turn of the nineteenth century, though interpreted a step further that the rise of industrialization and colonial violence might mean that, finally, yes, the world *is* coming to an end shortly, because for how much longer can this hold, really?

Utopian groupies on the other hand, like Young, like Macdonald, like me, are also responding to these same things, but perhaps the main difference is that the groupie remains unconvinced that there is one single clear way out—and so the traveling, gathering, observing, appreciating becomes crucial, in terms of making a broader provocation in our political and spiritual imaginary, but it does not lead us home. In Young's case and in Macdonald's, there are some clear similarities not just in their subjects, but in their positions and time periods, and the exigencies that both produced: they are both writing from a period of major economic depression (the edge of the 1940s and the years following the Panic of 1837); they are both twenty years away from national Black liberation efforts, through war or protest, and they can both see the way the powers that be are doubling down in their present on the status quo. In 1941, Marguerite Young saw fascism in full swing, and she suspected, even in that early moment, that something as horrible as the Nazi death camps were happening. Macdonald, in his early adulthood, had watched what happened to the Jews in Odessa. They could both see the kinds of lies that the strongman was telling about progress. They traveled in order to know what other options there were. The road they traveled was not an exit from society, but a hoped-for on-ramp to a new one—or, to use Young's words, it was a bridge they walked in good faith but which also might disappear before they reached the other side.

utopianotes
Mount Lebanon Shaker Community

I roll up on the long muddy road to Mount Lebanon, New York. It's winter. Sunset freezes the ground frost into a tight layer of ice. My car cracks loudly over it as I pass the entrance sign: SHAKER MUSEUM | MOUNT LEBANON. The property is full of original Shaker-style dwellings—big, tidy, rectangular two- and three-story multifamily farmhouses, wooden shakes painted clean white. Some of the houses have interpretive signs at the front porch describing their histories, and others look currently occupied by modern tenants, which I have no explanation for. I pass a dwelling that, for instance, has two kids' bikes resting at the bottom of some stairs.

I park and walk around. Most of the buildings are closed up for winter. I grab a brochure from a weatherproof box outside the original washhouse: Mother Ann Lee left England in 1774 with her followers for New York, where Shaker communities emerged all over the countryside soon after—of which Mount Lebanon, established in 1787, became the most important for its ability to maintain some contact and commerce with the outside world. Through a life defined by ecstatic prayer, celibacy, pacifism, egalitarianism, and expert craftmanship of brooms, bonnets, bentwood boxes and chairs, the Shakers set about living this communal life as a force that would eventually purify earth into a celestial paradise. The last Shakers left Mount Lebanon in 1947. But a guy named John S. Williams had spent the previous decade traveling to the few surviving Shaker communities for research purposes, and had acquired artifacts, so he bought the property and turned the carcass of this old community into a museum.

I pass the cookhouse, the schoolhouse, the workhouse—but the more I lurk around their edges, with their clean, high angles—the more I'm able to confirm that most of the houses are in fact inhabited by private residents. The brochure says, "The Abode of the Message, a Sufi community, occupies buildings that were once part of the South Family. Other original Shaker buildings are now private homes." I see Christmas tree lights in the bottom floor of one house. A teenager stumbles out of another, with two giant dogs on leashes. She glumly walks them around the perimeter of the oldest and largest fir tree in sight.

I pass an old tool shed, a vertical barn bright red, the "sisters workhouse" (Shaker life was sex-segregated in all things except for spiritual fellowship). Finally, I approach a behemoth half-crumbled stone barn, several stories high and long missing a roof. Behind the barn lie acre after acre of recently chopped-down trees. In some cases, the trees have been literally taken out at the root, mulched, mutilated by giant CAT tire marks. I continue on, tripping over the pulp and felled trees, until it is almost completely dark.

LIVING

When I returned from Rochester, Sweeney and I took a three-day retreat to the Millay Colony in the Hudson Valley. The Millay Colony, a nonprofit arts organization that operates on the late poet Edna St. Vincent Millay's former "gentleman's farm," had granted me an artist residency a couple of years back, and I'd later been selected to serve as a juror to admit the season of residents who followed me, for which the compensation was a free stay on the premises during the off-season. The offer included access to a room and a studio for me and a guest in either Millay's old Sears barn or the single-story main building, which, when Sweeney and I arrived in the dark that night, was edged deep in snow.

We had driven up the Taconic State Parkway to get there. I'd felt utterly alone as I looked west toward the foggy blue of the Catskill Mountains on the other side of the Hudson River. The Forester was full of trash: Rockstar cans, old coffee sludge, bills, a porcelain plate with a bit of old toast crust stuck to it. I hated the car. I hated that Sweeney didn't take care of it. I hated the smell of rot. I hated that at the end of these three days we were going to be back in a suffocating apartment in Woodlawn, looking toward the same life we'd been living for the last two, going on three, years—where I would be continuously in motion in order to make ends meet, and Sweeney would be continuously in motion taking care of his father, who we hadn't been more than a few minutes from since he first had the strokes. This three-day retreat was supposed to be our first vacation.

I chose a small room in the main building to set up shop. I wasn't quite sure where to start, and so I began by stitching together notes I'd amassed for an essay about The Corresponding Society, a small press that Sweeney, I, and a community of friends had started when we were in college, which operated out of the large basement apartment we all lived in and called "Gates"—but eventually the notes all started running together, and I wasn't sure what it was I even wanted to say or think about that time period, especially as it related to the "research" I was doing for the "book." I gave up. I opened a generic-style textbook about American utopian movements by independent scholar Jyotsna Sreenivasan that I had grabbed impulsively from the Fordham library, which I was flipping through at random—and which itself seemed an almost arbitrary compendium of examples, with chapters that were arranged alphabetically, like an index turned into a table of contents:

Amana Colonies
Amish
Ananda Colonies
Anarchism
Antislavery Communities
Bellamy, Edward
Bible Communism
Bishop Hill
Bohemia Manor
Brook Farm and Fourierist Phalanxes
Brotherhood of New Life
Bruderhof
Buddhist Communities
Burned-Over District
Camphill
etc.

In the next room, Sweeney was hammering away at his dissertation—a study about the theology of grief during the Dark Ages: when his dad had ended up in a coma two years earlier, Sweeney started this project about how in the wake of the fall of Christian Rome, grief was considered blasphemy, a holdover belief from the Stoics, reinforced in the letters and writings of elite bishops and statesmen at the time, and especially in state-sanctioned art. Dark Age-era visual depictions of Jesus make him look like an unblemished emperor, standing in front of, rather than nailed to, the cross, fully clothed, wearing a crown, radiating light and muscle. But by the beginning of the medieval era, several hundred years later, Christianity is *all* about grief and suffering—grief and suffering are at the center of the story, and this is made especially clear, once again, in the art, which is still basically state-sanctioned. So what happened during the Dark Ages, those several hundred years of political and social chaos? How did we move from stoicism to emotion? Sweeney had read thousands of books—to my count, literally something like two thousand books and articles—between the time his dad went unconscious and now, trying to answer this question. He wasn't sure yet.

At night in the Millay Colony kitchen, we'd nurse a bottle of tequila and soda and stay up late talking until we'd become terse, and then I wouldn't want to have sex; or we'd stay up late writing and go to bed at different times. When I would look at the months in front of us, they rolled out in a gray dribble. The time at the Millay Colony was supposed to be a reprieve from our constant caretaking. Sweeney's family members had pitched in to cover our three-day absence from Woodlawn, though he still had to drive a half hour to the town of Chatham to get cell service for a dozen calls a day from doctors, aides, insurance companies. I cooked our dinners and otherwise read on for the next two days, in my little borrowed studio, extremely depressed, hoping the feeling would pass.

On the last day, I went for a walk in the snow, in the meadows above the main building: I passed by Millay's former home, a white 1860s farmhouse; her clapboard writing cottage in the woods; the large enclosed victory garden that the groundskeepers still maintained; the trail that led to the headstones of her mother, husband, and Millay herself—a hard-living, cool as hell bisexual artist who'd died of a heart attack at fifty-eight in her home. In the decades after her death, Millay's sister worked with an arts organization to transform her property into this artists' residency—where artists could apply with a body of work and, if admitted, enjoy an uninterrupted month of time, space, and prepared meals in the company of six other residents during the spring and summer months, thereby preserving Millay's legacy and keeping the overhead low for a nourishing and communal, if temporary, existence for tired artists. The organization calls the off-season work-trade visitors like me "Winter Shakers," a term coined in the 1830s and '40s when all of the Shaker communities in the northeast would shrink in the summers, as people defected and returned to the cities or their families, or to frolicking and fornicating, whatever, and then when resources were scarce again in the winter, the colony populations would dramatically inflate with "Winter Shakers," those suddenly pious pilgrims, out of work and looking for food and shelter.

I hiked to the highest point on the land, a clearing that overlooked Harvey Mountain, where Millay's old clay tennis court lay crumbling apart. I had come here for a residency during the first summer after Dan's coma, in 2016. My grandmother died in Seattle unexpectedly the day before I left the Colony, and I had sat, in that wet summer sun up here on the tennis court where I could get cell service, listening to the final half hour of her ragged breathing over speakerphone. I stood now in that same spot and wept. I felt hopeless and endlessly angry at Sweeney, and I stumbled back into the main lodge, crying, kicking snow off my boots, making a declaration I had made many times before.

"We can't keep going on like this," I said, my blood pressure already dialed up. "I need something to change."

Sweeney was sitting in the common area at a series of card tables he'd jury-rigged together, his face obscured by the book stacks.

"What can change?" He edged his head out from behind a stack and straightened his back. He gathered his hair into an elastic and scratched at his beard. "I mean, what do you *want* me to do? *Not* take care of my dad? Literally, then no one is—then my dad is in a nursing home forever, or dead."

"But there's gotta be—like—*another way.*"

"Like what?" He looked at me, exhausted. New lines were forming around his eyes. Two empty beer cans sat by his boot.

"I don't know." It was a very old fight, and a very old posture of helplessness. "I feel like I'm dying—or like I just need to pause."

As usual he asked me what other ideas I had, and my ideas were, as usual, the same: we could move to Brooklyn so I could be closer to work, or take a semester off and live on rice and beans, or rent a place in the Catskills to lower our overhead, leave our jobs and figure out a new livelihood. Each of these were met with the usual litany of obstacles: too expensive, too risky, too insane, too physically far away from his dad.

"And what about me?" His face had hardened against my words. "You think I *like* spending forty hours a week on the phone with evil bureaucracies just so my dad won't die? I'm doing everything I can—and my dad is miserable, and you're miserable, and I feel like I'm failing no matter what I do. You've gotta just buck up. *Life is only harder from here on out.*"

I stared at the snow out the windows. It felt like a Bergman film. I could feel myself drifting away.

When I thought of the past, I saw Sweeney's heart-shaped face across from mine in a coffee shop on Myrtle Avenue in the spring of 2008, when we were twenty years old, overwhelmingly in love, poring over the Word files we'd gathered and printed out for a new literary magazine we were going to start with some friends, which—all aspects created in haste—at that moment had a very weird, spare cover design, just these inscrutable calligraphic letters spelling out CORRESPONDENCE, and which would become the flagship output of The Corresponding Society.

When I pictured the future, I saw myself alone or with someone else, casually using phrases like "my *first* husband." The furniture in the common room looked cheap and threadbare. Sweeney tapped his pen, waiting to get back to his work.

I stopped crying for long enough to give an ultimatum: we ask his family for more sustained help with Dan, which means that he has to relinquish some responsibility; we start doing couples therapy once a week, which his graduate student health insurance will pay 60 percent of; I teach one less class the following semester; he stops drinking during the weekdays for three months; I, in exchange, will refrain from pressuring him for a plan to move for one more year.

That night, I dreamed I was a passenger in the car driving up the Taconic State Parkway. I looked out my window and saw the Catskill Mountains across the river—dark blue rock—and they started to speak to me. Each blunt peak started to light up from the inside, as though ribbed with a colored neon bulb, revealing a glyph of some kind on each mountain face. The glyphs were giant and chiseled into stone, each a different color.

I didn't know what any of it meant, only a vague sense that the mountains were talking to me.

The first time we sat on the couch in therapy, I felt like we'd created a bend in the space-time continuum, an interdimensional wrinkle. I recognized him, sitting there next to me in his combat boots and plaid button-up, his long, messy hair pulled back in an elastic and his wiry black beard climbing up the side of his suddenly vulnerable-looking cheek, but he also looked remote, like someone in a movie. The light was low. The couch was brown. I felt sympathy for this man sitting next to me, some other person's husband to whom my heart was open. I was listening to him as though at a distance, talking about how tired he was, how responsible he felt for everyone's well-being. How were we going to get out of this? Where were we going? We lacked sharply a shared imagination for the future like we'd once had, and which had, I think, been the bedrock of our relationship—the most powerful thing that had kept us together these last ten years.

Then, a month after we started therapy, we stayed up all night talking about heaven.

We were driving from Baltimore. A friend's husband had committed suicide. Her husband's photographs lined the walls of an old church where the memorial was held in the neighborhood near Maryland Institute College of Art, where they'd lived together. Sweeney and I, and our friend Lina, were barreling back to New York up I-95 after the evening service, quiet and sad. On an impulse, Lina offered us each an Adderall somewhere in New Jersey and then the three of us started to talk about heaven: What is it? Where is it? What are the different things people mean when they say it, or think it? Can you believe in an afterlife but not believe in God? We started to talk about the TV shows and movies and harrowing religious institutions that had formed our ideas of heaven. Sunday school, CCD, *Angels in America*, *Six Feet Under*, *What Dreams May Come*. We got stuck on the Jersey side of the George Washington Bridge in standstill traffic at around midnight and I kept snarking to Lina: This is the afterlife!

Sweeney and I dropped her off and then drove the rest of the way home to Woodlawn, continuing to talk all the way about heaven, about how frightened we were by the ideas of heaven described in our childhoods. We teleported from the car to our kitchen table and kept talking, about all of it, and talked about our marriage, our fights—we talked as calmly as psychopaths, as though we were out of time, as though those fights we were referring to belonged to some other couple. We were enjoying the thought experiments. I felt elated, unburdened. We'd made a clean tear in reality and stepped into it, strangers on the same path. We lit a candle and worked at the kitchen table with the lights dimmed. Later, we had long, slow sex until dawn. In the morning, we went to his late grandmother's house in Westchester to help clear out her belongings. His aunts and uncles were getting ready to sell her house.

In her bedroom, we found a vintage hat box shoved under her dresser which contained worksheets from a Catholic marriage encounter workshop from the late 1970s, as well as lots of literature on the fertility awareness method (she'd even tracked her cycle for several months in pencil), and pamphlets, and also couples' worksheets where she and her husband, long-passed-away grandpa Leo, both put checkmarks next to "Feel lonely, like you don't know me."

utopianotes
Gospel Flat Farm

We are twenty-one, on summer vacation from college. Sweeney, our friend Robby, and I have been hitchhiking around the West Coast for a couple of weeks, camping and occasionally peddling copies of *Correspondence* Vol. 3 at readings we'd scheduled beforehand in various towns. We're now planning to stay for a few days with the Murches. They run Gospel Flat Farm in the secluded and dreamy community of Bolinas, California. The whole family—several of them—subsist almost entirely off of a cash-based, honor-system farm stand near the main road that runs through town. They plump up the produce daily with harvest, and somehow that keeps everything running. The rest of their income comes from a mobile education and food processing center called the LifeBoat, which operates out of a rusted WWII lifeboat they found in the bushes at the edge of their property when they first cleared out the brush.

As Sweeney, Robby, and I bump over Mt. Tam in that tiny charter bus we had to track down in a grocery store parking lot at the edge of Marin County (it is the only way to get to Bolinas without a car), we listen to the other passengers tell stories about the Beats who used to live there. We tunnel through redwoods, looking out over the bay, and then back down around salt marshes full of herons. When the driver asks where we wanted to get off, we say, "The Murches?" We are, you see, arriving at the farm uninvited—these Murches have never met us. We'd only met a Murch brother on the road a week earlier while we were hitchhiking who had given us this address and told us to just show up. There is a whale rib at the front drive. A Murch cousin waves at us as we approach, our clothes smelling like shit, our backpacks full of copies of *Correspondence*. We give him one. We tell him we met his cousin. He says, "Oh, yeah—we were expecting you guys. Welcome!"

These few details remain: the tap with homemade wine; the wild turkey meat the grandparents share with us; the bee swarm that chases us across the onion crop, and the hours of picking onions; the trees swaying overhead when we walk to town, then to the beach; the fight Sweeney and I have in the guest house one night; Robby patting me on the shoulder on the front steps; the giant block of Tillamook cheese we slice from for breakfast; the YouTube video of First Aid Kit singing that cover of "Tiger Mountain Peasant Song"—first time we see it. It was 2009. The old lady we hitch a ride with to get out of town.

HOW TO START A SOCIETY

A year before Dan went into a coma, I was sitting in the Center for Career and Professional Development at my alma mater, Pratt Institute, where I was currently adjuncting as a freshman composition instructor. One benefit to that otherwise exploitative contract labor upon which the neoliberal university system depends was that I had access to free life-coaching sessions with a campus career counselor. I was already burnt out, working four jobs and not sure what a next step would be, especially since I felt as ambivalent about a career trajectory now as I had at eighteen—other than writing and other modes of storytelling, but those things didn't ever feel like a career. The thing is, I had never really wanted to teach, nor seen myself as being a particularly capable teacher, but in the early twenty-first century, there was a surplus of need for cheap professors and I, with my MFA, was now qualified to fill those roles, so that's what I ended up doing.

Sweeney and I had moved back to New York a few months earlier, after I'd finished grad school in Wyoming. Meanwhile, Sweeney was struggling through his first year of a PhD in theology at Fordham University in the Bronx and wondering if he should drop out and go to law school instead. He'd been meeting up with his dad at diners lately, who was trying to talk him off the cliff of his depression—"*I* never wanted to be a lawyer," Dan would say, slipping Sweeney some more Klonopin across the table. Then he'd grin. "Let's have a cigarette," and if I had joined them for this meeting, we'd walk out to the parking lot to smoke. We didn't know how profoundly the three of our fates would invert the following winter. But a sense of urgency haunted the edges of the frame all the same.

"Close your eyes," Deborah, the life coach/career counselor said, "and picture a time when you felt really happy and safe."

I closed my eyes. "Gates," I said.

"Great," she said. "Tell me about Gates."

It was a surprising, almost ridiculous-feeling answer. Did I mean it?

What was "Gates"? Quite literally, it was the moniker my friends and I gave to an apartment building we lived in during college, from the aughts to Occupy: a ratty but regal, blond-brick late-neoclassical seventeen-unit building on the corner of Gates and Franklin Avenues on the edge of Bed-Stuy, Brooklyn. Gates was a literal location, but it was also a metonym for being twenty years old, shorthand for a moment in my life, a corner in a neighborhood populated by my closest friends, the site of the Gates Salon, and the birthplace of our small press.

I remember approaching Gates for the first time as a guest, in the warm early fall of 2007: walking down DeKalb, then onto Classon, left onto Gates, right down to the corner of Franklin, then standing before that large five-story complex, bathed in the dirty yellow sodium lights from the street. I was going to the Gates Salon, a biweekly reading I'd heard about from one of my new classmates. And that was the night I met Sweeney, and everyone else.

I went to the Salon every other Thursday for a couple of months. One night, Sweeney called my name, sheepishly, from one of the bedrooms. I stood in the doorway, proud, suddenly feeling my power, in these tall rust-colored polyester pants, feeling that I might hold out at the threshold a bit longer just because I could. He smiled at me from his sideways position on the bed. For the next few months, we lay in that bed, swirled in the sheets, talking into the dark until it was light, and a while later I moved in.

Over the course of four years, I lived in three of Gates's seventeen units, a good chunk of which was the large, dark basement apartment with about four cats, where we continued holding the Gates Salon every other Thursday without fail, and which acted as a hub for everyone else we knew, including our professors and strays and travelers, and where we also enacted a day-to-day life of dinners and writing and talking and fighting, espousing deep beliefs in art and truth and love—etc. On some Sundays, Greg baked a loaf of bread for dinner, which, if it was warm outside, we ate on the patio—the "patio" which was more like a garbage chute. We also destroyed our neighbors' quality of life, all around, with indiscriminate parties and yelling and music, and for this we will hopefully be forced to suffer a similar fate, for a longer duration of time.

So this is what I meant when I, in the Center for Career and Professional Development at Pratt Institute, answered Deborah's question with "Gates." It's embarrassing to say, every time I say it, because it was also just college, where these sorts of living situations are possible—and here I was back at my college as an employee. Arrested development notwithstanding, I was still genuinely troubled by the fact that college seemed to me the only sort of mainstream cooperative living acceptable in middle-class America, where one could live in a close community, and see each other regularly and organically, and where our lives were not entirely governed by an isolating nine-to-five job. It's embarrassing to uphold as a particularly happy moment in my life because it's so common, like, "Oh, college was fun and free? Big whoop, ya fuckin' baby."

But I was sitting in Deborah's office precisely because something about that life—I wasn't sure what yet—had provided an instruction or an ethic for me at twenty, and I now felt trapped by a limited set of options: I was back in the city where most of my friends still lived, alone now in their own apartments, tied to the subway lines that would get them most efficiently to their godforsaken jobs, and where even the slightest bit of social contact required huge amounts of effort, planning, and money. So I could choose to pursue a career, and form a life around it. I could become a radio producer. I could be an adjunct forever. I could get a book published and leverage that for a full-time teaching position, in some other city, in a bottlenecked market. All of these options felt hollow to me—I had never dreamed of jobs, I had only ever worked as a means to live. I sat across from Deborah and I kept talking of freedom, openness, the plains of the Laramie prairie I had recently left behind, the view from behind the Walmart where the town turned into rangeland. She told me to think of that openness, that prairie, that big space, every time I touched a doorknob, every time I literally opened a door. Let the doorknob prompt me to close my eyes and think of that big space, and work from there.

The lack I was communicating, at twenty-five years old in the Center for Career and Professional Development, is a lack somewhat unique to the upper classes, in a global context at least: I grew up thoroughly American middle class; my parents, and grandparents, and great-grandparents were musicians and teachers and social workers and janitors. But the kind of togetherness and community I was grieving is an upper-class longing in that there are plenty of people who live in community like this already—Indigenous people, poor people, rural people, people who have formed tight social fabrics in dense urban centers and remote steppes. I am not one of these people. I was, it turned out, of the people who go to college and start careers and become couples and disappear into houses.

The thing I was, and am, questing after is in a way quite simple: I wanted to remove wage-earning from the center of my own life—in the way that it currently determines where I live, who I live with or around, when I can and cannot spend time with loved ones and friends, when I can and cannot write, when I can and cannot be of service to other people. I'd like to do this in a way that helps others who'd like the same thing to join in. The way toward lower overhead, toward less reliance on wage-earning, is it seems through collectivity—whether that's collective ownership, communal living, appliance shares (cars, washing machines)—I am open to any scale. That love and community and opportunities for restorative justice might come out of that is a bonus, and not a guarantee. The basic desire is to not have to work as much, not have to have a career, and to be around people I like more often, and more easily.

I went home that night and finished the last episode of *Friends*, which I had spent a few months rewatching, in order and in its entirety, ten years after it finished airing, while Sweeney snored loudly beside me. I cried. It was not a good show, nor a good finale. But something about the way it marks the end of adolescence, the end of early adulthood, the end of an era, so neatly and so visibly for all the characters involved—all of them packing up Monica's huge apartment—highlights really how that doesn't happen in real life, how you never get to say goodbye to an era, let alone with other people standing next to you as you do it, as though you're watching a parade go by, together. Instead, it's gradual, people peeling off to go live elsewhere—but in my case, most of my friends didn't have kids or careers, or aspirations of such either. So what the fuck were we doing? It seemed, as I watched that final shot of them—Monica, Chandler, Rachel, Ross, Joey, Phoebe—walking down the hallway, their backs to the camera, blurring out on their way to the suburbs, that to walk away from the possibility of ever living lives that close together again was actually a moral evil.

Every other Thursday for five years we convened the Gates Salon, and people just showed up. There were our friends of course, many of whom attended regularly for years—our friends and their friends. And maybe some person off the street that Robby grabbed. Or our neighbor Carol who had suffered greatly a few years earlier in Tribeca watching her fiancé jump out of the burning Twin Towers, and who was now mentally out to lunch. It might be our professors from Pratt, or occasionally a slightly Brooklyn-famous poet who would pop in, usually just one time to sneer at what we were doing.

We were aggressively pretentious, but completely sincere. We were so deeply nerdy, so committed to the writing, to the art, to commenting on each other's work, to listening—that we cultivated a situation that I find more remarkable in retrospect than I did then. Every other Thursday night, from approximately nine o'clock to midnight, sometimes longer, thirty to forty mostly twenty-somethings sat silently in a living room and took turns reading their work to each other. The overhead lights would go off—replaced by the dramatic underlighting of our secondhand cracked Target floor lamps. And we would read, we'd read all night, all jammed into the room—sitting on the floor, on chairs, on the couch, on laps, everywhere. The ethos—the rule, even—was that no one could disrupt the reading until every last person who wanted to read had done so. Even the least conciliatory among us, Lonely Christopher, was usually the one to hold fastest to this rule. He'd say, "Does anyone else want to read?" Even if it was one o'clock in the morning, even if we'd been sitting there all night, in a cloud of cigarette smoke and forty-ounce bottles of Ballantine Ale, we would carry on, clapping and laughing, if one more person wanted to read. Then, when all the readings were done, we'd break into a party, people drifting into clusters or dancing or shouting or fighting, and I'd find myself sitting outside on the bench with someone talking until dawn.

The continuity and endurance of the Gates Salon formed the idea for the small press. We called it The Corresponding Society (named in part after the London Corresponding Society, an eighteenth-century federation of reading and debate clubs committed to democratic reform). We started putting out a perfect-bound biannual literary journal called *Correspondence*, which was made up mostly of the writing of the people who came to the Salon. We published them in printings of five hundred and would sell them at readings we'd host at bars and coffee shops all around the city, with insanely long reader lists—maybe five or six or eight readers. We'd have parties and fundraisers. We went on a cross-country tour with Vol. 2., and a hitchhiking road show with Vol. 3. Somehow by the skin of our teeth, through a thousand dysfunctional "editorial meetings," we'd put out new work. Eventually we started putting out chapbooks, too, which the generous folks at Ugly Duckling Presse would help us letterpress, for free, and which we would bind by hand, lazily, at our filthy coffee table.

Meanwhile, our daily lives continued. But what was that daily life like, in my romantic memory? I remember panels of aluminum foil falling down the apartment walls like curtains. I'd sit on the ratty recliner and marvel at my friends. Robby wore a felted hat and held a wormy cat in his arms. Bottles of Ballantine Ale littered the large kitchen table. Greg had baked two loaves of warm rye bread. Someone asleep in a repurposed office chair, and someone else reading Wendell Berry poems aloud as the rest of us listened or didn't. I'd sit with Amber on the roof, painted silver, on the cracked plastic bench, draining a six-pack and watching the sun set over the Williamsburgh Savings Bank.

Then the oysters. The big, clear bags of oysters that Greg brought from Chinatown, and the 750-milliliter bottles of Yellow Tail Chardonnay and fresh bread and my spinach salads with the soy sauce and lemon and salt dressing. Amber and Chanelle being around, though not living there, to talk and read—long nights spent writing poems back and forth, lying on the carpet, drunk at the patio table, heckling or being heckled, then later tucked into bed, passing a book back and forth.

Violets littered the kitchen counter. Chanelle had not yet become an herbalist, but was already beginning to identify and harvest edible plants she could find in our trash heap of a courtyard, or around telephone poles on Franklin Avenue. We tried to plant lettuces in the clawfoot bathtubs outside, and had great days of doing it, though nothing grew. Sweeney appeared aboveground at the entry gate at the end of each workday at the library and then came tumbling down the stairs in a metallic clang—the way his legs moved, under his very straight back, always looked like a Ken doll's—hurtling toward me to pick me up and kiss me and fly me around in a circle, my legs wrapped around him like he was a goddamned returned soldier from WWII.

My memories are mostly ensemble-like. Greg walking through the door with a thirty-pack of PBR over his shoulder like a stereo playing music. He had just come home from five months in France. "I missed you guys!" Sweeney constructing a desk in the back corner out of two-by-fours, having just finished helping Chanelle rig up the last of the teepee in the living room—something a student of industrial design had made and donated to us. Robby running into the courtyard with a bag of moldy onions, squash, and potatoes he'd rescued from a dumpster. Lonely Christopher saying something mean and funny from a dark corner, sipping a Ballantine. Robby playing music all night, Joanna Newsom or just "Great Gate of Kiev" over and over and over again, with one candle burning on faux Shabbat. Me feeling grateful that everyone was finally home.

Then came more and more stragglers: Topper, who could afford only a thin rice porridge that he ate daily, or what we fed him, while he was hanging out doing mushrooms in the living room or busking at Port Authority to get back to his girlfriend in Indiana. The French woman who slept on our couch. Jody while he wrote the first of what would be *The Mountain That Was a Hill*. Chanelle in the teepee. Dana in the borrowed back room.

One late summer, a few of us saw the play *Twelve Ophelias* performed in McCarren Park Pool, and then, in my memory, we all piled into Sweeney's Geo Prizm, picked up Matthew without much explanation, and drove to Pennsylvania. Robby's brother had a show he was going to perform in Quakertown in a couple of days, and we had nothing to do that weekend. So Robby, Chanelle, Sweeney, Matthew, and I headed onto I-78 and showed up at a tract of ticky-tacky apartments at the edge of Allentown, where a party was already in full swing. The next day we floated down a river, and then got on the rolling pastures of County Route 309 to Quakertown, and that's when I remember looking out the window at the rolling golden farm-land, and beginning, all of us, the first conversation of many about how one day we would all buy property and start our own school.

Someone was reading *Black Mountain College: Exploration in Community* by Martin Duberman. We became obsessed with the idea of starting our own anti-institutional institution that would sustain our material lives. We took special pleasure in the stories of poet Charles Olson's having taught a class called The News, which would run for upwards of twenty-two hours at a time, partly because he was hopped up on amphetamines, but also because most of the students were, too. Plans and projections about "the school" would become a significant feature of our lives together, for the rest of college, and for the next ten years, even after we were all living in different places, embarking on careers. Eventually the conversations did not have to do with an actual school at all, but where "the school," like Gates, had become a metonym for whatever communal life we would make for ourselves in some distant future.

That said, there were problems, too. Around the time I moved back to New York from grad school, Sweeney and I were at a bar. I had just started teaching at Pratt. We ran into a former professor at the counter. "Oh my God," he said. "Sweeney, hi!" This professor and I had in fact seen each other once already on campus for orientation. We were now colleagues. "Jackson, Tom," he said, motioning to two of his friends on the other side of the room. "Come here—I want to introduce you to Sweeney." We stood there in this coffee shop, side by side, facing the three men, Sweeney laughing nervously. "Guys—this is Christopher Sweeney, one of our star students from years back. He's an amazing poet. He started a small press while he was at Pratt, and ran a reading series, and went on to get his MFA at Brown, and is now getting his PhD. And this," he gestured to me, "is Adrian. She's one of us now," he said, indicating I guess that I now worked at Pratt. "Are you still writing?"

I don't know what happened in the minute or two that lapsed while this interaction came to an end. Everything went white for me. A feeling of rage so complete I could feel light coming out of my eyes, but all of my responses were jammed in my throat. I just smiled and nodded until the three of them walked away.

"Did you fucking hear that? Did you hear what just happened?" I said to Sweeney, while I walked myself to the windowsill to take a breather.

"Yeah—I mean, what?"

"All of it!"

"Like the Corresponding Society thing?"

"Yes, and 'He ran a reading series and got his MFA' and '*Are you still writing?*' What the fuck. He didn't even ask about your writing. *You* don't even write anymore."

I hadn't felt this way in a few years, but it reminded me that I once had felt this way quite often, throughout college: overlooked and blotted out against the backdrop of the mythic poet men who absorbed all of our small public's attention, including mine. I had forgotten this feeling, or it had been eclipsed by how much I'd spent the intervening years missing my friends, like family. Because they were my family in even the ways that horrendous things are forgiven in families for the sake of a claim to safety or the good of the group or a sense of home. I had been forged in a deeply male context, at times a misogynistic one mostly in the ways it failed to imagine the feminine, so that the metric for my own greatness was held to a masculinity I would never possess: loudness, brute force, sparring, take-downs, ego, candor.

Suddenly, I remembered everything else, the unyielding force to conform to that masculinity, during the years at Gates, the strain of that, the exhaustion of trying to achieve legitimacy in their eyes or the eyes of our audience or professors for being smart enough or visionary enough, while also knowing by definition I never would be, and that no value would be placed upon the kind of communing I did with my girlfriends, my queer friends.

Even at the height of our powers, everything always seemed about to fall apart completely. The gate at the top of the stairs slammed shut, nearly rattling off its hinges. A graveyard of white particle-board furniture, cabinets slouching sideways from loose nails, gathered against the walls in the courtyard. The broken glass on Sweeney's grandfather's bookshelf sat in shards.

Each of us were always in the process of trying to figure out how to leave, move out, hit the road for a summer, get a proper apartment as a couple, whatever. We were constantly engineering "final" moments of our communal enterprises. The penultimate Gates Salon! The Final Gates Salon! And then three Final Gates Salons to follow! Vol. 4 of *Correspondence*, the final installment—no wait, we'll call it *Foreverland*! The file still sitting, unpublished, in our computers.

The building itself still looks unchanged today—except that the two- and three-bedroom apartments we rented therein in 2007 for $1,500 are now twice or thrice that price. And the ragtag kids who carried out a life in it are all over the place being professors, doctoral students, herbalists, artists, musicians, paralegals, educators, travel writers, social workers. And the Black and brown people that our presence had insidiously displaced, both at the time and later on, were further out in the edges of Brooklyn, the Bronx, the exurbs, other cities, such that now the inhabitants of Gates are people who have careers that earn them at least six figures.

The failures were plentiful: During those years, we summarily failed to understand ourselves as dynamic political subjects, though we could have said a lot of shit about the evils of gentrification and racism and capitalism, sitting on our busted sofas with beer in our hands. We were mostly just living the lives of a bunch of jaded aesthetes. We reasserted hetero-patriarchy in our social relations. Our mission was absent of any real ethical content. Looked at another way, we were just a bunch of privileged assholes in Brooklyn in the early twenty-first century, writing and going to school and partying and drinking and keeping our poor neighbors awake.

And yet—why did we cleave so strongly to calling our press a "Society"? I know that the name came from Greg's pet interests in eighteenth-century history, but once we were calling ourselves The Corresponding Society, it became us. It was gestural, aspirational mostly, but genuinely felt. To call a press a "Society" is to destabilize its meaning a bit, to immediately broaden the possibilities of what it was we did, even if we didn't do much. A society is incidental. A society can make journals and chapbooks and hold readings. A society has an infinite number of possible members, though it can also be exclusive. A society can include those who live in it, or have defected, or are somewhere in between. A society is a site upon which basically anything can happen, and in being called a society, that site simply becomes more visible and official than it otherwise would be. One time, when we took *Correspondence* Vol. 2 on tour, several of us were at a party and about five of us slept in one bed. In the morning, Katie said, "We should get an award for best use of a bed," and Jody said, "Best use of a bed by a *society*." That about sums it up for me.

Societies also fall apart, God willing, and falling apart seems to be an important, if not necessary, part of utopianism—which I suppose Gates has now entered the annals of, at least for me. Not because it was a utopia, but because it was about world-building. And when I say "utopianism," I guess, by this point, I just mean world-building as part of a communal enterprise, making something that you think is great, but is only paltry and provisional, and at its very best simply a gesture of futurity.

Other than that, what was it that I learned during these years, in the steamy filth of a Brooklyn basement in my early twenties? I learned to live in a mess that doesn't kill you. I learned about a kind of care or stewardship that does not need to come from one person or one family; I developed a sense of possibility—a sense of anything being possible—that I wouldn't be the same without. I loved all of the people whose names I will repeat here, and whose names I've already written or will write down at other parts of this book: Sweeney, Chanelle, Robert, Amber, Dana, Laura, Jenny, Robby, Lonely, Lina, Lily, Greg, Matthew. Going down to Jersey to sleep on a lawn for an 8:00 a.m. beach christening or over to Pennsylvania: hop in the car! We'll stop in Allentown for a party, a place to sleep, then go swimming down whatever the hell that river is tomorrow, before we get to that show in Quakertown, where the music, even then, won't ever be quite as loud as I remember it.

utopianotes
Webster Café

I have breakfast with Lisa at the Webster Café, a couple blocks down the street from New Day. Lisa and her father founded New Day together almost ten years earlier. She comes from a lineage of Filipino anti-imperial and feminist activism that her parents participated in during Marcos's dictatorship, in a country where the Communists and the radical Christians had long been a coalition. She is currently wrestling with what that lineage means while in the middle of pursuing a PhD in theology. It is only our second or third time talking together alone, just the two of us, though I have been eager to hang out with her for over a year. Almost immediately, somehow, we mutually disclose that we both are holding out interminably for a communal life, and maybe actually a commune—sheepishly. "I would literally give up everything, almost everything in my life right now, if an opportunity appeared to live in some kind of communal way," I say, mulling through, as I said it, what I might even mean by "almost everything in my life." I am not sure how this statement lands. "Oh, me, too," she says, wide-eyed. "I feel literally the same way." Our eyes lock. We are dead serious. We don't know what it means.

TWO

COMMUNE

utopianotes
Salt Lake City Temple Grounds

I go to the Salt Lake City Temple Grounds with my family and immediately lose track of them in the North Visitors' Center. When I head up the ramp to the second floor to find them, I see another family sitting before a giant statue of Jesus Christ surrounded by a semicircular atrium painted like the solar system. The family is eating McDonald's hamburgers.

LIVING

In the early spring of 2018, I was invited to Charlottesville to join a Virginia Festival of the Book panel of three women writers on religion. Sweeney decided to come with me. We'd just gotten Dan out of another stint in the hospital for a bacterial infection, and he was stabilized back at home. The car was clean. By the time we rolled into Charlottesville's city limits, I realized it was the first stretch of twenty-four hours that Sweeney and I hadn't fought in what felt like forever. In fact, we were actively taking pleasure in each other's presence as well as the view out the car window of the Southwest Mountains, one name of Virginia's claim to the Appalachians, the same range that the Catskills are a part of, such that everything, at least botanically, topographically, felt familiar to me as someone who had been casually visiting the Catskills for a decade. The violence and murder of the Unite the Right rally was only a few months old.

That night, we snuck into a ticketed event on Main Street, but cut out early to go to a drag show at the only gay bar in town we could find. Our Uber driver was a recently returned Iraq War veteran, no more than twenty-two years old. We arrived at a crappy building at the edge of town that looked like a deserted highway tanning salon, but when the bouncer let us through, we found ourselves in what seemed like possibly the most diverse place in the city—at least in terms of age, race, and class—as LED strobes played across our tired bodies. Sweeney bought us Jell-O shots. We watched the performers sing Lana Del Rey and Whitney Houston. Later we played pool in the back room, taking turns telling each other specific qualities that we loved about each other under the cheap green glare of the disco ball.

I woke up in the middle of the night at the Comfort Inn around the corner with the weight of a terrible familiar pain in my abdomen, over my right ovary.

•

The next day I was late to the panel. I was giving a short talk on my book *And Your Daughters Shall Prophesy*. The other panelists were the writers Diana Butler Bass—who'd just released *Gratitude* and memorably said that day, "When men write memoir, people call it theology; when women write memoir, people call it a diary"—and Karen Wright Marsh, who'd just released her book *Vintage Saints and Sinners*. She and her husband, Charles, run an interfaith community organization called Theological Horizons out of a community space called the Bonhoeffer House—which was where the reception was going to be held.

Sweeney and I moseyed on over to the address we were given and found ourselves in front of a giant neoclassical mansion on a street full of mostly frat houses, all similarly styled, at the edge of campus. Karen waved at us from the wide-open doorway—so wide open at that moment it looked almost to me as though a wall had been removed—and we walked inside the bright entryway. She started to give us a tour, as guests from the reading gathered and snacked around a long, wooden table in the living room: "Over here is where the lecturers speak, and over here is where we have our Tuesday afternoon Vintage Saints and Sinners conversations . . . There is where we do Friday Community Dinners . . . and there's Charles's study," she said, gesturing to a room with packed bookshelves up to the ceiling, "and upstairs," pointing to a giant staircase, "are our bedrooms and stuff." She smiled beneath a head of long blond-gray hair and dark eyebrows.

"Wait—the Bonhoeffer House is also where you *live*?" I said.

"Yes," she said, grinning. "Yes, the reason we could live here and raise our kids here is because so much of the house is written off for the organization. C'mon."

We joined the people in the party parlor: friends of Karen's who'd come to the panel, but also a multi-faith cadre of neighbors, colleagues, high school students, families, people who enjoy the Bonhoeffer House's programming and wanted to come by for the cheese. A squad of college-aged girls rushed around picking up our plates and glasses, with their various tattoos and septum piercings. "I hired them for the day," Karen said. "They're from the intentional community down the block."

One of her kids, now twenty-five and living in Brooklyn, was home for the weekend and walked into the party. We started chatting. I asked both him and Karen what it was like to grow up in, or raise kids in, that space—where there was a regular spate of gatherings, public talks, discussion groups, community dinners, workshops, etc. I looked at him, then at Karen who was looking at him pointedly with her hands out, like, *Go ahead.* He darted his eyes around and finally exploded with "Well, it was a lot of *this*—like, being put on the spot!"

"OK, OK," Karen said, "Sorry."

I liked that her kid seemed annoyed in only a very ordinary way. It seemed to me, if you're actually able to talk openly about something you struggled with in the past as a family, then it must not be that bad.

"But," he said, "it was kind of interesting to have people around all the time—and awkward when we'd like, come downstairs in our pajamas to a roomful of people. And my dad hides out in his office a lot."

"Yeah." Karen shrugged. "Charles is actually pretty antisocial. And he always wants to work, ya know, so he closes himself up in his study. I mean, it was *his* idea, too, to start Theological Horizons! Back then, he was all, 'Yeah, community, man,' but twenty years later it's still sort of hard for him."

I could hear the girls from the intentional community jetting around in the kitchen behind the wall, clattering dishes, laughing.

When we got back to Woodlawn, I got my ovaries examined by a new gynecologist. I hadn't seen a doctor in years. She was a tough Russian lady in her forties, with jet black hair and red lipstick. "You have two dermoid cysts, one the size of your fist." She made a fist. "Do you want to have kids? Yeah? OK. Do you have a partner or a boyfriend? Yeah? OK. Well, you should get on that then. *Yesterday.*" She wrote me a scrip for birth control, to stop me from ovulating for a bit and take the pressure off my ovaries, which I never filled. She told me, if I didn't want to go on the temporary birth control, then I should get pregnant now and have the surgery later. Or I could have the surgery now and cross my fingers I wouldn't lose an ovary or both in the process. I drove myself to Carvel and bought a mint chip ice cream cone, even though it was cool and gray outside. I decided to not make any decision at all.

I had one more book event of the year, a visiting writer invitation at Phillips Exeter Academy in New Hampshire. Within five minutes or so of sitting down to dinner, my host, the writer and religion scholar Tom Simpson, told me he did doctoral work at University of Virginia in Charlottesville. I asked if he knew the Marshes. He did. I told him about arriving at the Bonhoeffer House: the masterful way that the nonprofit provides funding, fellowship, living room, a para-academic and community-building apparatus, outside the university, and outside of a particular sectarian faith community, *and* a place for the Marshes to literally live.

Tom listened. We were sitting, at that moment, in the Exeter cafeteria where we'd helped ourselves for free to a delicious smorgasbord of food, including a slab of freshly prepared whoopie pies. We were surrounded by high schoolers and other faculty. Tom began to tell me about how about how he, his partner, and their two kids all came to live in a dormitory on campus, another model of communal living that is not altogether repellent to me.

He'd left a tenure-track position he held in Wisconsin, "Mostly because we needed community." He took a bite of the braised veggies. "Yeah, we had two little kids at the time, and I was working all the time, and we lived in a crappy apartment complex far off from campus where Alexis was stuck all day with the kids and trying to figure out what she wanted to do. She also had a master of divinity and had formerly been a pastor for a congregation, but cut out of that scene after a lot of dispiriting sexist stuff. Ya know, I'd come home, and she'd be like, *I can't live like this anymore!*"

Now, for the last ten years, Tom and his family have lived on campus. It sounds like a small apartment-style situation, and sometimes Tom has to assume RA duties and solve issues, fights, drug use, whatever, in the boys' dorm. And they can eat in the cafeteria, or not. It seemed like a nice way to live, at least for a while, at least for ten years.

•

I visited classes, did a public reading, had lunch with the interfaith student group, helmed by the young queer school chaplain, Heidi, in the old Phillips chapel. Then, Tom booked me, Mercy Carbonell, and himself a reading at the Word Barn for the final portion of my stay. The Word Barn ended up being a giant venue in an old barn on a tract of land upon which also sat a cute farmhouse where Sarah and Ben Anderson lived with their two kids and dog. They ran events at the Word Barn, and also produced the Portsmouth Music Festival. Ben had done a lot of the work on the barn, including a little bar in the corner with a tap of local deep citrusy IPA. His combination of both social aloofness and communal attentiveness to the operation at hand reminded me of Sweeney. Sarah was warm and dynamic and hilarious and let us snack in her kitchen beforehand: me, Sweeney, Tom, Mercy, Heidi. They partnered with the local bookstore to have a mobile sales table at the front door, and the seats were filled to the brink with local residents from this rural area.

Above the venue space, there was a little loft where Sarah held writing workshops, and I thought: this could be an easy model for a residency or a retreat space, a set of buildings upon which a life could be made. They were about ten minutes from town, where a whole bunch of their friends lived and their kids went to school. Sometimes Sarah picked up a semester here and there at Exeter. All us readers hung out, drinking and lolling around the Word Barn after the event, and it wasn't until then that I realized these were all really good, deep friends who travel together, labored together doing relief work in Sarajevo in the 1990s and early 2000s, celebrate birthdays, get drunk. Later, Sarah and I stood over her kitchen table shoveling chips and guacamole into our mouths, talking about the night, their life here, how she hoped we'd come back.

My friend Anna Moschovakis—the poet, translator, novelist, and Ugly Duckling Presse collective member—joined me for a beer one night in Fort Greene after our long days of teaching at Pratt. I asked half-jokingly if I could informational-interview her about the life she'd made for herself up in the Catskills. Anna and I were colleagues, fellow adjuncts, but before that she was my professor when I was a student at Pratt, and the person who helped my friends and me, including Sweeney, launch *Correspondence* and the larger project of The Corresponding Society back before I'd even turned twenty. So we had known each other for a long time, but had only recently become friends. I sipped my brown ale. I talked about feeling stranded and stretched at the edge of the city where we lived, and she answered my questions about her life in the western Catskills, the way it felt like home now, though it had taken years of loneliness and eavesdropping in village cafés for her to build up a community of friends. But now she had a robust world up there, and loved it, even if the commute was tricky, expensive, and required couch surfing. But I, who live only on the edge of town, am also couch surfing for days when I'm down in Brooklyn, and when I get back to Woodlawn, I don't feel as if I've arrived home—but rather at another weird outpost. Then she dreamed out loud: "We'll find a place, you and I, here in Brooklyn, with four or five other adjuncts who live outside of the city, and we'll have a shared Google calendar—and we'll have six plates, six mugs, six forks, six sheet sets, just enough for everyone to use, to keep it covered at cost. There will be enough of us that our rent will be super cheap."

We left the bar. She pulled her black coat tighter around herself. I kept dreaming.

"A cheap one-bedroom, maybe," I said, "with bunks, or something barracks style."

"Yes," she said. "And we'll have the freedom to hang out with each other, if we want—but it'll be understood, too, that we can just be invisible to each other, if we want, and work in silence, be alone, ya know?"

As the days began warming up, I sent her a glib text asking if she'd figured out how we'd do it yet—and, to my surprise, she had.

And so three days a week I lived at the henceforth Adjunct Flophouse, a beautiful boarding-style apartment with a bathroom in the hallway, a communal living experiment in Prospect Heights where Anna, a variety of other adjuncts who lived outside the city, and I embarked on a semi-communal living experiment born of not wanting to burn out in the gig economy and the neoliberal university system.

The very first night we got the keys, we bought altar candles at the bodega since we had not yet paid the electricity, and we laid them out along the dark red scratchy pub carpet still lining the hallways. We slept on fold-out mats. The light that came through the windows in the morning was beautiful. There were optimally angled windows everywhere.

In a way, like a fool, I found myself holding out for the existence of the per-fect home, of finally getting home or going home—so much so that I cried without fail at the most saccharine songs about home, songs like "Coun-try Roads" by John Denver and "Marathon" by the Heartless Bastards or "Home" by Edward Sharpe and the Magnetic Zeros, or "Sitting on the Dock of the Bay" by Otis Redding, who is not even heading home, is only thinking of it, far away at that moment but intact, waiting for him in Geor-gia. I don't feel like I have a "home" I can even sing to in that way, a point of origin to which I can return, in reality or nostalgia—not a childhood house, both of which are gone now, not even really a city, partly because of how profoundly my own hometown has changed over the last decade, rendering it nearly unrecognizable. So home, to me, is a fantasy, but a fantasy which I believe will eventually take on materiality.

I kept wondering, though, if it's any good to fix my gaze on the perfect horizon—the stick with which to beat the present. I don't want that. I don't know what I want. How will we make money? How much money could we reasonably expect to make if we stopped relying on the city for employ-ment? How will we not just isolate ourselves to death? "Look to the com-munity you already have to build the community you want"—where the fuck did I get that store-bought line? Anyway, there is no plan, per se—the hope is that *we are the plan* (my friend Kate had said this to her husband-to-be in her wedding vows when I officiated in Portland that summer).

But honestly, what hope is there for utopia if I'm still scrambling around for a cigarette on a Monday night?

utopianotes
minutes from a meeting

I. Desires
  a. Investment purposes (i.e., save money by putting it in land)
  b. Create a residency or multi-purpose artists' colony
    i. But something we can also live in/on
  c. Live with lower overhead, to support our own creative projects
  d. Possible associated revenue generator (i.e., school, shop, B&B)
    i. Running a hotel (shared equity/ownership?)
    ii. Camp?

II. Location
  a. Near rail and/or able to commute to the city

III. Different fiscal models
  a. Club model with "right of refusal" (re: buying & selling, down the road)
  b. "Buckey Mountain" model
  c. "Neighbor" model (subdivided parcels)
  d. "Be our own rich uncle" model

IV. Different property types
  a. Several close-knit parcels
  b. Private residences with one shared communal space/building
  c. Old hotel? Big raucous house with many rooms?
  d. Camp/Summer camp/Revival Camp??
  e. CAMP CAMP CAMP CAMP CAMP

V. Money?
    a. $500,000 property = $100,000 down (20%)
    b. Everyone provides $10,000 depending on type of use
    c. Where does the money come from??

VI. Next steps?
    a. Talk to Calliope
    b. Talk to Anna about Bushel
    c. Talk to a broker

RULES IMPOSED:

No guns

Attention to aesthetics, i.e., new construction can sometimes be ugly

1½ hours from the city, max.

Bathtub in the backyard

THE BRUDERHOF

I sent a note through a general query form on the Bruderhof website, re-questing a visit to their Fox Hill community in the foothills of the Catskills. In the query I said, stupidly, that I was "writing a book about utopian movements" (a very groupie-ish reveal), and the woman who wrote back to me said that while I was welcome to visit, I was not invited to write about them, and that they did not understand themselves as a utopian anything. So, I wrote her a long reply amending my initial bravado, trying to explain that I was not a journalist nor an academic, that autobiographical narratives were my primary medium, the way through which I explore a large question I have, and that I am using the word "utopian" very broadly (I mean, the tag-line on their own website is "Another life is possible"). And I shared that I was not just peering into the Bruderhof as a skeptic, but was bringing to the visit my own deep spiritual concerns—that were forming in part from my relationship to New Day—about living in community as a religious conviction. My correspondent demurred, making no promises, but offered the opportunity to talk more about it and get to know each other when I arrived.

The Bruderhof formed in Germany during the cultural upheaval following WWI, out of the heterogenous ideologies and communities of the German Youth Movement—essentially the German hippies of the 1900s to 1920s, defined largely by similar aims as their American counterparts later in the century. The German Youth Movement was broadly made up of what we might call today back-to-the-landers, pacifists, draft dodgers, leaders of simple lives interested in reviving German folk culture, communal anarchists with a searing critique of what they understood as their parents' generation's bourgeoisie Protestantism. (Of course, by the 1930s, the German Youth Movement was conscripted into Hitler Youth, the way all cultural institutions were absorbed by the Third Reich.) One particular community of these German hippie-Christians eventually became the Bruderhof, led by Eberhard and Emmy Arnold. Eberhard was jaded by his work as a Protestant

minister in a country where the church and state were so institutionally in-
tertwined. By the end of WWI, he felt moved by the German Youth Movement's "translation of ideals into practical action," writes Anna Neima in
The Utopians. "He knew that many of those involved were not Christian:
Catholics and Protestants played a role, and so did pagans, Zionists, anarchists
and naturists. But he dreamed nonetheless that he could persuade all these
idealistic young people to follow Jesus, that the youth movement could become a perfect vehicle for Christian socialist revolution." After one particular
visit to a secular commune outside Frankfurt in 1920, Eberhard and Emmy
moved from the dream of a roving, mobile caravan of evangelism to setting
up a rural commune themselves, which they called the Bruderhof, "brother
home."

They started as just a bunch of friends in their twenties and thirties,
living communally in the German countryside in a giant rented farmhouse,
practicing a way of life drawn largely (as per usual) from an interpretation
of the book of Acts. Then they opened their doors to fellow travelers. In
The Utopians, Anna Neima describes the early makeup of the Arnolds' commune as a place where "Evangelical Christians shared sofas with anarchists,
army officers rubbed shoulders with artists and journalists. The conversation
was tense, the air filled with cigarette smoke." She says, "The majority of
visitors were young . . . their interest fueled more by a generalised desire to
make the world anew than by Christian conviction. Among them were the
bohemian participants of the youth movement, with their signature long
hair, colourful clothes and backpacks; the clean-living members of various Christian organisations . . . [as well as] writers and artists; First World
War veterans who were haunting the countryside, unable to settle back into
their pre-war lives; expectant single mothers who had heard about a refuge
where no one was turned away; and a sprinkling of the misfits and eccentrics
drawn to utopian endeavours in any age."

She highlights the major influence of international exchange going on
during that moment, in the first Bruderhof commune, where "people came
from England, Holland, America, France and Switzerland out of simple
curiosity; some came determined to join the Bruderhof for good; others—
like an international group of young Zionists who would go on to start a

kibbutz in Palestine—wanted to learn about the practicalities of communal living. The Bruderhof looked fondly on the kibbutzniks as fellow religious idealists . . . The arrival of these foreigners, particularly those from 'enemy' nations, filled the Arnolds with the hope. The community was, Emmy said proudly, taking steps towards 'a new world—a new age in a new spirit of reconciliation.'"

During this time, Eberhard found out about the Hutterites, a radical German Anabaptist community that had migrated to North America in the seventeenth century due to persecution and had been there all this time: Eberhard's mind was blown. *How is it that no one had told us*, he thought, *that there are Germans sharing our same theology, out there in the wilds of the northern Great Lakes region!* Eberhard deputized himself and a small group of individuals from within his community to go visit the Hutterites in Michigan, during which time they were "convinced," came back to Germany, and announced that they were becoming Anabaptists. This included a stricter interpretation of the theology of "all things in common" they had been innovating up to that point: they became even more staunchly anti-state and committed to mutual reliance, renouncing labor-saving technologies, and assuming more essentialist gender roles. What had been an egalitarian arrangement between the sexes now prevented women from voting in community matters. Their clothing changed—women started wearing plain-clothes dresses for modesty and covering their heads.

The years of (and preceding) WWII brought massive changes. As the Third Reich began to cement power in the 1930s, the Bruderhof went into exile and sought respite in Switzerland, then in England, and later—when most countries were not willing to shelter German nationals in exile—they migrated to Paraguay, where there were also a contingent of Mennonites, another Anabaptist religion. During this period of exile, their own theology and culture transformed under all these changes, and during the Paraguay years, they fell out of communion with the Hutterites, and it was then that the Bruderhof culture really formed as a distinct entity. During this period, women once again were participating as equal members of the organization. And though the exile years were full of struggle and famine, following the war, they were eventually able to form several communities (or "hofs") primarily in New York and Pennsylvania, where they still exist today, each one housing two to three hundred people. The movement has just celebrated its hundredth year of existence.

Like most communitarian movements and Anabaptist sects that center the book of Acts in their spiritual beliefs, the Bruderhofs prioritize their commitment to the community as a fundamental tenet of their existence. They have a fully shared-purse economy. Today, they support themselves with a few cottage industries, which every hof contributes to some aspect of: a company called Community Playthings, which produces wooden children's toys; another called Rifton, which manufactures equipment for people with physical disabilities; and a publishing house called Plough. Everyone shares equally, on a rotating basis, in the labor of these enterprises, as well as the labor of maintaining their daily existence—laundry, farming, cooking, serving, building, cleaning. Though today they are no longer in communion with any particular religious organization, their life does still look a bit like other "simple" Anabaptists (the Amish, Old Order Mennonites, Hutterites), but the borders of their orthodoxy are looser: the Bruderhofs smoke and drink alcohol, in moderation, and they use all kinds of labor-saving technology, excepting things like personal cell phones or computers (though these are available in the community). And they are not separatist—anyone can join.

I was drawn to the Bruderhof particularly because of the tension they modeled between a penchant for orthodoxy and adaptation when it came to their theology and culture, which had both somehow changed a great deal and remained coherently in existence for multiple generations.

Because of this, they are particularly open to outsiders. They don't missionize—but if someone feels called to join, they have multiple channels by which people can reach out and arrange for both short- and long-term stays as a form of discernment.

I was hosted by a woman named Laura, the woman I'd been corresponding with, who—as she put it—came from "the outside" thirty years earlier, when she was a graphic designer living in D.C. She met me in the parking lot, by the dining hall, which sat at the end of a long, wooded driveway I'd turned onto from a foggy rural road. In a way, Laura was kind of exactly what I expected—a small, strong-looking woman with white hair, in a kerchief and cape dress, sitting on a rock. I awkwardly waved out my car window, and accidentally rolled it up while doing so. When I got out of the car, I tried to shake her hand, and she tried to hug me—then I tried to hug and she stuck out her hand. She stood so close to me she saw my suitcase packed for the weekend tucked into my backseat, and asked if she could take it for me, but I said, no, no, "that's for later" cryptically, and she said, OK then, and we were off to a weird start. I didn't want her to know that my husband was coming all the way up to meet me in the region the following afternoon, but would not stay with me here. I figured it would prove that I was just a tourist of the worst kind, which I suppose I was.

As we walked up a tidy stone path, she told me that the third- and fourth-graders were making tacos on the lawn outside the laundry building—they had prepared tacos for the day's laundry crew. There were a dozen or so kids, overseen by their summer school teachers, presiding over card tables on which the taco makings were carefully laid out.

"That's one of the best things about being here," Laura said. "You just drop off your laundry, and then the next day it comes to your door all clean and folded. It saves so much time for mothers to spend with their kids."

It was weird for her to say this because she knew that I knew that she had no children—and I think she knew I had none, either.

But on the other hand, she was right. Imagine a world where food and clothing and education and healthcare and housing and fiscal security were not a question. What kinds of relationships with your kids, spouse, neighbors, workmates would be possible, that otherwise aren't in a culture built on individualized or atomized survival? What kinds of daily feelings might you experience, weightless of stress, pressure, performance, time? What kinds of passions and ideas would you be free to explore—and, I guess, *would* you be free to explore, or is that itself burrowing back into the territory of individualistic behavior that the Bruderhofs exist in resistance to? If you came from the outside, would you get bored? Would you, say, have time to write a book? It did seem to me, immediately, a Bruderhof convert would already have to be living in a somewhat countercultural way in order to get footing and purchase in the pace and expectation of life here—you would have to have been tempered by a life that had taught you about radical self-abnegation already, at least a little.

Then again, while the American communes of the nineteenth century were met with similar questions from the outside, utopians were often having a lot more fun than their worldly contemporaries trying to survive bitterly against the tide of industrialization and rural alienation. I thought of something that, in his book *Paradise Now*, Chris Jennings writes about the nineteenth-century utopians: "Except for the Shakers, who felt theologically compelled toward tranquility outside of their raucous prayer meetings, most of these communities kept up a dizzying schedule of contra dances, lectures, card games, seances, philosophical debates, cotillions, history lectures, picnics, stargazing expeditions, concerts, plays, tableaux vivants, boating trips, baseball games, oyster suppers, and croquet tournaments." And this was true for the Bruderhofs today.

The day was divided up into different parts, and everyone was on an extremely organized but easy-paced schedule. Laura and I walked up to the schoolhouse, where the kids were playing in the yard with their minder, and we visited the school library and the classrooms (where some special-needs kids from "the outside" were made room for, too). We walked by the meal hall, where an older man greeted us. When I said I lived in the Bronx, he replied jubilantly, "Wasn't that young socialist just voted in for the primaries yesterday?" Then we gathered organically for noon meeting, in a circle of chairs and benches that were already set up in a grassy clearing under a big maple tree. Without any sort of open signal, people began to file in from all different parts of the large compound. When we were all seated, everyone sang hymns in beautiful multi-part harmonies, German springtime hymns, and we said prayers and petitions. Announcements were made. A man came up and gave a three-minute meditation on the love he feels for this community especially in times of need. Then we adjourned. There was no minister.

My host, Laura, took me on the path back to her dwelling. There were a variety of dwellings all over the giant tract of land. They looked sort of like 1990s tract housing, but extremely tidy, usually two or three stories tall. Three to four families lived in the smaller ones, and six to eight in the larger. Every floor had a communal kitchen, and each family had their own living room, but then bedrooms and bathrooms were spread out all over the building, so there were always people to say hello to in the hallways. Laura and another woman named Dorothy were a "family" as older single women, with a twenty-five-year-old single woman "adopted" into their family—at least until or unless she gets married. We had lunch in their living room, surrounded by books and pottery that Laura and Dorothy had made themselves, as a hobby in their free time. What did we have, so quickly assembled? A little bread, cheese, chicken salad, fruit? Dorothy cut apples into a bowl while we talked for a pie she'd be cooking that night. I told them about New Day Church, about Sweeney and his dissertation, about Dan, about Sweeney's tireless caretaking of Dan, to which Dorothy remarked, "That's a testament to his strong faith." Laura pulled a glass carafe from the fridge. "I love my cold brew," she said. "You want some?"

After lunch, we walked the path to the Community Playthings factory. It was a cool, gray day. We passed people of all ages, on their way back to various modes of work following the lunch hour. Most if not all were barefoot, though all the women were wearing long skirts and blouses, or long heavy smock dresses with blouses underneath, and kerchiefs. The men wore mostly jeans and t-shirts, or ordinary button-downs. Laura asked what I thought of *The Benedict Rule*, a book by contemporary neoconservative Catholic Rod Dreher, who argues that Catholics need to sequester themselves from the world (I hadn't read it, but I knew of it), and then later mentioned how much they had helped counsel Shane Claiborne as he started his community, the Simple Way, in Philadelphia. "I couldn't live how they live at the Simple Way, though," she said, kind of laughing, and I was not exactly sure what this meant, but I figured it was because their community was quite messy and anarchic compared to the incredible order of the Bruderhof. She told me that some folks from the Bruderhof recently collaborated on a talk down at the Dorothy Day House in the West Village. "With the Catholic Workers?" I asked.

"Oh, yeah," she said. "We work with them a lot."

The Community Playthings factory was so organized, so efficient. There were a hundred rounded plastic hooks for people to hang their coats upon walking in. Across the warehouse floor, happy barefoot people worked on packaging for the toys, sanded down wooden blocks, assembled wooden children's play structures, slowly, thoroughly, old women and young women, men, boys, the whole lot. Laura and I assembled and packed wooden truck sets for a couple of hours, with a woman named Suzanne who'd joined the movement as a former back-to-the-lander in the late 1960s. Her husband walked by with a dolly carrying one of their hottest items: a mud table. Suzanne told me that, back in the 1960s, she and her husband had bought a piece of land with a friend in Vermont, with the intention to become totally self-sufficient. "My daughter was born there—she didn't even have a birth certificate," she said. But then the friend eventually bailed on them, and they were cold and alone in the woods, and the vision didn't come into being. We pumped out industrial tape, slapped on shipping labels, taped boxes. Laura wanted to give me a sense of the daily life here, so she carried out the work with me, but I could tell this wasn't her normal job—although the idea is that everyone does every job, even if you're a guest.

Later, she led me into a different part of the building where their publishing house offices exist. Plough puts out books and a quarterly magazine. She brought me to a giant pillar they created for the recent BookExpo at the Javits Center in New York, where she'd invited people to put a sticky note on the pole naming a book that had changed their life: "Seems like a lot of people had their lives changed at thirteen when they read *Catcher in the Rye* or *To Kill a Mockingbird*," she marveled. In the Plough offices, people of all ages filled orders, took phone calls, did computer work, accounting, marketing, editorial, etc. And then there was a boardroom with a library, and that's where I started to see the continuities that had been slowly revealing themselves to me all day: on the shelves were Shane Claiborne's *The Irresistible Revolution: Living as an Ordinary Radical*, Erik Reece's *Utopia Drive*, several books about Dorothy Day, different volumes of Clarence Jordan's Cotton Patch gospels from Koinonia, things I had been reading piecemeal that summer and had never seen gathered in one place. Laura walked me through Plough's own library of titles, which included writings and authors gathered from a variety of radical theologians who had nothing formally to do with the Bruderhof movement: collections of Óscar Romero's writings, Daniel Berrigan, Wendell Berry, plus lots of writing from and about their founders and history, the Arnolds.

Clare was basically, it turned out, the creative director of Plough, though she seemed extremely hesitant to claim a title because the Bruderhof ethos of labor was that no one's identity was bound up in one job. She put the magazine to press, organized the production calendar, developed sales relationships, and managed an internship program. Everyone I passed greeted me, talked to me, wanted to know more about why I was there. At four o'clock, there was a coffee hour—which are elaborately orchestrated three times a day at all the different work sites (the laundry, the kitchen, the farm, the school, the factory)—and we all went outside on the lawn outside the factory, and carts were brought out holding coffee and tea, water, and maybe some kind of powdered sports drink. We had fifteen minutes to sit on the benches and visit and rest under the trees. I drank hot coffee from a white mug. I heard stories of people from the community being regularly dispatched to perform humanitarian aid and work in refugee camps all over the world, which, Laura says, "We can do so easily. Organizations like us because, well, *no one has a job*—so we always have people available." The Bruderhofs understand themselves as a service community, constantly at the ready to mobilize any of their two thousand members worldwide to volunteer in humanitarian aid organizations.

I also listened to how one family recently went to Koinonia—Clarence Jordan's radical multiracial Christian commune in Americus, Georgia, that's been there since the 1940s—to help with a service project for several months; another visited communities all over the Northwest. I was beginning to realize that there was a lot of mutual exchange and common knowledge among all of these movements that I had thought of, until this moment, as discrete and separate and cut off from one another.

We walked around afterward, past other dwellings and trails, then had dinner back at Laura's house—while all the families of the 220-person community also had dinner, all at the same time, in their own units. It turned out that a lot of people only live in their dwellings for a few years at a time, sometimes more, sometimes less. People move, or get reassigned, about and between the twenty different outposts throughout their lives—which are primarily in New York, Pennsylvania, England, Germany, and Australia. I am not sure who decides when someone moves.

We ate dinner back at Laura's dwelling with Dorothy and the twenty-five-year-old. Laura poured us a bit of box wine in one of her handmade mugs, laughing: "What can I say, it's our Franciscan poverty." We ate a delicious dinner of braised veggies, a green salad, a kind of savory North African stewed meat porridge. I struggled to describe to them my own religious background, as well as my religious present. New Day, which felt so powerful to me earlier that day, now felt sort of remote, like, what *does* it mean to gather only on Sundays? How was my life actually being upended by that weekly observance? How can I say I believe in something as radical as the gospel and not be living a life of all things in common? It took no time at all for me to feel this urgently, for my own life to feel quite pale and un-thought-through in comparison to what was going on here, despite how foreign and alienating it felt to me.

Laura and Dorothy started to talk vaguely about politics: they were devastated by Donald Trump's election, but skeptical that Bernie Sanders would be able to successfully campaign against him in 2020 or that there was anyone else who might run in his place. "And we just *couldn't* support Hillary," Dorothy clucked, but didn't say why. The only media they referred to having recently read, though, were books published by Plough, and *Plough* magazine. Dorothy said she found it particularly difficult when visitors, women in particular, would come and comment on their dresses: "I like what I wear," she said. "I'm free! I don't have to think about it! And I like being a woman, and being known as a woman." Laura complained about a story where a visitor had remarked on how German the Bruderhof culture was. "I mean, what's so German about it? It's just some old folk songs we like to sing is all." But, I thought though did not say, it is *so* German. The music, the dress, the food served in the communal dining hall, the wooden children's toys, and the powerful level of order at every sector of daily life. And then, maybe it goes without saying, but this community was almost entirely white. And it wasn't lost on them.

A lot of people I encountered felt the moral crisis of the homogeneity. Laura talked about this—a lot of folks did. Laura put it: "If you've come from a life or a family where you've never had anything, or you've had to fight bitterly for what you have, and then some white people come along and say, Give it all away! I mean, *I'd* be suspicious." But the community has no current strategy for rectifying that or dealing with the fact that folks who are even going to have the wherewithal, time, safety, etc. to join a community like this are going to be white. Of course, neither has the private art college I currently teach at prioritized these questions for its 150-year existence, or many other communities and institutions I participate in, for that matter.

A weird thing about me—something I begin to remember, as the day wears on, has always been true—is that I seem to be able to pass in extremely conservative or otherwise orthodox religious spaces, whether that's a Lakota Sun Dance or a white complementarian evangelical church service or here with the Bruderhof. And it's not just that I pass; there is something I do, some way I hold myself that makes me not just open and available, but complicit: The Bruderhofs are conservative in their social practices, definitely anti-gay (though no one talks about it), and essentialist in many of the divisions of labor. They ask a lot: that you divest everything you own, all assets, upon becoming a member. That, for the rest of your life, you share the two cars, you give up your phone, laptop, TV, all of it, though there are fiscal provisions made if you eventually decide to leave the community, and you can return later, too, after a period of discernment. Where are the artists, the rebels, the weirdos, the queers? Where are the loud women, the fey men, the two-spirited? Where do they go? This question is at the heart of things for me, though I don't ask it, and this has something to do with why I allow people in these situations to assume I share all their beliefs: no matter how conservative or heteronormative or white many of these utopian communities I'm interested in are, I'm continually drawn in by the ways that they attempt, on a day-to-day basis, to overturn the neoliberal individualistic healing and living modalities. There is something irresolvable in my openness to that, so regularly turned into complicity.

As I thought about these things, I also listened to myself continuing to tell Laura and Dorothy about my own conversion into evangelicalism when I was twenty, and I skirt around the fact that I had left because of the social conservatism; I listened to myself talk about New Day, and realize how little of myself I'd actually given to that community since I'd joined.

The twenty-five-year-old, who had been mostly silent, talked about her most recent mission trip to a refugee camp in Lebanon, her decision to stop eating meat, and as she downed a second cup of hot coffee—the sun setting behind her out the window—how she was looking forward to joining the other twenty-somethings tonight for an evening of construction on a new dwelling. "We're installing toilets tonight," she laughed.

Why was I there? I wanted to know, if I'm being honest, whether I could show up somewhere, and not just sit around thinking about these things purely in the abstract. I wanted to know I could talk to people, make contact; I wanted some self-confidence in my inquiry. I thought about other writers, other utopian groupies, who would go for a week, or a month, often or sometimes almost joining, and they needed to do that in order to say anything of substance about the life there, in order to be able to describe it. I don't know that my task or my interest is to be able to describe faithfully or comprehensively any of these communities' daily lives—I certainly couldn't begin to describe the Bruderhof. In a way, I don't think I could do that kind of writing without being a tourist, no matter how long I stayed. And if I stayed, then I wouldn't write a book about it, or include it in a book. My task has really been about wanting to know that such things have existed, still exist, and beyond that—again—what was I doing here? How much time should I spend questing for information, performing "research," and how much time should I spend living, spending time with family and friends, eating healthy, actually exercising, making concrete plans for the next phase—or is it folly to think that any of these things are separate tasks?

Or maybe it was exactly as I said to Laura in my query: when I have a big question, or a knot in my esophagus that feels like a question, it gets threaded into everything I do—and if I'm not writing, I'm not really thinking, so I write to think and write to live, and then I talk to people about the writing. What does it mean to belong to a radically inclusive, multiracial faith community in the twenty-first-century Bronx and still have a life that feels totally conventionally isolated by capitalism? There was a kind of joy, delight, or something in the idea of New Day's utopianism, and then there was a hollow thud in my mind when I thought about how much all of us at

New Day still lived alone, still had to work our godforsaken jobs, away from our kids and our friends and our ailing fathers-in-law, how much people are shamed if they are not working much or at all.

After dinner, Laura, Dorothy, and I drove on a muddy road to the other end of the compound to have tea with what they called "a proper family," the Wilsons. We arrived at a spectacular nineteenth-century farmhouse that had been, on the interior, similarly converted into a communal dwelling with three living rooms and multiple bathrooms and bedrooms outfitted throughout. "Preservationists would have a fit," Laura laughed. "I think you'll like the Wilsons, though." It was interesting how proactive she was in putting me in touch with folks to speak with, especially considering that she had been very clear that they were not yet going to give me permission to write about my experiences there.

The Wilsons greeted us and brought us into the hallway.

"You have such a beautiful home!" I blurted to Don Wilson, who smiled tolerantly and said, "Yes, isn't it? And best of all, it's so *communal*," lest I forget that no one lays claim on any particular structure here.

His wife, Maureen, came into the entryway to greet us, too. She was a beautiful, tall, northern European–looking woman, who I realized I'd met during the coffee hour, and who was funny and wry when we chatted. She swept us into the family's living room. Their fifteen-year-old daughter sat in her smock dress, talking to her adult sister on a landline.

Don and Maureen were lifers, born-Bruderhofs. Maureen's father had joined the movement after he'd been conscripted into the Civilian Public Service as a conscientious objector during WWII, which is how quite a few Americans joined the movement during the twentieth century, it turned out. Most of the CPS men were coming from the Historic Peace Churches, mainline Anabaptist churches mostly: Church of the Brethren, Quakers, and Mennonites, though there were other denominations and faiths represented as well. Don Wilson's family, on the other hand, had ended up in the Bruderhof in a more unusual way.

His family's story started with a secular commune that his father and mother started together after World War II, after his father was discharged from a CPS camp. The commune was called Macedonia and had been in Clarkesville, Georgia.

"Here they were," Don said, "living in this old farmhouse out in the middle of nowhere, during McCarthy-era America, and the cops come to storm the place: Let us enter, in the name of the law! And then they do. And ya know, there's people sleeping on the back porch and whatnot, and the cops think they've stumbled on some commie hotbed. And this woman, sleeping on the back porch, getting stepped over, this woman of high Southern breeding, says, 'I say, are there *any* gentlemen here?'"

Laura and Dorothy laugh at this line—"Oh, Elizabeth," they say, because, I guess, they know this story, and they knew Elizabeth personally, this particular woman from this story, because she, this woman that the cops found sleeping on the back porch at Macedonia in the 1940s, eventually joined the Bruderhof. All the people at Macedonia did.

Don continued: "They were trying to live in a way that—well, they were trying to make a kind of life that doesn't lead to war. That's it." It was a multi-faith project, with people from a variety of backgrounds, though no one was particularly observant in any tradition. They farmed. They are the ones, he tells me, who started Community Playthings—which only became a Bruderhof enterprise when the two communities merged.

At the time that Macedonia was eking out its existence, the Bruderhof had just begun migrating from Paraguay to their first North American community in Rifton, another town in the foothills of the Catskills. Some of the folks at Macedonia heard about the Bruderhofs and invited them to visit them in Clarkesville. "And on that visit," Don said, "half of the community at Macedonia were convinced, converted, and half of them were not. And so they decided to separate everything evenly, down to the last piece of flatware."

Then Don began to cry. I couldn't believe it—I did a double take. Hadn't he already told me that they eventually all ended up back together again, in Rifton? But the residue of the breakage—I got it instinctively. It is the kind of thing I've been steeped in a lifetime of grief about: the family, the community, breaking up. Even though the story ultimately ends, twelve years later, with them all reuniting as Bruderhofs in New York, and even though Don wasn't even born yet during the Macedonia years, he tells this story as though it is the saddest story of his life: a community amicably, lovingly, divorcing.

So the old members of Macedonia carried on, at half population, on their multi-faith communal living project, making children's toys (though now the company was shared with the Bruderhof), and slowly there were ideological rifts and people leaving and all of that, so they decided maybe they did all need a theological agreement of some kind, in order to preserve the community. They corporately decided they would do a survey of all the world religions and decide on one. They stocked up on holy texts—the Bhagavad Gita, the Qur'an, the Torah, the Bible—and then sat down in the living room and opened up the book of Matthew and that night, Don said, "They met the person of Jesus Christ." That was that. They didn't even get to the Bhagavad Gita. Or so the story goes. They all converted and connected back up with their lost Bruderhof comrades and moved to New York and joined their business together.

This couple, the Wilsons, had themselves connected with other Christian intentional communities a few years back, when the Bruderhof actually sent them on such a mission, which happens from time to time: they were given the community credit card, a budget, and one contact. Their job was to go out and connect with other communities, develop other contacts. They stayed with several different communities over the course of a few months, including non-Christian ones. Maureen said, "It just goes to show how there's so many different ways to follow Jesus."

Don was speaking in awe: "I mean, we just kept meeting more and more people living in community. It was incredible. In Portland, we smoked cigars with the Adsideo community. Up near Olympia, we stayed in a tiny house colony. It's just like, there's this whole, robust world of people living together in these amazing communities, like flowers growing up through cracks in the sidewalk, it's wild, and no one knows about it. No one's writing about it."

What I realized then was that all of these different communities I'd been reading about lately—Koinonia, the Catholic Workers, Englewood, Simple Way—all knew about each other, and not only that but were in communion with one another. It seemed, in fact, from my one day with the Bruderhof, that most organized radical Christian communities in the United States actively collaborate and support each other, despite the ways in which I, someone from "the outside," understand them each to have drastically different lifestyles and theologies from one another, so much so that I assumed they could never get along.

In fact, I'd assumed all this time that the decision to live in a radical and somewhat closed community must also require a refusal of some kind, a need to convince yourself that this was not just a way to live or to believe, but *the* way. And so the idea of interfaith or intercultural collaboration seemed out of the question. The irony is that that level of dogma, the kind I assumed that people like the Bruderhof lived with, is really a dogma *I* live with. It is perhaps I who have convinced myself that there is only one way to live and only one way to believe, and that it is this dogma that propels all the daily actions of my life: going to work and paying rent and being isolated and buying shit and continuing, day in and day out, to make those same choices.

Breakfast at Laura and Dorothy's, and presumably in everyone else's household, was at 6:00 a.m. sharp. I set my alarm for 5:45 and lay in the dark for a few minutes to get my bearings till about 6:05, when Laura knocked on my door to make sure I was awake. It was misty and gray outside. After breakfast, Laura and I met in a small office room with another community member, a man, who helps run Plough. She invited me to tell them both more about my "book project," and, exchanging glances with one another, they decided that they'd like to read whatever it was I ended up writing before it went to print. Then I went to work in the Community Playthings factory until lunchtime in the big hall—where the whole community prayed, sang, and ate, and bowl after bowl after bowl of freshly prepared vegetables from the farm and sausages were passed down the dozen rows of tables.

A girl sitting across from me was turning seven that day, and so everyone sang happy birthday and she was given a bowl of ice cream, which was vexingly served as a tower of cubes. The other children around her were happy and relaxed and playful, in a way that I only ever see when the adult world that frames them has meaningfully included them in the daily goings-on. A group of second graders who had just returned from a weeklong camping trip approached a mic as a group and told a story about how they saw a bear. I've honestly never seen such high numbers of happy, relaxed kids.

After lunch, Laura walked me back to my car and we hugged goodbye. And on the road toward Newburgh, I caught up like a hurricane with what had gone on in "the outside" in the thirty-six hours I had been away: Justice Kennedy, for one, had announced his retirement. Draconian anti-LGBTQ legislation had been upheld in the Supreme Court. Texts and emails came in like an avalanche after I parked in a gas station to buy a phone charger. I leaned against my car under the wet spring sunlight, listening to my heart beat.

Sometimes I wonder: what if I realized at a young age that I wasn't going to do anything creative at all? Instead of hoarding time for writing, I would spend my days helping people, all the time, till my hands fell off. Not because I am good, but because that was where my energy would drift, in my tendency toward self-abnegation. Or I would spend my days fretting and asking everyone if they're OK, if there's anything I can do. I would stand in the kitchen sending plates out to the people I serve, a household, a homeless shelter, a church, a commune, a compound. Listen to me, though—am I saying that if I weren't an artist I would be more self-giving? No. I would be a bee, or I would be like a bee; that's my tendency. It's a hard knot, a kind of wheat-paste-colored feeling—the idea of my life not as an artist—a dry, tan mush or the color of peasant clothes. Oh my God, I see now clearly what it is I mean: if I weren't an artist, I'd wear plain clothes, I'd be at the Bruderhof, living for the community, working in the toy factory and the magazine office, dining with all my brethren every day and praying, sitting in the common room with Sister Dorothy, and putting together simple feasts and going back to work when I am called at 2:45 p.m. I would be in pale blue clothes with a pale kerchief pinned over my head, sometimes letting it down when I got hot, with little hairs flying about the crown. I would wait on that rock by the parking lot for the young woman coming in from out of town to see what it's like to live in harmonious existence with 220 people, where the beet greens are always fresh, where the networks of people are always growing, where they can always supply people to go work in relief efforts because no one has a job. Where the laundry is dropped off in the morning for the laundry people to do, whoever it is that day, and at night it returns crisp and smelling fresh, and you know that all is working and all is well. It would be that muted color I'm thinking of—that mushy, taupe, wheat-paste color I think of when I think of this existence, though it would not be an unhappy one. The color is reflective of the way people collectively disappear into a group which has agreed to disappear into each other, to lose a self for the fruits of a good life, or a right life. Who cares about what you make, or what special thought you have? All vocations are yours. Everyone drinks coffee. All the children cared for, all the adults rested and articulate, everyone working at an easy pace because we don't need to produce more than we can ship off or consume. Basically, what I am realizing is that I would be an Anabaptist Old Order Mennonite, I would still be in Pennsylvania, where just three generations earlier many of my ancestors had been for hundreds of years, living communally in Lancaster County since the 1630s.

What am I bringing to the idea of being an artist, though, in this thought process? Am I asserting that it is something that happens individually, with an audience? Something that's necessarily *not* group-oriented? Who's to say they aren't artists at the Bruderhof? Laura and Dorothy make pottery. That last morning I worked in the factory, I watched a dozen men lovingly sanding in a hypnotic rhythm each of those individual wooden building blocks getting ready to be shipped to kindergarten classrooms all over the country, all of them careful craftsmen.

There is an inheritance of self-abnegation in me: a long, long line of Anabaptist Christians living out communalism and poverty in rural landscapes, outside the city, defined fairly strictly against urban life and modernization. But then there is its opposite: I also, in a different line of descent, come from plunderers, colonists, who came to the beautiful, "virgin" forests of the Pacific Northwest to build utopia for white people.

utopianotes
The Aurora Colony

Sweeney and I visit the Old Aurora Colony—now Aurora, Oregon—on our way up to Portland. Aurora is a dusty cow town now, just outside the state capital of Salem. It is also the pinot noir capital of the world.

There are a couple of buildings that still stand from the Colony's early days in the 1850s—one is this big white multifamily dwelling, a frontier Victorian which houses most of the museum's artifacts. It is cool inside from the heat, and totally silent. An older woman sits at the desk. She asks if we'd like to watch the video. We are the only guests. We sit on a wooden bench, and after some technical difficulties, the 1990s-era video wiggles onto the screen: from 1856 to 1883, fifty-four families, mostly of German and Swiss descent, left their commune in Missouri to create a communal colony in the "second Eden" of Oregon. A great deal of the Aurora members were Harmonist defectors from Father Rapp's third and final commune of Economy, Pennsylvania—the last encampment he set up after New Harmony. They built Craftsman homes and schools, farmed grain, ran a very popular hotel, and had a notorious brass marching band.

Even now the video, and the other interpretive materials, go through a lot of trouble to avoid the word "commune," saying instead things like "Christian communal colony." It makes sense: they didn't have a shared purse; they lived in mostly separate houses (though they had shared spaces for meetings, religious gatherings, and cooking). They did practice communal confession (from which the leader was exempt), and they did have a charismatic leader (exempt also from manual labor), but otherwise they seemed to be functioning just like an old town—which was what it eventually became, when they dissolved the commune.

It was the first designated historic district in Oregon. It was "the most significant communal society that existed west of the Rocky Mountains in nineteenth-century America." Afterward, the docent tells us to go ahead and ring the old church bell on display in the second room. She shows off the music boxes some of the former colony members collected, at great cost. She hands us a brochure, printed with the silhouette of a fictional female avatar: *Walk with Emma—YOUR self-guided tour of Historic Aurora.*

THE ANCESTORS

I remember coming face-to-face with my first ancestor at my Grammy Evelyn's eightieth birthday. I was five years old, and the family had booked a lavish party downtown at the old Multnomah Athletic Club. Toward the end of the night, my father brought me to a large, framed photograph in the foyer: a big, gruff man with wild mutton chops and a jaunty bow tie, next to whom sat a tiny, tight-lipped woman. "That's Captain Couch," he said, "your great-great-great-great-grandfather, and the first person to bring people to Portland by boat." I stared into Captain Couch's face, straining for a sense of attachment. He looked back, grim, maybe gassy, and mute.

We do need to get one thing out of the way: I wouldn't be here thinking about utopia if it hadn't been for some white people who had a lot of money in the nineteenth century, and an idea about creating heaven on earth, in Oregon, away from whence they came. Oregon, even then, had long been laden with ideas of a white Eden, ever since the Lewis and Clark Expedition—particularly for commodity barons and nautical capitalists in places like Massachusetts and New York, entrepreneurs and boy-dreamers wasting away under the weight of their growing fortunes. Those were my people. Sure, there were other white folks who ended up in the Northwest on the Oregon Trail, pioneers pursuing the promise of verdant homesteads, but a lot of those people were poor and already pretty far west when they began their journey, in the heartland or the Rockies or the high desert. Captain Couch's journey was just classic manifest destiny.

I hadn't thought about these particular ancestors for a while, until a special communion service during Lent at New Day Church got me considering them in a different way. One of the assistant pastors gave the sermon that morning, preaching from a passage in Revelation. He began with a story about coming home one day from high school with a library book about Santería, which his grandmother immediately threw into the trash can, warning him to stay away from witchcraft. For the assistant pastor, a Black gay man, his grandmother's reaction embodied the fear that ran through his entire Afro-Caribbean family around claiming or even acknowledging syncretic religions as a legitimate part of their spiritual ancestry, after generations of assimilation that their survival had depended on. And yet, it was through Santería that he found an important code to his past, and an aspect of his own connection to the divine, which would take years to return to. About Revelation, he addressed its author, the political prisoner John of Patmos, framing the book as a kind of code, legible only to those on the radical Christian underground as the Roman empire is falling apart.

Then he started talking about the TV show *Underground*, how it tells the story of the Underground Railroad as navigated by a series of codes, how for people of color in America, their whole ancestry has had to be encoded in things like songs and parables in order to be passed down and preserved from imperial intervention. So, John of Patmos, John the Revelator, is singing about the fall of Babylon, the fall of Rome, and then a new heaven and a new earth emerging in a show of awesome destruction. The power brokers clutch their pearls. *Well, what is this new world? What the hell does he mean?* Those on the underground know, and will know.

When he finished, the communion stewards, an ever-changing set of volunteers from the congregation, entered the cafeteria from the back doors and walked down the aisle between the stacking chairs, singing a soft Lenten song in Spanish. They processed to the front and separated into pairs: one person with a finger bowl of red wine and the other with a circle of unleavened bread. We all lined up. When I approached, the woman offering me the bread said, as she had said to all the other congregants before me, "The bread of life. This is your ancestors," and a cold shiver went through me. *My ancestors?* For a great deal of the people in that room, it was an empowering invocation—hailing from the Caribbean diaspora, being descendants of the Great Migration, coming from long and forcibly broken lines of descent created by colonialism and slavery. But for me, it was a little sinister, like, *Do you know who my ancestors are?*

·

So, a handful of these guys—Couch and others like him—showed up in the late 1830s to start building out the new ports in the Columbia River Valley, becoming both the region's premier businessmen and politicians. In 1844, before Oregon even became a territory, slavery was outlawed and all Black people residing there were required to leave: women were given three years to leave; men were given two. By the time Oregon formally joined the union in 1859, the legislature ratified a law that made it illegal for Black people to own property, live in, or even enter the state.

This was how they would make their little white utopia, in keeping with many of the other existing "utopian" communities at the time: *We will start from scratch because we believe this place we have staked ground is a blank slate, waiting for us.* Though rather than waiting for the end of the world—like the Harmonists, Shakers, and Millerites expected—these guys imagined they had created one. So they abolished Black citizenship, and they also erected enclosures around the river people who were already there, a massive heterogenous federation of tribes along the Columbia River, and they conscripted the Chinese to build the railroads which would undergird their businesses, before enacting Chinese exclusion laws as well.

Let's be real: whiteness is a moral crisis. Just being white already messes up my ability to write meaningfully about utopia, because it's like: You, white forebears, you dreamed of this fucked-up world—and now you want to escape it? Now *I* do? To make a faithful excursion into people who have made a heaven on earth in America, or tried to, or thought they were, I have to begin where I began, on a beautiful, tree-flanked hill in southeast Portland, Oregon, a state that—when it was founded, by the very intentions and investments of my direct ancestors—was never supposed to contain Black people. Of course, Oregon went on to be a place that was later characterized by wild visions of the New Age: radical progressivism, back-to-the-landers, separatist feminist communes, and the infamous Rajneeshpuram. But the wholesome culture of late twentieth-century white liberalism and neo-hippies I grew up with sits on the back of the most abhorrent exclusionary laws of the land. Portland is still the whitest major city in the United States. With a metro area population of over 2.7 million, white people make up 76 percent.

Portland, especially, seems to be the pinnacle of that utopian project that was the state of Oregon in part because of how top-down its creation was, versus the messier pluralistic creation of other large cities, like New York, which of course has its own barons and monopolists, but which, in its variety of vested interests, made room for surprise and for uprising. But in Portland's case, it was five to ten rich white guys, almost all of whom I'm related to, around whose fortunes and power the development of the city strictly took place for the first fifty years.

Captain Couch made the first of five "land claims" on what settlers simply called "the clearing"—a small wharf north of Oregon City, whose prominence as a port he hoped to supplant with his participation in building this new town. (The second land claim was made by a businessman, Daniel Lownsdale, also my fourth-great-grandfather on my mother's side.) These relations are eerily not that remote: Captain Couch was my Grammy Evelyn's great-great-grandfather, and my aunt reminds me that my Grammy had actually spent time, as a child, with Captain Couch's youngest daughter—an erudite bohemian who moved away to Paris as an adult. And she reminds me how Captain Couch's wife, Mary, was let off his ship in Panama and muled across the country to get to the Pacific port, packed with her three daughters in tow and all their stuff, to meet him on the other side. And then they settled in the hills above their land claim.

But it's not like my immediate relatives—my parents, my aunts and uncles, and so forth—are capitalists, nor do they wear the mark of their Victorian bourgeoisie heritage. Four generations later, everyone is now thoroughly middle class, and fairly salt-of-the-earth. They are social workers and gardeners and union officers and musicians. Some went to college, and others did not. What happened? When I look at my family tree at the turn of the twentieth century, I do notice one thing: they all started to have daughters—daughter after daughter after daughter. Women disrupted the flow of power and the consolidation of wealth, as the money that trailed behind them was put into the hands of dudes who were not businessmen, often older men, who made decisions with that money that had nothing to do with the particular family legacies of their wives. What did the lines of descent mean in the white utopia once the heirs to that white settler wealth began to dissipate? For one, we got instantly poorer, as a family line, generationally speaking, moving to the East Side, living off our fathers' wealth till it dwindled, marrying the wrong guys, our houses getting smaller and smaller, till we'd disappeared into the landscape.

My Grammy Evelyn—whose eightieth birthday we celebrated at the Multnomah Athletic Club under the portrait of Captain Couch all those years ago—was the last vestige of Blue Blood culture, the last person to live in Portland Heights, looking out at the land, thinking proudly of all her great-granddaddies to whom she promised, spiritually, to preserve their legacies. Don't get me wrong: she was dutiful, not stuffy. She was a cool lady, very smart, sassy, arch, civically minded, twice divorced and independent as hell, but she had an agreement to work out with their ghosts, and I guess so do I.

Most of the white settlers in Oregon were ideologically against slavery, or against slavery in the abstract—but only in as much as they imagined a white Eden where the question of Black enslavement was, in their minds, moot. So slavery was outlawed by the provisional government in 1844, and provisions were put in place that required those slaveholders who had come into Oregon to free their slaves at once. And then the provisional government immediately instated a draconian law ordaining the punishment of any Black people—including those who had come to Oregon freely—who refused to leave during the allotted removal period, called "Peter Burnett's lash law." The "lash law" ordered public flogging for all violators, about which Burnett himself, a judge on the supreme court of the provisional government, said, "The object is to keep clear of that most troublesome class of population. We are in a new world, under the most favorable circumstances and we wish to avoid most of those evils that have so much afflicted the United States and other countries." While the law was rescinded within a year of its ratification, and supposedly before it was actually ever enforced, it sent out a most clear and violent message.

Already, in that language, the ideology lays itself plain: we mean no harm; we are simply certain that we have made "a new world" which is

uniquely ours, under "the most favorable circumstances" of white supremacy. This kind of reasoning reasserts itself over and over again during the
last half of the nineteenth century as politicians struggled to maintain their
social order in a quickly changing world. In a public reflection a few years
later in 1850 about the exclusion laws, congressional delegate Samuel Thurston stumped, "[It] is a question of life or death to us in Oregon. The negroes associate with the Indians and intermarry, and, if their free ingress is
encouraged or allowed, there would a relationship spring up between them
and the different tribes, and a mixed race would ensure inimical to the
whites; and the Indians being led on by the negro who is better acquainted
with the customs, language, and manners of the whites, than the Indian,
these savages would become much more formidable than they otherwise
would and long bloody wars would be the fruits of the comingling of the
races. It is the principle of self-preservation that justifies the actions of the
Oregon legislature." Everything about this speech is enough to make you
puke. I sit with it now because it articulates white supremacy so precisely,
heightened by Thurston's absolute best attempt to use logic. Self-preservation! It's astounding, the level of self-delusion at work here—what the hell
do they think it is they're preserving? They speak as though they have been
camped out here for eight thousand years.

In 1857, the territory's legislature submitted a new and more precise exclusion clause to white voters which included a proposal to legalize slavery.
While voters overwhelmingly decided to keep Oregon a "free state," they
did double down in equal positive numbers for the revised exclusion clause,
and those were the laws on the book when Oregon was incorporated into
the union in 1859: Black people were forbidden from being in the state,
owning property even remotely, or entering into business contracts within
the state of Oregon. Again, there was little to no real enforcement (and
all attempts to pass laws that would legalize enforcement were killed by
either voters or legislators), but I suppose that is because by the 1860s, there
were so few Black people in the state or attempting to move there that the
citizens just didn't see any use—the laws had already done the work they
were looking for, which was to shun, separate, and create such inhospitable
conditions for Black people that none would try to cross the boundary. The

white voters might have looked at the enforcement clauses on their ballots and thought, *But, my God, we're not monsters!*

Francis Pettygrove, one of the two politician-businessmen who gave Portland its name—and who possessed one of the five neighboring land claims next to Captain Couch—said in a public address toward the end of his life in 1880, "It fills my heart with joy to see the great city where I once saw dense woods." There is continuously this sense that they, the white settlers, understand themselves as having arrived somewhere unoccupied, totally their own, where there were only "dense woods" before them, and little else than virgin potential.

Near the end of that decade, the exclusion laws were loosening, especially as cheap labor was needed in the state's now thirty-year-old emerging industries. The supremacist ideology really started to make itself explicit, ironically, after the Civil War, as public figures were fumbling to explain why they and their now defunct laws were never anything like those hateful, evil Southern racists (i.e., *But, my God, we're not monsters!*). In 1889, John McBride, a lawyer and former Oregon delegate, echoed a general sentiment (so familiar) that the exclusion laws of the mid-century, which he acknowledged were de facto coming to an end, were never borne of racial hatred: "Some believers in the doctrine of abstract human rights interpret this vote against admission of free negroes as an exhibition of prejudices which prevailed against the African who was not a slave, but I have never so regarded it. It was largely an expression against any mingling of the white with any of the other races, and upon a theory that as we had *yet no considerable representation of other races in our midst*, we should do nothing to encourage their introduction. *We were building a new state on virgin ground; its people believed it should encourage only the best elements to come to us, and discourage others.*" (Emphasis mine.)

Although the Fourteenth Amendment made the exclusion laws legally inert, the laws were nonetheless not repealed from the state's constitution until 1926—a decade that was met by a raging uptick of the KKK's presence and activity in Oregon, as reported by historian and journalist R. Gregory Nokes in his book *Breaking Chains: Slavery on Trial in the Oregon Territory*. (There is evidence that, in the 1920s and '30s, Oregon was perhaps the largest hotbed of KKK activity in the country.) And the rest of the racist language that riddled Oregon's constitution, so steeped in it as it was, remained until 2002. Unsurprisingly, Black people today make up only about 2 percent of the state's population.

But overplaying Portland's whiteness, whatever restorative justice it's supposed to do, has long been a way to further ignore the Black communities that were there, are there, and in many cases have been there all along.

In 2015, Walidah Imarisha embarked on a year of Black regional history lectures all across the state of Oregon. She was routinely threatened by neo-Nazi and white supremacist groups to not show up at whatever college or small town she was next scheduled for to share with residents what had happened in Oregon: the exclusion laws, the lash law, the flood at Vanport, but to share also that Black people had always lived in Oregon—even during the brutality of the nineteenth century, and in higher and higher numbers in the twentieth. She talked about the Golden West Hotel, a central hub of Black civic and leisure life in Old Town Portland, still standing today. She talked about the legacy of the Black Panther Party's Portland chapter, one of the longest living chapters in the country, which started a variety of free clinics and after-school programs, all of which are still there; she talked about Albina and Alberta and Mississippi, all historically Black neighborhoods in the city which, as I was getting ready to move to college in the early aughts, were the sites of the first major gentrification campaigns in Portland, a testing ground for the all glass and brushed steel buildings that would become ubiquitous across the East Side by the end of the decade, proffering artisanal coffee and fine food and folksy music venues at high costs for an ever-approaching tidal wave but not-yet-arrived new class of twee white people.

When I was a child, my dad took me on a short drive up to Council Crest. He told me it was "as high up as the clouds," the tallest point in the city. I was looking forward to the logistics of this, balancing on the clouds and so forth, wondering whether they'd be able to support our weight. I was concerned, but happy to figure it out once we got there—and I was doubly disappointed to find that Council Crest was just a very tall butte, cloudless, which provided a view of the whole city, including all of the nearby mountains: Mount Tabor, Mount Hood, Mount Rainier, Mount Adams, and, on really clear summer days, the jutting caldera of Mount St. Helens. The winding road that encircles the butte is lined with old-timey lampposts. I remember my dad telling me that this was about a mile away from the neighborhood where he spent his childhood, "Portland Heights," the West Hills, its white peaks, a section of the city I hadn't spent any time in till that moment and, over the course of the eighteen or so years I would live in Portland, have rarely been to since. We East Siders could see the West Hills from wherever we were—our backyards, parking lots, the tops of our garages. It was a remote and forested part of the city, one we felt apart from, full as it was of ancient mansion houses. I don't remember fully understanding until that day that his people had been up in the West Hills, and that he and his mother—Grammy Evelyn—were the last to leave.

Council Crest is now a public park that sits at 1,073 feet above sea level. It's a beautiful park that's situated as a fulcrum to the most powerful white settlers' homes in the nineteenth century. From 1907 to 1929, it was host to an amusement park, the "Dreamland" of the Northwest, designed by a Coney Island architect, complete with things like the "Barrel of Fun" and an elevated trolley track constructed by what was then Portland's burgeoning transit company. A decade prior to the construction of the amusement park, a group of Congregational ministers had collaboratively landmarked the spot for the public as a commons, and in doing so made up, whole cloth, an origin story that would lead to the park's name: the butte, they said, used to be an intertribal "council" site for Native Americans in the area. There has never been any evidence to substantiate this claim.

It makes sense to me, though, that they needed this story to pave meaning into their own use of it: because if, in their minds, it was once an intertribal council site, in a time so remote and no longer in use, then they could understand themselves as picking up the mantle of a tradition. They could imagine themselves as continuing a tradition rather than starting one out. They could use that story as a way to convert the "Doctrine of Discovery" into a story of fraternal mutual aid, rather than genocide.

But just thirty years earlier, down the hill toward the Willamette

River—in the area that would eventually become what is now known as the South Waterfront—city officials had created internment camps for the local River People, the very people those ministers had created this story about, readying them for their removal to the Grand Ronde Reservation: the Chinookan, Multnomah, Cascades, Clackamas, Tualatin, Tillamook, Salish peoples, and more than twenty other tribes and bands. So, while the River People were enclosed in a reservation, white people made up a dream about how they were continuing a rich tradition of intertribal council up on a hill.

For the most part, prior to the arrival of white settlers, the people who had populated the lower Columbia River basin lived in multifamily plank houses, in communitarian societies that figured into the "dense forest" that made up what is now Portland. These societies were brutalized by removal campaigns and European contagion. According to a city planning document on a West Quadrant/Central City development plan, the authors note that "by the time Portland was founded in the mid-1840s, introduced diseases had reduced the area's indigenous population by as much as 90 percent. By the late 1850s, encroachment by white settlers and forced removal to reservations had further devastated indigenous societies." In 1856, the Grand Ronde Reservation was put forth by a combination of treaties and executive order, and all of the confederated tribe members—sixty-one tribes in all—were forced from their ancestral lands in a murderous winter march to the allotted acreage, where none of them had ever been. The people who were rounded up and held in a relocation camp at South Waterfront were from the surrounding tribes in the immediate area—but many tribes within the federation were pushed up from the southern coastal lands and Mount Shasta hundreds of miles away.

A few years ago, Portland's transit authority authorized the construction of a pedestrian and bicycle bridge called Tilikum Crossing—which would also aid in a new light-rail line—that leads directly across the Willamette from the neighborhood I grew up in to the South Waterfront where those internment camps once sat. On either side of the crossing are two basalt carvings by a Chinook artist, Greg A. Robinson, of the confederated tribes of the Grand Ronde community.

The carvings are called *We Have Always Been Here*. They are done in a traditional Chinook style; one is a five-foot pillar depicting a *tayi*, or chief, with his people in the past, present, and future, and the other is a six-foot-diameter medallion depicting the Morning Star with her children, encircled by coyote. At the dedication ceremony, accompanied by tribal members and elders, Robinson said, "It's much less about me having my art here as it is about having a permanent testament to the survival and ongoing culture of the Chinookan people that still live here in the Portland–Vancouver area." It is not a memorial to the past, but a marker that grounds the present in reality.

In his introduction to *Wasáse: Indigenous Pathways of Action and Freedom* by Taiaiake Alfred, the Blackfoot scholar Leroy Little Bear emphasizes three times the importance of place as a referent in Indigenous life. The writer Jennifer Kabat, my friend and fellow resident of the Adjunct Flophouse, pointed me to Little Bear's writings one afternoon on a walk around her home in the Catskills, while we were talking about my family's colonial hold on the Pacific Northwest. Little Bear names other core elements of indigeneity, too, such as the idea that there is "constant flux/motion, that all of creation consists of energy waves, that everything is animate, that everything is imbued with spirit, that all of creation is interrelated, that reality requires renewal" but reiterates over and over that "space is a major referent." The arrival of Europeans, of course, changed all those dynamics. "They are the interference," he says. "They are a people . . . with no collective ethos. In other words, they have no common spirit and beliefs that hold them together. What is common to them is a very strong belief in individuality and material gain." And most dangerously, perhaps, white Europeans, specifically Anglo-Europeans, lack space as a major referent.

The British people who were the main colonizers of this continent are acultural in an indigenous sense because the history of Britain is one of successive takeovers by foreigners. The effect of these successive takeovers is to erase any semblance of indigeneity to the land from which they came. A lack of culture results from unrestrained freedom, which is best explained by the Calvinist school of thought. Calvin himself explained: "When that light of divine providence has once shown upon a godly man, he is then relieved and set free not only from the extreme anxiety and fear that were pressing before him, but from every care." In other words, cultural prescription and circumscription do not enter their minds. Expedience is the operative mode.

As soon as I started in on this project, it seemed obviously true and obviously ridiculous that the utopian communities in the United States made by Anglo-Europeans were just very pale recreations of Indigenous life. While those groups usually didn't intentionally aid in the destruction campaigns against American Indigenous people, they were nonetheless part of the imperial arm whether they wanted to understand that or not. It's like those fresh-faced utopians arrived, in New York, Ohio, Illinois, Oregon, crested over the mountaintop, and shrieked, *We have found the land of milk and honey!* while a few miles down the road was a battleground where a thousand Indians had just been murdered by the government, thereby freeing up a homestead for the Shakers or the Harmonists to build a commune on. *How convenient, a perfect plot upon which to enact our experiment, our totally novel, never-before-attempted, God-ordained experiment in simple communal living.* It seems to me that so much white (and functionally Protestant) utopianism really reads like Anglo, or more generally white northern European, people who have no sense of their own indigenous culture or history, which sort of explains why, say, you don't really hear about Irish or Italian people starting utopian communes in nineteenth-century America, or Russians for that matter, or Finns. There are exceptions, of course—for instance, in Oregon there was a nineteenth-century Jewish proto-kibbutz called Am Olam, as well as several Old Believer Orthodox communities dotting the rural outback. The main difference I'm underlining, I guess, is that the white European people who did have a sense of their indigenous or folk culture usually carried it with them in their migration to the United States in a way that structured their community lives. The ones that lacked this sense tended toward imperialism, or utopian communities, or both.

Which leads me back to the question of ancestors, and that morning at New Day Church when I was invited to invoke mine. The gruesome irony is that I actually have access to an extremely comprehensive genealogical record—I can, for the most part, literally call on each of my ancestors by name going back to the first seventeenth-century arrival—but there is no sense, in that fastidious record keeping, of an indigenous or folk culture that the act of genealogy might be preserving. Absent any cultural preservation project, then, the precision of that genealogical record looks more like an attempt to *create* something. Like the beginning of the Old Testament, that endless list of begets and begettings, a fastidious genealogical record like my family's sounds more like the act of building a precedent, a people, or a race.

I guess what it is making me think is that the founding of Oregon, and all the laws enacted to ensure it was a primarily white encampment in this "virgin rainforest," a whole state, was a way that these rootless English Protestants were trying to create an indigenous culture for themselves.

In his book *My Grandmother's Hands*, somatic therapist Resmaa Menakem premises his analysis of white supremacy as something that lives in the body. Somatics is a practice that roots recovery from traumatic experience in bodies, specifically nervous systems, rather than the brain or the mind as the object to be interminably corrected, healed, or retrained. Menakem turns the lens of somatics onto white supremacy, reframing it as "white-body supremacy." He says that "when the English came to America, they brought much of their resilience, much of their brutality, and a great deal of their trauma with them." He comes from the position that, despite decades of social movements that have sought to "teach our brains better to think about race," racialized violence perpetrated by white people unto Black and brown people hasn't really abated "because white-body supremacy doesn't live in our brains" and "our bodies have a form of knowledge that is different from our cognitive brains." His assertion: The English settlers brought forms of torture and violence to the Americas that they had been exacting on each other for centuries: whipping, branding, flaying, stocks, gallows, slavery, bioengineered starvation, disease, human collateral at the altar of capitalism and industrialization. It's not that the white body, Menakem is clear, is deserving of its own special sympathy that in some way outshadows the violence it has gone on to cause, but he's inviting a brute reckoning with the force of unmetabolized violence that lives in our very cells. That ancient brutality was mobilized into centuries of repression, projection, unmitigated, so that not even moving to the edge of the last frontier, looking out at the deep waters of the Pacific, creating a world where all you see is the mirror image of your own blameless white self looking back at you, saying, *Me? You can't possibly mean me? I'm good. I'm a good white person*, could save you from it.

Consciously or not, this is what a lot of the other white European utopians came to build in America, or found themselves building in the nineteenth century, or later on, too. They were dredging themselves from the slime of a violent empire and trying to simplify the means of production, simplify the world down to a single element, because they could not square their understandings of God or heaven or the good life or the eschaton with all of this trauma, all of this horror, all of this will toward torture and conquest, coursing through their veins like the River Styx.

utopianotes
Lost Valley Intentional Community

I'm seventeen, and my friend Maggie and I have both graduated from high school early. The week after our commencement ceremony, I get my first full-time job at a paper goods store and feel miserable, and she leaves Portland for three months to study permaculture at an intentional community outside of Eugene called Lost Valley. She shaves her head. I take a Greyhound down to visit her, winding in and out of the old-growth forests along the Cascades. The community is arranged in a clearing of evergreens as a collection of portables, yurts, and a shaggy redwood mess hall. Someone tells me that the property was bought in the early 1980s from the Shiloh Youth Revival Movement, a loosely organized collection of hippie Christians who splintered from the rangy theologies of the Jesus People. Now it is populated by secular eco-warriors and ardent practitioners of nonviolent communication. Everyone I meet is barefoot, and speaks so softly I can hardly hear what they're saying. We eat communal vegan meals, drink blackberry beer, sleep in a field of purple thistles, rinse off in the outdoor shower, and prepare breakfast outside in the sun. The next afternoon, we go swimming at Fall Creek, and then up the road to the annual Oregon Country Fair, a fifty-year-old festival that, for three days, hosts parties, music, camping, and a barter economy under an umbrella of Renaissance fair–style makeshift stalls made of tree branches. We see Rob Brezsny give a speech about pronoia on a tree stump stage, and watch a queer folk band from St. Louis sing about sycamore roots pushing through the neglected sidewalks of that old city. We run barefoot through the dirt from attraction to attraction all day, eventually ending up in a dance party in a field under a rainbow parachute, where we find one of Maggie's comrades from Lost Valley, who winces at us as we shout about all the different things we've seen that day. "Hm, well, I've just been letting the universe guide *me*," she says, as she whirls back into the crowd of bodies.

THE BIG MUDDY RANCH

I grew up taking for granted that utopian visions were possible. Most of my peers and I descended, in one way or another, from the mid-century back-to-the-land, environmental conservation, and New Age movements that found their spiritual home in the Pacific Northwest and parts of California throughout the twentieth century. In elementary school, our annual fieldtrip was to the salmon ladder at the nearby Bonneville Dam, where we learned about ecological and indigenous social destruction wrought by the infrastructure, and the measures that state was taking to reverse the damage. In high school, the kind of thing we did was borrow someone's parents' 1986 Volvo to drive across the Willamette River to the wooded land trust behind Lewis and Clark's campus where a student-led intentional community had developed, and where we sat by fire pits or drum circles or went naked into a cob sauna, and maybe drank a beer. There were intentional communities everywhere. Or there were enough casual references to them that their existence seemed ordinary and reasonable.

Tellingly, I think, my experiences of teenaged unrequited love are marked indelibly by the crossfire of these weird social conditions, bound up in a daytrip I took with a crush to a hot spring on an Indian reservation. When I remember it, way in hindsight, I remember stopping for ice cream, the sunlight rippling on the surface of the Columbia River, the Buena Vista Social Club on the car stereo, talking about this herbalist gynecologist he knew and how I should talk to her, if I wanted. He was a cob builder, and talked often about his plans to buy some land outside of Portland—not far from the Salish reservation we, two white teens, were about to trespass onto—where he could develop an ecovillage that he and his friends and his family could live on, but which would also sustain itself through eco-tourism. We arrived at the gate and parked. He led me over the reservation boundary. We hopped on rocks in the woods for a while, hiked in secret along the river in the growing dark, my heart pounding, and finally made it to the springs. We stripped naked and jumped in, then lay on the cold rocks above the water till the stars came out. I loved him, but he didn't love me. He talked a lot about cob.

Oh, the wonders of cob—good Lord. Instead of listening to young men go on and on about sports or video games, it was about the wonders of cob, how they would save the world with cob, a natural building material made of soil, water, and straw! We'd sit around and bat our eyelashes, watch them play instruments, smoke weed from giant bongs, all of it. The patriarchy was still intact; it just looked different than it does some other places.

One night I was making out in the grass at Sunnyside Park with that same cob builder. And he paused suddenly and yelled, "Mark Lakeman! That's Mark Lakeman!" There was Mark Lakeman, a minor local celebrity cob builder, repairing a cob gazebo the city of Portland had commissioned him to build next to the jungle gym. He'd rolled up to it in the dark on his bicycle with a toolbelt. I remember only his shadowy outline, and my own painful feeling that our make-out time was running out. The following week, Mark Lakeman came to my high school social studies class to talk about the Beehive Design Collective, the anarchist sustainable architecture group that had been commissioned by the city to build a variety of things, including that gazebo. These different spheres of life being hooked together by utopian dreamers was not so unusual.

For the most part, in my memory, everyone I associate with these scenes is white. The exceptions were the gatherings and properties connected to the Whitedeer family, a Lakota spiritual community my dad became a part of when I was a kid. The Whitedeer hoop was made up of people following what the head medicine man, Bill Whitedeer, called "the Red Road"— both those whose ancestors were indigenous to North America and non-natives, including Anglo whites like my dad. They gathered for ceremonies, vision quests, sweat lodges, *yuwipi*, and an annual Sun Dance, all of which I joined my dad for variously between the ages of twelve and eighteen. But the Whitedeer family gatherings, even the high-desert compound where the Sun Dance was held, weren't really communes—they were networks of mutual aid, organized by the Lakota principles of community life and spiritual practice. However, what was unusual about Bill Whitedeer's vision for his community—he being native to the Rosebud Lakota-Sioux Reservation in South Dakota—was that it was multiracial.

Bill had had a vision back in South Dakota, after he was recovering from the trauma of Vietnam: the way forward with Spirit was to build a multiracial community around practicing ceremony. The Whitedeer multiracial community was intended to be a corrective, to eventually become a powerful enough community where folks could begin to unplug from capitalism and live more communally, in and around the Sun Dance acreage, but then Bill started to bureaucratize things a bit, and then he died, and then the larger paradigm-changing vision of the community—and the nascent network of intentional community that had formed around it—began to thin out. But between the Whitedeer community, Mark Lakeman and the like, cob builders, intentional communities, cooperatively owned cafés and all-ages music collectives, citywide composting, and people who wandered into the woods to live in the branches of sequoias in order to save their lives, these were some coordinates of the cultural map I grew up in.

All of what I'm describing, though, was just the I-5 corridor of Oregon—and not the character of the rest of the state, which is huge and rural and looks a lot more like the lunar high deserts of Wyoming than the verdant rainforests of the coastal range. The rest of the state was quite conservative, full of farmers, ranchers, loggers, and even whiter than its blindingly white cities. But it is rural Oregon that saw one of the largest utopian experiments of the state's—not the mention the country's—history.

In the fall of 2015, the Washington Family Ranch just outside Antelope, Oregon, found itself unable to go forward with an expansion to its luxe compound. Already, it had water slides and club houses, zip lines and go-carts and, like most nondenominational ministries, lots of multimedia equipment. The ranch is run by Young Life, an evangelical Christian organization based in Colorado Springs that works with impoverished or at-risk teens. The Washington Family Ranch, located in the sparsely populated high desert of north central Oregon, is the eighty-year-old ministry's biggest camp in North America.

Young Life has been pushing to expand the ranch since the late 1990s, after they were deeded the ranch by a Montana billionaire looking to unload an otherwise barren and unprofitable piece of land. But the state of Oregon has continually placed restrictions on these plans, and citizens of the tiny neighboring hamlet of Antelope are wary, too.

That's because this particular ranch has been site of tension, in one way or another, for the past 120 years. During that time, the land has been the site of a fatal shoot-out between white settlers and Native Americans, and also a movie set for the 1975 John Wayne vehicle *Rooster Cogburn*. More notoriously, it's been the site of the New Age "city" Rajneeshpuram, home to thousands of ecstatic, red-clad followers of the guru Bhagwan Shree Rajneesh. In 1984, a few of these disciples ended up carrying out the largest domestic bioterrorism attack in U.S. history.

The property was first settled as the Big Muddy Ranch. "The Big Muddy," as it is affectionately called, sprawls out over sixty-four thousand acres of dusty hills, covered by sage and juniper and a wandering steer here and there. Kentucky settler Howard Maupin founded neighboring Antelope in the 1860s, where he worked as postmaster and operated the stagecoach.

Shortly after he arrived, the U.S. military signed a treaty with the Paiute Indians which forced them out of the mountains surrounding Antelope and into reservations further west. When Paiutes started defecting from the reservations not long after, in resistance to the exploitative treaties, Chief Paulina was among those who set out to reclaim their territory in the Blue Mountains.

One night, Maupin, reinforced by a posse, shot and killed Chief Paulina just outside of Antelope, and in some accounts is said to have tacked his scalp above the stagecoach as a warning. When a Paiute medicine man found out about the murder, he came to Antelope and put a curse on Maupin "and his land forever."

Over the following years, the ranch served as a cattle and sheep concern and, eventually, a new stop on the stagecoach line. Then, for a good deal of the mid-twentieth century, the Big Muddy Ranch was dormant as American rangeland practices shrank to outsourcing and Big Ag.

In the 1970s, Katharine Hepburn and John Wayne found themselves tromping around the Big Muddy Ranch filming *Rooster Cogburn*, a tepid sequel to *True Grit*, the story of a hard-drinking, disgraced U.S. marshal questing to get his badge back, accompanied by his "spinster" sidekick seeking her father's revenge. In that great American tradition of reenacting the history of the West, Hepburn and Wayne took the law into their own hands, battling bandits and road warriors from the fortress of a homestead.

Later, when the followers of the Bhagwan Rajneesh bought the property and stories began to spread of tensions with the locals, *People* predicted "a showdown stranger than any the Duke envisioned." Eventually, the site of the old Big Muddy Ranch became the infamous utopian city Rajneeshpuram.

For a time in 1984, Rajneeshpuram was not only the fastest growing city in Oregon, but potentially the fastest growing city in America, according to the *Chicago Tribune*. At its peak, there were between two thousand and three thousand permanent residents, though it was built to house six thousand, and around gatherings and festivals the population reportedly rose into the tens of thousands.

But just a year later, this intentional community met its dramatic end when its two most powerful leaders, the Bhagwan himself and his fearsome spokeswoman, Ma Anand Sheela, were charged variously with immigration fraud, conspiracy, attempted murder, and organizing the single largest domestic bioterrorism attack in the United States.

The Bhagwan and his disciples arrived in Oregon during the summer of 1981, having already developed a strong following in his ashram in Pune, India. Many Westerners were drawn to his philosophy, which mixed Buddhism and continental thought and encouraged the practice of free love and meditation. In an attempt to elude tax evasion charges, the Bhagwan deputized one of his devotees, Ma Anand Sheela, to scout a place for them to expand their community to the United States.

The two thousand or so disciples who arrived in Oregon immediately began building permanent housing—small outbuildings and tents, and then more lavish quarters for the "enlightened one" himself. They got to cultivating farmland and setting up security details at the front of the ranch near the main road. There were daily devotional gatherings, meditation sessions, and "encountering sessions," where the philosophy of free love was often practiced. And the Bhagwan began collecting Rolls-Royces, in which he'd be chauffeured daily through the gauntlet of his devotees.

Within three years, they had become incorporated as an Oregon municipality: Rajneeshpuram. At the time, the *Chicago Tribune* ran a profile on the community, describing a "technologically impressive, ecologically sound 2,000-acre city with an airport, shopping center, hotel, disco, restaurants, a blackjack casino, transportation system, newly built dam and lake and near self-sufficient agricultural production" staffed by the hardworking, red-clad devotees who lived in simple cabins and A-frame tents. The Rajneesh also bought up, over time, one-fifth of the property in the neighboring town of Antelope, which included in its sweep a general store and a café that they reintroduced as an all-vegetarian spot called Zorba the Buddha.

Needless to say, the residents of Antelope weren't happy about this massive influx of disciples. And the state of Oregon began to level complaints and lawsuits against Rajneeshpuram's unsanctioned use of land and lack of building permits. Plus, by then, Rajneeshpuram had its own police force that, in addition to patrolling the compound, also patrolled the streets of Antelope armed with Uzi submachine guns.

Many of the more aggressive occupation efforts were allegedly fueled by the Bhagwan's mystic spokeswoman, Ma Anand Sheela, who by then had been given control of much of the activity of Rajneeshpuram.

There was a Rajneeshee hotel in downtown Portland, where there was a bombing at one point. A lot of their attempts to expand the kind of building they wanted to do out near Rajneeshpuram were stymied or challenged by the uniquely powerful conservation laws at work throughout the state that protect the old-growth forests and complex ecosystems of the region, much of which is controlled (as is the case throughout a great deal of the American West) by the state government.

In an attempt to gain voting power to have sway in decisions about land use in Wasco County, where Rajneeshpuram was located, Sheela and other higher-ups arranged to bus in thousands of homeless people to vote. They also carried out a mass salmonella poisoning of eateries in a town called The Dalles, the county seat. Rajneeshee delegates surreptitiously drizzled infected liquid into the Taco Time salsa bar and other restaurants, a strike which left 751 people infected and successfully stifled voter turnout on election day.

Eventually, Sheela and her henchmen were charged with a variety of crimes, including attempted murder. The Bhagwan was charged with immigration fraud (from arranged marriages) and conspiracy, but fled to India after being let out on bail. He settled into a quiet life with his disciples there, in a new ashram, dying of a heart attack just five years later. Sheela served prison time, eventually was granted an early release, and now runs an assisted living home for aging and special-needs adults in Switzerland. When *Wild Wild Country* came out on Netflix in 2018, the whole country had something like a freaky love affair with the story of the Rajneeshees, and especially with Ma Anand Sheela who is, I think, the true north of that documentary's story and spectacularly represented as a cutthroat genius villain of operatic proportions.

After the Bhagwan and Sheela skipped town, thousands of residents in Rajneeshpuram began to evacuate, many of them remaining in the Northwest, or particularly in Portland.

When I was growing up in Portland, it wasn't uncommon to meet someone's parents or know someone who knew someone who'd been a Rajneeshee or lived in Rajneeshpuram or had some kind of connection to the utopian city. One of my best friends' dad worked at an industrial metal shop and says now, casually, that the Rajneeshee contracted them to build several massive trucks and single-handedly kept his company in business throughout the recession of the 1980s. My parents' neighbors were former community members. My high school boyfriend's mom used to babysit for a couple of erstwhile Rajneeshees. A lot of these people were hippies of the variety that eventually filtered back into the civic life of the region, becoming somewhat unrecognizable from the other ex-hippies who'd found themselves there, with kids and government jobs, in the nineties and early aughts. There was just an ordinary proximity that folks had to the weird utopian experiments of Oregon.

Young Life acquired the Big Muddy Ranch through the Montana billion-aire Dennis Washington, a mining and construction magnate who ranks at 105 in the *Forbes* list of richest Americans. He had purchased the Big Muddy in 1991 for almost half the price the Rajneesh bought it for, and then he sat on it, unsure of what to do because of all the land-use restrictions that had emerged around it in the previous decade. For a while, he and then governor John Kitzhaber talked about turning it into a state park, and then a youth correctional center. When Young Life did finally acquire it, it was still what *The New York Times* called "the first ever New Age ghost town."

Young Life began to develop the same piece of land into their own compound in 1997, a $300 million "Christian ranch" where inner-city kids were carted to lavish water parks and rural splendor for summer fun and worship.

When Young Life got the land, it seemed, at first, like it was going to be a technical challenge to engineer their dream ranch on the land. But they had a few lucky breaks. The *Statesman Journal* reported that the camp's plans to build a man-made lake were stymied by the fact that the arid environment would cause evaporation at ten thousand gallons per day. But then the group happened across a natural spring below the new swimming pool that pumped exactly ten thousand gallons a day. Moreover, when the camp's sports field needed a large quantity of sand to prevent mud, someone tooling around on the property found a huge sand deposit.

And finally, when they couldn't decide what to do with the Bhagwan's lavish former quarters, "a 1997 range fire decided matters," wrote the *Statesman Journal*. "A finger of the fire raced down the ridge and torched the residence, the only one of 300 Rajneeshpuram buildings to burn."

In the same article, a Young Life camp leader at the Washington Family Ranch marvels that "this place is a gift," and a camper, having just completed the ropes course, professes that "God's grace definitely changes lives at Washington Family Ranch."

Young Life had to push for several years for clearance to develop forty more acres of land. While the state legislature did eventually pass a bill to rezone the land, another land management agency stepped in and set up rules that limited capacity and sewer system connectivity.

The latest concerns drift more to the delicate ecology of the high desert, the preservation of Indigenous artifacts, and not wanting to set "a precedent for circumventing the land-use process by making accommodations to special interests," in the words of Representative Mitch Greenlick. Many of the fifty or so Antelope locals are ranchers, after all, whose livelihoods depend upon that sweeping rangeland.

It would just be a run-of-the-mill land-use squabble, so typical of the rural American West, were it not for the fact that many of the current residents still remember having been run out of town or poisoned with salmonella by Rajneeshees, or that John Wayne had blessed the land with his cowboy boots, or that the Paiutes had paid for it with their blood.

utopianotes
St. Jude's Day

I'm at a St. Jude's Day party in late October 2018 at a new friend's house. I'm greeted by a beautiful woman I've never met before. Her name is Pareesa, and she shows me to a bowl of green glitter which, she instructs, I should smear on my forehead while standing before the altar candle to make an offering to that tender Patron Saint of Lost Causes.

Toward the end of the party, she asks if I know Anna Moschovakis, a poet who also works at Pratt, for whom she's been doing some assistant work as of late—in fact, she's just come from the Adjunct Flophouse this evening, where she was working with Anna on spreadsheets. "Do I *know* her?" Pareesa and I become good friends, almost immediately. She's an Iranian-Louisianan painter, and currently in between jobs as an artist's assistant and a gallery docent. We meet up for drinks and I tell her about my obsessive and sort of stagnant quest to develop a more communal life, and find that we share this aim. A couple of weeks later, she sends me an email while Sweeney and I are holed up in Edna St. Vincent Millay's old barn on the off-season in exchange for another work trade. Pareesa is, at the time, working for an aging public intellectual named Charles Ruas, who had once interviewed every cool and fringy artist and thinker of the 1970s as a host on the Pacifica Radio Network. She is digitizing his interviews, and has come across one he had done with Marguerite Young, who had written tomes and tomes about utopia, and who had also spent some summers reading Shakespeare aloud to an elderly former patron of Edna St. Vincent Millay's in the 1930s, and *had I heard of her?*

LIVING

I did molly for the first time just after my thirtieth birthday, in my living room with my old friend Robert. We talked about where we hoped to be living in a year, his recent heartbreak by a ghosting guy, and then watched Cher's new music video of her "S.O.S." cover on a continuous loop: a multiracial squad of women lurk around the industrial edges of L.A., conspiring to help a down-and-out friend who keeps shrugging off their advances for help and communion. Cher is nowhere to be seen; instead, each of the women, sometimes collectively, lip-sync her voice. Robert burritoed himself in a white cotton quilt on my couch, while I sat in my open window chain-smoking and peeling back the connections between my hope in utopian experimentation and my belief in God.

I said that night, to Robert, that my sexuality felt "deeply communal," but I wasn't sure what that meant. It wasn't the first time I'd said it, either. I had in fact said the same phrase out loud earlier that day to a room full of people. Prior to meeting up with Robert, I'd spent the afternoon at a New Day Church–organized "growth group" for womyn and femme-of-center. My friend Lisa had been facilitating these monthly meetings in the living rooms of different members' apartments all year, and they were the kinds of gatherings where we spoke pretty openly about sexuality, where a statement like "my sexuality feels deeply communal" was probably among the least remarkable admissions of the day, but I had struggled to elaborate then, too. With Robert, now, I tried to think it through: The erotic can show up in so many forms other than sex, and when I thought about my modern fantasy of pre-modern society (bear with me), anywhere in the world, I imagined that the erotic was often found in the goings-on of daily life: growing food, harvesting, hunting, living so close to one another, eating together, seeing each other through ceremony and season. But the horror of living in a system that, as Audre Lorde writes in "The Uses of the Erotic," "defines the good in terms of profit rather than in terms of human need, or which defines human need to the exclusion of the psychic and emotional components of that need—the principal horror of such a system is that it robs our work of its erotic value, its erotic power and life appeal and fulfillment. Such a system reduces work to a travesty of necessities, a duty by which we earn bread or oblivion for ourselves and those we love. But this is tantamount to blinding a painter and then telling her to improve her work, and to enjoy the act of painting." Like everything under capitalism, the erotic is atomized to certain acts and certain kinds of relationships, conscripted into patriarchy's pleasure, and then there is suffering, boredom, loneliness, lies. Families break apart. I supposed, as I coughed smoke out the window, that I still did believe that marriage was good. Sweeney walked in and laughed at me sitting on my perch, and we kissed. "I like him," I said. I continued: I really still did believe in marriage, at least when the marriage or the married people are connected to a larger community which their marriage helps to bind and stabilize—not to create a network of other marriages, necessarily, but to create other kinds of relating to each other for which the marriages act as a support beam in a more diverse infrastructure of single people, orphans, pirates, sluts, hermits, cousins, aunts, your own children, and the children of other people. Other than that—if marriage is just a way to be alone with someone else forever, drawing offspring into that loneliness, then why do it?

I started organizing my endless utopia notes into dedicated journals, which I committed to have with me at all times and which I hoped would help me live. And the notes, and drug adventures that began to happen here and there—adventures which I had spent my whole adult life afraid of embarking on, not because of physical side effects, but because I was afraid of what might be inside of me—began to open up, or force more open, my latent desires. A week after the night with Robert, Sweeney and I met up with an old friend for drinks in Midtown, and then ended up walking from 2:00 a.m. till dawn, from Hell's Kitchen to Grant's Tomb, where we watched morning wash over the Hudson. In the deepest part of the cool dark hours, on those damp sidewalks, we talked about love and sex. We listened to every word the other said. We made our way home. I peed in our bathroom next to the frosted glass window and picked up my phone sitting on the sill. A text from Robert had been waiting there unread for several hours:

"Isn't it crazy how present day you has been present for every day in your life?"

"Yes," I texted back.

Then I wrote some delirious utopianotes:

Anyway, also if only a few times in the rest of my life, I'd like us to have sex with other people, who would love it, and whose own marriages or relationships might benefit from it, too. Not like the Oneida Community, no program or anything. Just as it presents itself. If a magic psychic told me right now that I was about to enter into a really sexy time for a few months, I'd be very excited. I'd like to have different kinds of sex: communal sex, friend sex, funny sex, molly high sex, first date sex, nervous sex, me, Sweeney, other men, some women. It's more than that though. Just a more communal life would be fine. With me and Sweeney providing sexual excitement for people who need it, as a bonus or ancillary project. Now I've got to go to sleep though. I am enjoying being 30—I would like to go a little further into the pleasure of life.

Sweeney and I had spent years, long before Dan's strokes, talking with our friends about different kinds of cooperative living arrangements—and while those conversations were beginning to reemerge in our lives, it was difficult to zero in on a timeline or a situation that worked out for the various people involved in those discussions. But Dan was beginning to be more independent, and more family members had stepped in to help out with quotidian tasks, so when summer came, as promised as part of the post-shingles ultimatum all those months ago, Sweeney and I started talking about what we might want to do next.

Buying something on our own felt outrageous, but we started to timidly look anyway, to see if there was some way we could make a move independently that might inspire, over a longer period of time, other people to come make use of the land—or a ramshackle compound—with us, or even a place where we could comfortably bring Dan, too. We had virtually no money with which to do this, just a bit of savings and a large school-debt-to-income ratio, but we hoped that a live-action-role-playing approach to real estate speculation might yield something eventually.

Sweeney and I booked our first appointment with a broker for a five-acre parcel on Oswego Road in Pleasant Valley, New York, that we had no way of affording. I started to wonder as we neared our destination how much this story I was wending my way through, this odyssey, might just be the story of middle-class aspiration, going to college, getting married and buying a house, in spite of my hopes of visions to the contrary. As we turned off the county route to the narrow road which runs alongside Oswego Creek, we passed a blue historical marker, which described this neighborhood as once belonging to an early nineteenth-century Quaker community, though it uses the term "Society of Friends." As we snaked up the road, all the architecture around us dialed back in time: the blacksmith's house. The common well. A tidy, single-story meeting house which is now privately owned. And then the property we had come to see.

Walking around it, I found myself still focused on the metric of its malleability, the way it could make a home for us and a home for others. There was an apartment above the old garage, a covered pavilion by a "plunge pool" in the creek, raised beds and a victory garden off in the woods, a conspicuous fairy ring in the lawn and toadstools everywhere, the sound of water, cool and dark. Beyond the creek was a steep bank of woods that blotted out the late-fall sun overhead. The house itself was tiny. "Do you have children?" the broker asked.

Sweeney and I got free tickets from a friend of a friend to see *Light Shining in Buckinghamshire* at the Public Theater, which was all about the different strains of theological and political radicals from around the time of the English Civil Wars—the Diggers, the Levellers, the Ranters, and the Quakers among them. An eighty-five-year-old Black woman dressed as a Quaker quoted Joel midway through the show: "And your sons and your daughter shall prophesy!" The director, it turned out, was Rachel Chavkin, who was the director for some of the most transformative theater I had ever seen, from a troupe called the TEAM, going way back to when I first moved to New York at eighteen years old.

Robert, Amber, and I went and saw their operatic *Particularly in the Heartland* at PS122, where a man playing RFK in someone's Kansas dreamscape gets assassinated over and over and over again. We were nineteen years old. The cast had invited the audience to join them across the street for a drink. We ran across to the bar and ordered Guinness, and Jessica Almasy, one of the actors, came up to our table and talked with us. At one point she said, "Listen—I hope the opposite of your wildest dreams comes true—'cause it'll be *better*."

Things started to change. One night Sweeney and I were on our way to meet up with a woman for a date together, something neither of us had ever done. We sailed far down Brooklyn's Atlantic Avenue in the hazy December sunset—warm enough to have the windows open as Brownsville and Bushwick flew by, scream-singing to "Reinventing Axl Rose" by Against Me! a punk band that neither of us had really listened to since we were teenagers but which we loved. I remember feeling, finally, almost a year after the shingles, after what had felt to me like the end of the road—the end of our relationship—I looked at Sweeney in the sun, singing this song, and we were nineteen years old, racing each other under the Brooklyn–Queens Expressway, and we'd been right all along.

Let's make everybody sing
That they are the beginning and ending of everything

Sweeney and I went to a New Year's Eve party at my friend Anna's house in the deep of Delaware County in the Western Catskills. She lived in a huge Victorian home that she and her now ex-husband had been renovating together for the last ten years. It was gorgeous and simple, with elegant curling banister staircases, many bright, yawning rooms on each floor, with soaring ten-foot ceilings. A beautiful porch facing south. And the house was full of friends that night—friends at the kitchen, snacking, drinking, dancing to records, dissolving thimbles of weed coconut butter onto our tongues. I realized that I knew half of the people at her party from my time at the Adjunct Flophouse, where, unwittingly, I had apparently been developing a community of people up here in this county.

The next day she took us over to the Bushel Collective community space, in a former Masonic lodge on Main Street in Delhi, New York, where she and a group of five other local and transplanted residents were in the process of relocating their nonprofit. They'd started as an experiment a few years earlier in a rented storefront down the street, inspired by the form of traditional rural meet-ups and urban pop-up storefront experiments, creating an all-volunteer-run space interested in "growing community and discourse through programming in the arts, agriculture, ecology, and action," offering gallery exhibitions, readings, musical performances, town halls, classes, and anything else that the community brings to it. The ground floor of the former lodge, which Anna was managing thanks to an investment from family, would provide the collective with an affordable home into the indefinite future. The building had suffered a fire and repair was going slowly, but the bottom floor was almost ready to be unveiled: a gallery, a library, a performance space, a gathering space, a future community kitchen.

Then she took us to a house just up the road from her own, which she was also caretaking. We rabbited up a steep muddy road, up up up to a mint-green manufactured home. Anna and everyone in the surrounding community called it "Frank's Place," named after the eponymous former owner who'd died not long before. "Frank's Place" was a three-bedroom, non-winterized double-wide that she was in the process of turning into a three-season "Upstate Flophouse" for artists and educators, seasonal farm workers, and communal dreamers. The house sat on thirty-five acres of woods and hayfields, threaded with trails, and she was hopefully imagining—she said, as she walked us through the empty rooms, looking out onto the mountains—a landlord-less future for the place, in which people could plop down living structures and share equity.

On the car ride home to Woodlawn, Sweeney scratched his beard, go-carting down the Taconic State Parkway in a contemplative daze, and said, "Ya know what we should do? We should just propose to Anna that we'll rent that place for the summer, and then figure the rest out from there."

I scheduled to have my ovarian cysts removed. I sat in the St. John's Riverside hospital room with my paper gown and medical-grade socks, wiping my entire body down with antiseptic towelettes. The Tappan Zee Bridge had been dynamited down the day before, and we could see its collapsed form from the window. Sweeney kissed me and played the Robert Blake song "Sweet and Easy," and then "Didn't We" by Jim Page, an anthem for the critical mass riots that disrupted the 1999 World Trade Organization convention in Seattle. I was wheeled slowly out of the room on a gurney through the green corridor of the operating room, and put under anesthesia. When I awoke, my gynecologist, the tough Russian lady who takes no prisoners and who'd performed the operation, was standing by my bedside, smiling: "It went beautifully," she said.

"Do I still have both my ovaries?" I said in a morphine daze.

"Yes," she said.

"Oh, that's so great."

And then, I'm not sure if I hallucinated this or not, she smiled, gave a little tender laugh looking down at me, and touched the back of her index finger to my cheek, like she was my mother.

Our new friend Pareesa arranged for us to meet her best friends—Alyssa and Zach—at a bar, and halfway into the night she said, "OK, the reason I brought you all here tonight is so we can talk about utopia!" She gave us index cards to sketch our ideas on. Within one week, the five of us were all hanging out regularly, having dinners, going to plays, dancing at an Iranian New Year's party, having multiple weekend-long hangouts at our place in Woodlawn. On Easter Sunday, Alyssa, a long-lapsed Catholic, corralled us to a four-hour mass at a cathedral in the West Village, during which I lit my hair on fire with a vigil candle.

Sweeney and I kept LARP-looking at houses and properties, pretty rabidly, finding one in Sullivan County, the southern foothills of the Catskills, which had a huge Victorian home on it, plus two one-bedroom cottages, a studio apartment above the garage, a giant horse barn, a ghost pond surrounded by willows, and several acres of land. We drove out to meet with the broker, ready to pretend we had money, talk to her as though we were just another young white couple looking to buy a house in the country—rather than disclosing that we only imagined buying this house with no fewer than three other people. We walked through the house, which seemed like it could easily be turned into a two-family house. By this point, we'd begun to talk at considerable length and seriousness with Pareesa, Zach, and Alyssa about buying a piece of property to build a low-er-overhead life on together, a life that is less entirely organized around waged labor, where we could make art, raise children, keep the door open to the outside.

We were going to move up to Frank's Place for the summer, either way. Around this time, I began to envision a situation that Sweeney, too, had been seeing in his mind's eye: a kind of federation of communal outposts that ran between Brooklyn, the Bronx, the lower Hudson Valley, and the Catskills. We felt high on possibility.

But already the pitfalls were obvious. Way more than the vagaries of communal living and making is just the devastating segregation of the way a group like this forms: stratifying and further isolating ourselves especially along the lines of class and education level—and not because anyone is barred entry, but because even these ideas and desires are classed, are modi-fied by our own backgrounds, feelings, or experiences of power and access.

At some point that season, we got really into anarchism again, for the first time since we were teenagers. Somewhere in the hang of returning to Against Me!'s discography and other early-aughts music that came out of the Battle of Seat-tle, and stumbling into David Graeber's work, and beginning to reflect on the communities that had always meant the most to us, a different understanding of anarchism formed than the one marked by the crust punks of our younger days. It wasn't so much like swearing allegiance to an ideology or dropping out of participation in electoral politics—it's just that I remembered or discovered for the first time (I'm not sure which) that anarchism or anarchist thinkers possessed the most compelling vision of the future for me, whether or not it was actionable or the makings of sound policy. The political and social vision of anarchism, the primacy of both individual freedom and consensus process, of mutual aid and pleasure, which much later I read Graeber describe as "a kind of faith" in *Fragments of an Anarchist Anthropology*, even if it's outsized, is what makes civic participation feel worthwhile at all. And anarchism had, I realized, a kind of eschatological vision of the world I identified with—that required planting seeds and dismantling systems you would never live to see the fruits of, but required your participation in this life nonetheless.

I also finally read *Caliban and the Witch* by Silvia Federici. I'd been meaning to read it for a long time, partly because so many more of my students had read it, and I was growing too embarrassed to admit I had not. It may sound ridiculous, but at least I'm being honest. I noticed that Sweeney had checked it out of the Fordham library and it was somewhere in his own dissertation reading stack. Our apartment had some 1,900 books checked out from the library, a combination of Fordham's collection and inter-library loan. We should have been arrested. Anyway, I loved this book and it helped bridge my thinking.

Caliban and the Witch tells the history of how the sixteenth- and early seventeenth-century transition from northern European feudalism created a vacuum where a more communalistic society tried to emerge, before capitalism created the grounds for the witch hunts—as well as chattel slavery, waged labor, and the Inquisition. Federici argues that, while by no means paradisiacal, feudalism allowed for the vast majority of European men and women to exist, in the private and public life, with virtual parity, and to preserve shared resources, "commons"—such as forests, meadowlands, quarries, lakes, rivers, canyons—for the free use of the peasant class. When the Black Plague decimated the continent's population, European recovery saw a brief period where the worker—male or female—retained a great deal of economic and social power, narrowing the class divisions that had once separated the lords from the serfs. Then the ruling class doubled down. During this same period, we saw the rise of the transatlantic slave trade, which included poor European whites and Indigenous South American people, and in those Caribbean plantations where all of these people converged, complex multiracial alliances and families formed. Then the English Civil War raged for thirty years. By the 1650s, however, the diminished ruling class had done a variety of things to thwart the development of the communalisms that were emerging both in Europe and in the Caribbean: In Europe, the creation of private property essentially eradicated any idea of "the commons" and de-collectivized the peasant class into nuclear units; waged labor did a similar thing, increasing the value of the individual laborer into a fiscal unit; and with the disappearance of "the commons," women, and more specifically the womb, became the commons, the site of "primitive accumulation," the source of producing new, future laborers who could accrue wealth.

Basically, capitalism wouldn't have worked if it hadn't been for the expropriation of chattel slave labor and the labor of the womb. In order for that to happen, the role of women in sixteenth- and seventeenth-century European society had to go through a change. Women were barred from a slew of professions in which they'd traditionally worked, especially midwifery and medicine, which undergoes a branding change at this time to an innately male profession. The church and the state, for virtually the first time, start to intervene into the reproductive lives of their subjects: the first-ever modern moral and legal debates and inquisitions emerge around the use of birth control and abortion, further controlling the use of "the commons" (women, wombs). In the Caribbean, race emerges for the first time as a concept that determines the conference of wealth and property, legitimate heirships, and slavery is articulated as befitting only a single race of people, as well as being a hereditary condition. Strict laws emerge around interracial marriage. (Although, in South America, there was already a sizable and growing mestizo population.) At a certain point during the English Civil Wars, the enclosure of the commons, Federici would refer to the emergence of the Beguine movement—which was essentially convent-style centers of living for women but unaffiliated in any official way with the Catholic church. Of course, organizations like these were seriously threatening to the social order and the authority of the church. There was a spiritual dimension to these communities, but also a practical one as women were being run out of their homes, property, families, people dying of the plague, etc. Then they started to burn witches.

•

I came home one evening around this time, and Sweeney was listening to Tracy Chapman's self-titled album on repeat, as he had been for days at that point. He had just finished the conclusion to his dissertation. Something had been set loose in him by the writing of it. He had arrived somewhere he wasn't expecting to arrive. He was sitting on our roof-deck, covered in ash, an empty beer can by his knuckle, in the dark, smoking, with this manic grin. "I get it," he said, looking at me. "Everyone's just trying to get free."

We took Pareesa, Zach, and Alyssa out one afternoon to the property we'd looked at in Sullivan County and ended up holding the broker hostage there for three hours as we waited for different parties to show up, including Uncle Joe, the engineer. In that time, our three hours of hemming and haw-ing, the price of the property dropped from $750,000 to $350,000, because the three old ladies who had to get this weird piece of property off their hands were anxious to let it go. We poked around the other buildings, crit-icized the weird yellow and hardwood kitchen, admired the rows and rows of fresh peonies about ready to bloom out in front of the house. We asked a million questions. There was so much potential there: sites of future studios, houses, a seven-thousand-square-foot horse barn that could be *turned into anything, can't you see it?* The way all the houses just look toward each other across the lawn, *can't you see it?* A fire pit and gathering space erected in the center? Even through Sweeney's and my manic, laissez-faire optimism, we had a hard time trying to convince Alyssa and Zach that we could feasibly share the one house, and my own sparkling vision began to fade. I could see it now: one day, that house might have two infants in it at the same time, crying through the night, dirt and devastation, agitated and tired young parents. Plus, the red carpets were ugly and would be expensive to replace.

Afterward, we went to a little bakery nearby that served Polish food, and we got three Polish sampler plates to share, and Zach said he felt "ter-rified" in response to Sweeney rubbing his hands together and saying, glee-fully, "So, we gonna buy this place or what?"

utopianotes
Adjunct Flophouse

The natural light inside the Flophouse is spectacular, illuminating the white walls and rumpled linen comforter gathered around my feet on the bed in Room C. I've just received my post-op update. Pleasing news all around. The pathology report describes the larger of the two ovarian cysts (RIP), both teratoma, as benign and having contained, among other things, hair and "two tooth-like structures," which is exciting.

I jam my backpack with supplies, teach all day, and then drive up to Northern Westchester Hospital, where two minutes before midnight my sister-in-law gives birth to her beautiful son. My sister-in-law ventured through twenty hours of labor like a veritable birthing goddess and still let us into the room to say hello and pat his little shoulder and his pruney beautiful hand. I keep thinking about my new nephew's face, and everyone's faces in that hospital room. I keep thinking about how all the ages and all the ancestors before us are etched onto our faces, even at a half hour old, maybe especially at that moment, and so we walk into a room with a just-born baby, and we just lose it because the immensity is unfathomable. Everyone is in tears, especially the dads, and especially Dan, who has been wheeling around the maternity floor with a plastic button on his shirt that says "Grandpa," telling everyone he passes, "That's me now!"

Between Diana's giving birth and my recent teratoma, I have been reflecting much on how insane it is that such mystery, lacunae, and erasure still shroud women's/femme health, bodies, my own anatomical literacy. How is there still so much surprise and confusion involved in caring for a woman's body? OK, that's Pollyanaish. I have at least a cursory answer to why women have been systemically prevented from this and other forms of bodily autonomy. None of this is shocking or anything. I am the last person to think this thought. But where is the Land of Many Mothers, where this knowledge lives and is casually exchanged from generation to generation? When will we get there?

THE SIMPLE WAY

One Saturday morning each month, the Simple Way community in the north Philadelphia neighborhood of Kensington hosts an informal open house for fellow travelers. They found that they had to start doing this several years ago after their veritable figurehead Shane Claiborne published his book *The Irresistible Revolution*, which itself read like—or was at least interpreted by many as—an invitation to said fellow travelers, and people just started showing up to live there and join their good work: radical Christians, anarchists, utopian groupies, etc.

The main building on Potter Street looked like a ramshackle corner office or an old bodega, its windows papered over with job and apartment listings, referral services, phone numbers for various social welfare programs. The listings were regularly changed out, retaped by Maria, the resident social worker—who I met as soon as Sweeney and I passed through the front door. "Hi," she said, flashing us a big smile. Maria kept a rolling analog list of these services for the people of Kensington who don't have access to smartphones or who just don't know how to navigate the internet. She wore tiny all-black Vans and black slim jeans that day, and simultaneously marshaled volunteer action in the food pantry while helping to set up chairs for this info session in the living room we were getting ready to join.

It looked like the living room of a college apartment, with tidy mismatched secondhand furniture and chintzy dishes laden with snacks. Sweeney and I, plus three other visitors, had come for the open house, and we sat in the big front room on a collection of benches and folding chairs, facing our hosts, Caz, Katie, and Maria—three women in their early forties, each of whom looked to me that day like a tired stylite fighting off demons at the edge of their precious world: their neighborhood.

We each shared a bit about why we were there, what had drawn us to the open house that morning in north Philadelphia.

Among the visitors this day was a young man getting a master of public health in a one-year program at some school in Philly (I think of Professor Frieda Knobloch's insistence that "We need more people pursuing degrees in public health and divinity"). He was a Mennonite from Kansas, and just from his nervous, rapid speech patterns, the little downward lilt of his voice, the way he almost swallowed the entire sentence he just uttered, made me think he was from a fairly traditional community. Then a Lutheran pastor from Fishtown and a blowhard middle-aged guy from who knows where, who wanted to make sure we knew how involved he was with the Catholic Workers.

Caz, Katie, and Maria talked about the history of the Simple Way movement. But their interpretive moment began with laying out the story in Shane Claiborne's book *The Irresistible Revolution*—a book I had ended up with because Amber gave it to me, and a month later I had seen it on the shelf in the library at the Bruderhof community in the Catskills. The book tells the story of the Simple Way from about 1995 up to 2005, though lots has changed since then—Caz and Katie anticipate that this crowd's knowledge of this community begins and ends with that book, and they talk a bit about how the book drew people to them.

"One guy walked from Chicago," Katie said. "Knocked on the door, and I opened it, and he was like, 'I'm here! I'm ready,' And I was like, cool—ready for *what?*" He stayed for a few weeks and ultimately left. Another time a high-school-age kid ran away from home to join them, but his parents were relieved when he called them and admitted that their community was "lame" and went home. "We were a little hurt by that," she laughed.

The community, and its understanding of itself, has been in flux since the beginning. It has never been one thing. What began as six college friends who started a student movement that successfully stood ground to protect the one hundred women and children who were squatting in an abandoned Kensington Catholic Church that the city was trying to demolish, turned into six friends who bought a condemned house in Kensington for pennies and committed to live in intentional community for five years while they lived into their mission of continuing mutually caring networks in this neighborhood, upon which time they could renegotiate their terms. And during those five years, they developed relationships with their neighbors, opened a free thrift shop, turned their house into an open community space, provided annual back-to-school bags for local kids, long-table meals, street festivals, trash pick-up, holiday parties, and eventually a food pantry, run by themselves as well as a cadre of volunteers who were themselves recipients of the food. Everyone on Potter Street and the surrounding neighborhood felt some kind of ownership for what was being exchanged there. And at the end of those five years, the original six friends mostly disbanded, but had been supplanted by this larger, looser network of people—including folks who had always lived in Kensington and folks who had come to live there—and buildings on this block that they now called the Simple Way.

As a 501(c)(3) now, they acquired, in collaboration with members of the community, more housing and buildings on the block for one dollar from the city, and opened a huge community space—kitchen, common area, offices—which lasted until 2014, when it all burnt down as a result of an old factory catching fire nearby. By that point, Simple Way had tons of other mini-projects at play: magazines, sanctuary coalitions, after-school programs, an internship program, Shane Claiborne's movement of going around the country convincing gun owners to melt their artillery down to be remade into farm tools. They were also effectively aligned for a while with a growing tide of economically radical left white evangelicals. But all this activity revealed a drift from what was their original mission: to live a life of mutual aid with their immediate neighbors in this specific place.

"Ya know," Caz said, "Miss Sunshine down the street just wanted a place to come hang out and eat, and to play her guitar with a few people around—and we just weren't around enough anymore to spend time with Miss Sunshine. So something had to change."

At that moment, another community member, Miguel, burst through the side door from the food pantry—the room that made up the corner of the building which juts out into the corner-cut of sidewalk, which also has its own entrance. Miguel had just picked up a huge load of soon-to-be-expired food refuse from all the Acme franchises in town, in his white Ford F-150, which he'd back straight up onto the sidewalk now for us to unload into the pantry, its shelves, and its big industrial refrigerators: cheese, eggs, onions, apples, Oreos, Velveeta.

We returned to the living room, and they continued the history.

At that moment of existential drift, they decided to send all the other projects out on their own, as if cutting the ropes of several dinghies from a larger ship—even Shane Claiborne's public work and writing was a part of that sloughing off: *go start your own projects, organizations. Go do good work. We don't have to all be unified and operating under the same umbrella.* Meanwhile, they bought three more buildings, an empty lot left from the fire-burned building and turned it into a public green.

Then they started Simple Houses.

Simple Houses dispenses interest-free loans to an individual or family that wants to renovate a more or less condemned home in an economically depressed neighborhood to live in. The loan is backed by a larger organization, the Fuller Center for Housing, which was founded by the same couple who founded Habitat for Humanity. The Fuller Center backs the interest-free loan and the Simple Way holds the mortgage through Simple Houses, so that the individual or family who wants the house can pay toward that, interest-free, and eventually become the owner. Then the family and the Simple Way volunteers who live on the block have to work on improvement before they can move in, but the family ultimately hold the title themselves.

"How do you think about your own whiteness in this context?" the young Mennonite man asked Caz and Katie.

"Yeah," Katie said, "It's something we've had to think about a lot over the years and learn about, given the origins—like, we had to live through some experiences to understand what white saviorism even *was.* We're still doing that. That doesn't end."

They have four Simple Houses on the block now—Miguel, who was just orchestrating us in the food pantry, lives in one that he now owns and has painted in Eagles colors. Another is looking like it's not going to reach financial solvency, but "that is just part of the life," Katie said. The partnership with Fuller Center started from Simple Way's main mission to build "security," a city-block world of security and safety and permanence. "So the book bags," Caz explained, "are given out on the same day every year. And our food pantry is organized in such a way so that neighbors can expect the same foods, at the same times, every week." Katie stressed, though, that they don't view homeowning as a virtue—just something they want to make possible for people who do want it.

I liked Caz and Katie. They spoke like veterans of a war of white hope—which they came out of not jaded, just practical and humbled and older now than they were when they started. In their own history-telling of the community's life, they modeled how to evolve, how to be suspect of your own motives, how to keep the overhead low, how not to spin off into a bunch of discrete projects, but rather let those projects break off and become autonomous as they themselves grow. Staying true to the spirit of their original vision was crucial, but so was remaining loose and unprecious about it. Caz saw her role as director as just maintaining the ability for people to keep doing what they're doing, and keep doing the things that made them feel most alive. The organization is mostly led by women, the majority of whom are white; they all have roots in different evangelical movements, but they have been a part of this community now for many years, and their theologies have evolved a lot over the past twenty-five years. Caz said as much, yawning—and added that she had been up all night taking care of her toddlers.

As we exited the building, everyone on the block stopped to say hey to Katie or Caz or someone else, from their stoops or on the sidewalk. I saw Miguel talking to a neighbor outside his Eagles-colored Simple Houses home. There were alley gardens, streamers left over from a weekly Sunday street party, volunteers finishing the unload at the food pantry's corner-facing door. The sky was high and gray and blank as we circled to our last stop of the open house: a small community park they had cobbled together from a former burn site, replete with a firepit and a hydroponic greenhouse and a string of pretty colored cloth pennants hanging on the chain-link fence that encloses the green, which is locked. For insurance reasons, only Simple Way organization members possess the key.

I looked around. The houses in this part of north Philadelphia were largely street-level rowhomes, three or four stories tall, narrow, with little porches or stoops, all seemingly built in one fell swoop at the end of the nineteenth century and patched up under poverty during the groaning end of twentieth-century industrialism. They are stone, sometimes wood, often painted white or brown, some with decorative facades or box-seats in the second-story window—and a lot of them have been ravaged by sixty years of abject civic neglect and disinvestment. The houses faced each other on these extremely narrow, intimate, almost medieval-looking streets. Many of the houses were abandoned. As Caz explained, the way the neighborhood used to be set up—before deindustrialization—was that every other block or so had a factory, and around that factory were these houses, and a shop, a laundry, a church. If you lost your job, you just moved over, a block or two, and worked at the other factory, lived on *that* block. The old civic design she described struck me as ancient and feudal—tied as it was to industry—but also communal, maybe Soviet. That existence was likely tarnished and spartan and exploitative, but the scale of a full life lived on one or two city blocks seems also so humane to me compared to the high-tech atomization of nuclear family careerism. After deindustrialization, there was nowhere for people to work—so the houses emptied, or fell apart, the tax base shrank, the factories and storefronts and churches emptied out, trash collection ceased, buildings were lost to arson or decay, and the poor people who were still here were left to salvage what they could of the empire's dregs.

I found myself thinking about MOVE, another Philadelphia community of the recent past that had, for all intents and purposes, some overlap with the communitarianism of the Simple Way. But MOVE had seen a horrific end for which the city has not publicly apologized to this day. Ten years before Shane Claiborne and those white teenagers from Eastern University descended onto Kensington to put their bodies on the line for those mothers and children in the abandoned Catholic church, the Philadelphia police had, during a rapidly escalating shoot-out, firebombed the commune of the Black liberation group MOVE, on flimsy or otherwise unfounded allegations of disorderly conduct, illegal arms possession, and terrorist activity.

MOVE formed in 1972, and had been living out a growing communal life of Philly-based anarcho-primitivism combined with the Black Power tenets of mutual reliance in lieu of white supremacist capitalism ever since. They first organized as the Christian Movement for Life, and only later renamed themselves MOVE—which, they make clear, is not an acronym, despite the capitalization. It's a spiritual battle cry. Among their other causes, for which they regularly and almost exclusively demonstrated and protested, were animal rights and climate change. And while they were a Black liberationist movement, the community was multiracial.

By the late 1970s, MOVE had captured the violent attention of Philly city officials and law enforcement. In 1977, following an earlier standoff with police, they'd issued a statement hoping to bar future hawkishness, saying: "We are not a bunch of frustrated middle-class college students, irrational radicals or confused terrorists. We are a deeply religious organization totally committed to the principle of our belief, as taught to us by our founder, John Africa. We are not looking for trouble. We are just looking to be left alone." Part of MOVE's radical renunciation of capitalism meant that they spent a lot of time scavenging, foraging, composting, developing raw cuisine, being outside, keeping children out of public schools, not wearing clothes, and abstaining from any violence towards animal whatsoever—which included no neutering or spaying of dogs and cats, and no extermination of rodents. It included boisterous organized demonstrations at zoos, circuses, slaughterhouses, and industrial parks. It also eventually included not paying utilities. In 1978, the police lay heavily armed siege to their commune when members resisted eviction. A police officer was shot. Nine MOVE members were convicted of and imprisoned for his murder, where some remained until as late as spring 2020.

After their arrests, MOVE relocated to another commune in a middle-class neighborhood in West Philly. Racist tensions continued to escalate for the next several years with the police and the surrounding neighbors—especially as MOVE became more ensconced in the demonstration against the political imprisonment of their nine members. By all outside accounts, the new commune was ramshackle, with lots of unvaccinated dogs and cats, not adhering to garbage collection, reports of loud rows—these were the sorts of community complaints that the police leveraged for their ensuing intervention. When in 1985 the police, with the ATF, had developed what they believed was sufficient evidence of illegal activity, having carefully solicited and documented outcry from the surrounding middle-class community—which included charges such as the amassing of arms and terrorist activity—they lay siege.

On May 13, 1985, five hundred police surrounded the commune in a heavily armed SWAT team and demanded the arrest of several members for whom they had warrants. A shoot-out ensued—the police say it was started by MOVE, and MOVE members say it was started by the police—and when members refused to emerge from the house, the Philadelphia police dispatched a helicopter.

That afternoon, Philadelphia's finest hovered in that helicopter over the commune—a rowhouse attached to dozens of other rowhouses just like it, the neighboring occupants having been evacuated with the promise they could return in twenty-four hours. They bellowed into a bullhorn: "Attention MOVE: This is America!" And then the Philadelphia police dropped a military-grade C-4 explosive, which incinerated sixty homes, killing eleven MOVE members: six adults and five children.

As we stood on Potter Street, saying goodbye to our hosts, I felt frozen in horror by this memory, by the brutality of a system that had murdered all of these people, these children. I felt some kind of paralysis from being in such close proximity to the insane and evil disparities between a Black communal movement and a mostly white-led one, in the same city, just a decade apart. Simple Way isn't armed—but why would they be? Who would they be arming themselves against? Who in power even cares, or notices, that they're here at all? There's such a sick irony at play here. The kind of invisibility that whiteness constitutes in this culture—invisible because it is not othered—allows for the Simple Way's efforts to pass largely unnoticed, unlike the hyper visibility of a Black community whose basic theology and mission were largely shared.

There's something tricky about this dichotomy, though, which is that the kind of racist hypervisibility brought to utopian communities of color is extended as a lens only to magnify the fear and vitriol already projected by the looker. So while they remain noticed as a menace, their fruits are undocumented, because they are completely unrecognizable to empire. In Saidiya Hartman's book *Wayward Lives, Beautiful Experiments*, she thinks about what then must be done to record and remember the kinds of histories that go unrecorded, the histories that are illegible to or absent from the racist historical record. In her book, she engages the limits of the erasure of the academic archive and uses it in alternative ways, intuitive and anarchic and truer ways, to tell the stories of young women of color between 1890 and

1935 in northeastern cities, especially Philadelphia, the stories of their beautiful world-building, stories of their art and pleasure and freedom, against all odds, stories about which the archive has remained mute or condemning or obfuscating. Hartman notes in the introduction that "the endeavor is to recover the insurgent ground of these lives; to exhume open rebellion from the case file, to untether waywardness, refusal, mutual aid, and free love from their identification as deviance, criminality, and pathology; to affirm free motherhood (reproductive choice), intimacy outside the institution of marriage, and queer and outlaw passions; and to illuminate the radical imagination and everyday anarchy of ordinary colored girls, which has not only been overlooked, but is nearly unimaginable." And in this is the will to "explore utopian longings and the promise of a future world that resided in waywardness and the refusal to be governed."

Imagination comes with responsibility. I mean imagination as a corrective force, not as a tool of invention—of making things up whole cloth—but as a way to forcefully reread the evidence, to take great pains to turn the received interpretations upside down and start from there, especially if we're old enough to know now which histories and which communities were predetermined to be read or recorded negatively, or not at all, and which were poised to be valorized, tolerated, or treated as benignly quaint. Which isn't to say that there aren't plenty of reasons that utopian experiments and communal movements have a sinister gloss: the patriarchal exploitation and sexual abuse of the FLDS; the coercion of the Branch Davidians and the Children of God; the violence of Jonestown. The most obvious and consistent indicator of corruption and abuse, in fact, is the presence of a white male leader.

Sweeney had a conference to attend at Villanova the day after we visited the Simple Way. He was presenting on a section of his dissertation which was turning into a revelation that the religion of emotion and suffering and identification with the tortured, peasant Christ that emerged in force in the early Middle Ages was the remnant or creation of Dark Ages peasants whose devotional practices had been consciously stymied and which imperial leaders had attempted to squash—because they wanted their subjects to believe in a Christ that looked like *them*—but when they couldn't squash it, just co-opted it, hence the later emergence of passion piety. The centralization of grief, suffering, and mourning in the Christian tradition was, Sweeney was beginning to assert, made by poor people, for poor people, mostly women, who were like, *This story is for us, this God was more like us than like the emperor.*

While Sweeney was in the conference hall delivering his paper, I found an abandoned classroom and watched a documentary called *Briars in the Cotton Patch* on my broken-ass computer.

The documentary was about Koinonia, a purposefully, or at least as-pirational, multiracial Christian commune that formed on the outskirts of Americus, Georgia, in the early 1940s and still exists today. Koinonia, mean-ing *communion* in ancient Greek, started as an anti-racist communal farm by two white couples: Clarence and Florence Jordan and Martin and Mabel England—though Clarence Jordan was and has been generally regarded as the community's figurehead. Jordan became increasingly radicalized while pursuing his PhD in the Greek New Testament. During that time, he be-came involved in the struggle for paying Black and white teachers equally in Georgia, gradually drawing away from academia and condemning the white supremacy undergirding the white Protestant church, turning instead to fellow political and theological dissidents with whom to start a commu-nity. The intention of Koinonia was to develop a life structured around the couples' understanding of the gospel: holding all things in common, prac-ticing nonviolence, and living out a commitment to racial equality. In his book *The Beloved Community: How Faith Shapes Social Justice, from the Civil Rights Movement to Today*, historian and theologian Charles Marsh says that the members of Koinonia "understood the decision not as a withdrawal from the social order but as a way of demonstrating that racial reconciliation and beloved community emerged out of engagement in common life in a particular place."

For a number of years, Koinonia offered farm apprenticeships, hosted short- and long-term visitors, provided emergency housing, and facilitated integrated Bible studies, dinners, and other gatherings. In 1955, it opened as an integrated summer camp for children, though the camp quickly provided a structure for which a more permanent membership-based community formed soon after, operated by "shared purse." They maintained a robust set of crops and farm stands and supply chains that kept the commune afloat. And though Koinonia had developed strong relationships with Black neighbors and farmers over the previous decade, finding Black members was difficult. Though the community was a site for many long-term informal interracial relationships and collaborations, the official membership was entirely white until, at its peak population in 1956, they were joined by two Black members and a few Black apprentices who lived on the commune.

By the late 1950s, following the determination of *Brown v. Board of Education*, Koinonia's attendant farm stand and farm store were subject to routine attacks by the KKK—shoot-outs, firebombs, dynamite, Molotov cocktails. Groups from all over the country started to aid in Koinonia's protection, including people from the Bruderhof and Daniel Berrigan and Dorothy Day (founder of the Catholic Workers), who stood guard one night in 1957 during a shoot-out. Their farm produced, famously and most abundantly, pecans, and so they had to create a mail-order business for those since racist boycotts prevented them from selling locally.

The fate of the community was precarious amidst all the violence, and with the community now somewhat estranged from the organized civil rights movement. Jordan and most of the members of Koinonia were now vocal about their critiques of protest and marches, instead seeing the growing of their multiracial community of care as a more essential response to confronting systemic change. The idea for Koinonia, as in most utopias, was to live out the "city on the hill," to let the city-on-the-hill-ness of itself transform the world at large, rather than try to effect change through the existing channels, such as direct action to the legislative powers. Jordan had wanted Koinonia to be "a demonstration plot of the Kingdom of God," or, as Marsh intones, "a living parable of reconciliation, though [Jordan] never had a clear picture of how a Christian community of total sharing and racial equality would transform the social order." And so—unmoored from a larger civic community, and under major threat—the community was on existentially shaky ground, and their relationships with revolutionaries like King were fraying.

While many Koinonia members did not directly participate in the demonstrations and marches of the growing civil rights movement, they mutually regarded each other as fellow travelers. Jordan and Martin Luther King Jr. were, for instance, in correspondence throughout the decade about their theological commitment to Black liberation and racial reconciliation. They were also openly critical of each other: King found Jordan's commitment to the racial reconciliation "demonstration plot" of Koinonia shortsighted, and later myopic; Jordan found King's commitment to the modality of political change insufficient in the face of what he understood to be a crisis that could only be addressed by spiritual means. The failure of Jordan's binary thinking here comes down to a purist ideology that strikes me as very white. He fails to understand that the Black American church had always been a site of resistance, in the fact of its continued survival in the face of a violent empire, such that it never had the luxury of fantasizing that the political and the spiritual were separate.

Purism never holds for very long, though. But the reason I even know about Koinonia at all is because during the early 1960s, in spite of itself, in spite of its lack of intention about political coalition-building, Koinonia became a sort of clearinghouse for a diverse range of activists, radicals, people from peace churches (say, the Bruderhof, the Mennonites, the Brethren, the Catholic Workers), rabbis, and civil rights lawyers who came to Koinonia often not as members, but as fellow travelers looking for respite, retreat, rest, and contemplation, in a place where such activists could develop the work they wanted to keep doing when they returned to the outside world. Marsh says, "Koinonia makes nothing happen in terms of a familiar statistical-legal measure. Yet the movement in the South, like Bonhoeffer's resistance movement in Germany and Gandhi's *satyagraha* in India, depended on intentional communities dedicated to work, study and contemplation . . . where weary men and women found refreshment and restorative fellowship between the major campaigns." In this way, Koinonia became something more than it meant to, something different than what even Jordan had imagined, and perhaps something vital to the civil rights movement.

The political vision of Koinonia, much like the Simple Way, was about particularity, and the spiritually transformative power of living out reconciliation in a specific place, through the daily work of living and loving, and tending, with other people. Societal transformation was, they suggested, something that works itself out at that scale, but it seems obvious, of course, from this vantage point that this is not, and never was, a zero-sum game.

As I watched *Briars in the Cotton Patch* in the empty, fluorescent-buzzing classroom, I stumbled into an intersecting story I hadn't anticipated: Linda and Millard Fuller had a watershed moment themselves in their mid-twenties. They sold all their things and traveled around United States in their camper van, trying to find a community. They had two young kids at the time, strapped in the backseat, as they let their fortunes and careers dissolve behind them. They stopped by Koinonia to visit a couple of friends who were living there at the time. The Fullers' intention was just to have lunch. They ended up staying for five years. Later they started a program that operated out of Koinonia called Houses for Humanity, which allowed the organization to buy and hold land in partnership with poor or impoverished families in the immediate rural area surrounding Americus, and in doing so significantly aided in building up Black land and homeownership.

This enterprise became the basis for Habitat for Humanity. Eventually, the Fullers' worldwide vision didn't fit with the very localized vision of close, intimate Christian community that Clarence Jordan was building in Sumter County. So the Fullers left Georgia and built the organization into a larger global network, with offices and projects all over the world.

And, as always, there are all kinds of ironies, even hopeful ones: Habitat for Humanity opened its world headquarters in Americus in the 1980s and became the largest employer in Sumter County; the organization had interracial leadership and community collaboration; the uptick in homeownership it fostered massively increased the county's tax base—and so the once racist and deeply segregated county came together because they faced the opportunity to share in capital. A kind of wealth generated on the expansion of nuclear families and private homeownership, the opposite—except for the interracial alliance—of what Jordan and the early residents of Koinonia had hoped for, envisioned, and believed in.

And another tired irony: Millard Fuller was forced out of his role at Habitat in the early 2000s for workplace sexual misconduct and abuse—which is maybe not an irony at all, it's just the kind of thing that always happens, and is always happening because unless we actively and fully disrupt the way patriarchy organizes even the world's most altruistic projects, all things become sites where power can accumulate and do violence. Fuller spent the last decade of his life growing a new organization—Fuller Center, which, I had just been learning the day before, is the sponsoring organization that undergirds Simple Houses, the organization that gives the interest-free loans for smaller organizations to hold on to for individuals working toward homeownership, what I saw being carried out on Potter Street in Kensington.

Toward the end of *Briars in the Cotton Patch*, one of the current Koinonia residents says: "One of our biggest challenges I think is that we've become acceptable. When you become acceptable, you run the risk of becoming mediocre. Our greatest fear I think is we'd lose our prophetic edge, and we need to fear mediocrity more than failure."

Koinonia is still here, trundling along in a piecemeal version of its roots. In fact, when I visited the Bruderhof community that past summer, I'd spent some time talking to an older couple—the former back-to-the-landers who had later converted to the Bruderhof—and when I got home from that trip, I received an email from my host, Laura, telling me that Koinonia had been in need of extra help that season and so the Bruderhof had sent this couple to go join them for several months.

Near the end of his life, Clarence Jordan wrote in a letter to one of his sons, "This is what always baffles me—Koinonia is forever dying and forever living. We should have conked out long ago, but somehow others came in the nick of time. This half-born condition is agonizing, and I could wish it otherwise, but there it is."

What does it mean to be radical, to retain "a prophetic edge"—or to live in the agony of a project in a half-born condition? Half-born isn't so bad if you take for granted that the utopia is never far from its opposite, so to be fully born is to accept that the worst has already happened. If something ever feels or claims to be finished, then you can probably assume it's gone bad.

utopianotes
Benincasa

I drive to the Upper West Side one day after work. I park in front of a six-story brownstone with a mansard roof and a garden-level entrance. While it was constructed to be an ordinary upper-class nineteenth-century home, it was bought by the Catholic church at the turn of the century and turned into a convent for the Sisters of Charity, which it had remained for nearly one hundred years. After the church started to consolidate its real estate in the early 2000s, though, then nuns were turned out into the community, and this building sat vacant until three years ago, when a woman named Karen turned it into a commune. I ring an old buzzy bell, and then Karen—a remarkably young woman—throws open the door and welcomes me in.

The building is now inhabited by Benincasa, a radical Catholic community and host of the nonprofit organization the Daniel Berrigan Center, which itself is just the fifth floor of the house, but as such pays their rent through grants. They also host renegade liturgy on Sundays. Karen throws up her hands. "Yeah, I bless my own eucharist. Who the fuck's going to stop me?"

Karen sits across from me at the large plank table, running her fingers across her scalp. When I ask about the nature of the relationships between groups like hers, the Catholic Workers, the Bruderhof, she thinks for a minute, before offering that they all—these different radical American Christian group—have a set of "shared elders."

I paused. "Really? It's not the shared theology, the book of Acts, renunciation of personal wealth and all that?"

"Yeah, I don't think it's that thought out," she says, as she starts to prepare dinner. "Ya know, 'cause, like, Daniel Berrigan and the Bruderhof literally took a bullet at Koinonia while the KKK were shooting at the farm during the 1950s, so now they're all in communion forever. And we," she says, gesturing to the house, "are all the grandchildren of those elders, and so we all take care of each other in honor of them."

We eat lemon broccoli and homemade veggie burgers in the cool, clean kitchen—and talk about how Benincasa started. It took years of searching for a space, Karen says, literally knocking on the doors of parish priests all over New York City. She talks about how, going through the enormous and precarious labor of starting a radical religious organization, she now really empathizes with the formation of all the different Catholic lay orders. She recalls this stained-glass window depicting the plight of the American Dominican sisters: four women in a rowboat, rowing across the Atlantic, and arriving at the poor they'd serve forever: they opened an orphanage! Started a convent! She laughs. "They probably had to ward off all kinds of in-fighting and threats from the patriarchs at the time, especially about their disobedience." But now the patriarchs put them in stained glass, laud them, highlight the seamless divine plan that so smoothly put them on the path to their obviously, uncontestably good works, which we, the patriarchs, were always 100 percent in support of.

We laugh. We eat some more broccoli. Will Benincasa someday get subsumed into the master narrative of empiric Catholicism, a stained-glass fixture of three young people standing in the door of an Upper West Side brownstone inviting in the poor and weary, the tempest-tossed, or be forgotten? As we moved into the common room to read and pray, I feel, once there, this overwhelming call I often feel in those contexts, the presence of a pace, a life, that can accommodate all manner of feeling and work.

THE FARM

When we turned off the interstate, the brush started to thicken, and the trees bowed in the Tennessee heat. As we approached the three-square-mile piece of land that was The Farm—one of the few remaining hippie intentional communities of its size left from the late sixties—we began to see crudely painted plywood signs on the county road, with arrows, spelling out in broad elementary brushstrokes, THE FARM. Amber, Laura, and I had driven down from Nashville to Summertown on a hot Monday. We drove straight south, in a line, down those steamy flat highways of Middle Tennessee. Laura and I were visiting Amber for our second annual "writer's retreat." I was still working on the utopia book, Amber on a project about queer outlaws in film, and Laura on a poetry manuscript called *Heaven*.

I wasn't sure—never am—what our plan was, what questions I wanted to ask once we got there, but a couple of weeks earlier I had called The Farm's "office" and asked to arrange someone to give us a tour. There seemed to be only one woman who fielded these requests—her name was Vicki, and she was in the welcome house when we arrived, a cottage that was host to a small museum of historical Farm ephemera, including a pair of elaborately embroidered bell-bottom jeans which had affixed to them a note, under glass, that said "Donated by Vicki."

Vicki had arranged for community member Rose Crockett to guide the tour, so we waited for Rose at the welcome cottage, thumbing through silkscreened t-shirts for sale and looking at old photographs of big groups of happy-looking twentysomethings circa 1972 in the "museum's" cases.

Eventually, Rose rolled up in her red SUV and said, "Am I giving y'all a tour?" She had wild curly red hair, a tiny frame, and cute flare jeans.

"Is there a bathroom anywhere, before we get going?" I asked on behalf of my friends.

She squinted. "Uhhh . . . here? Uh, no not really. We just go in the woods. I have some TP in my car if you want it." She stared. I shrugged at

Amber, who gave me a "no way" headshake, and we got into her car with full bladders.

I thrust forty dollars to Rose—the website had requested that visitors compensate our tour guides—and without speaking, she stuck the cash in a cup holder.

The land that The Farm sat on was flat, sprawling, verdant, a mix of mowed fields and patches of forest. There was a wide main road for cars and golf carts, and then a whole matrix of narrow wooded paths deep in the trees where people's homes were. Rose was not, as she said, an "original Farmie," but her boyfriend was—and so were a lot of the people we passed on the road. People, she said, often left The Farm at some point, only to return later in life, maybe more than once. There is, actually, an annual reunion for former Farmies, which had just taken place and finished up two days before our arrival that day. I knew about the annual reunion from the documentary *American Commune*, directed by sisters Rena Mundo Croshere and Nadine Mundo, who grew up partially at The Farm and filmed the event of the 2012 reunion, made up of many young adults, as the coda. Rose refused to put on her seatbelt while we drove so the car beeped its safety alarm incessantly for the entire duration of our visit, to which she occasionally responded, "Those aren't *our* laws!"

She took us around the sites of The Farm's various cottage industries, which had been supporting the community since the beginning: SEI, which manufactured solar technology; the Book Publishing Company, its actual name, which put out titles on vegetarian cuisine, New Age thought, and many of community founder Ina May Gaskin's *Spiritual Midwifery* volumes; the mushroom spore operation; the soy dairy that makes tempeh; the offices for Plenty International and for The Farm's board, which were housed in two off-white portables plunked down in a sunny field—the others in dingy double-wides parked in the trees just off the road.

These various enterprises had been supporting the community since nearly the beginning, when The Farm was still a commune. Rose shuttled us to the community center—a modest, open-concept 1970s mess hall–style building—where we peed in the only public toilets on the grounds. Outside was a sawtooth building which made up The Farm School for about twenty-five kids, all of whom live in the community. "They get *a lot* of recess," Rose laughed.

As we continued on, looking out the car windows, in those Tennessee woods were clusters of little houses: pre-fabs, trailers, cabins, cottages, shacks, A-frames. Residents were walking, or rolling around on golf carts, or on horseback. Eventually we rolled up to a big metal original geodesic dome structure that remained from the old days, shading, among other things, The Farm Store. We got out and walked around.

"You should hear the kinds of questions people ask me on these tours," Rose said. "Like, 'Is it true y'all have orgies?' And I'm like, 'What, nooo! We're old! I mean, back in the early days Stephen encouraged free love and all that, but it was a bunch of young people. Of course, people were having sex! Probably orgies. But now we're an *old* community. I mean, we do have nekkid Wednesdays. So when they ask those questions, I say, 'Only on nekkid Wednesdays.'" She smiled to herself.

When she made reference to Stephen, she meant Stephen Gaskin, who—with his wife Ina May—started the community by evangelizing for a year in 1969 back and forth across the country in a fleet of painted school busses, with some followers, bent on buying some property and developing a community of higher consciousness. When they found their land in Middle Tennessee, right here, they pooled all of their resources together and rented for a while, then bought it outright—and from 1970 to 1983 about a thousand people existed in a shared-purse commune. Under Stephen's leadership, the community gathered for daily teach-ins out in the field above the river, where he would "preach" on a bricolage of Christian and Eastern religious thought, and he served generally as the community's spiritual adviser. He was eventually forced out of that position, in the early eighties, when the shared-purse commune model had gone full broke and reorganized itself as the more financially informal intentional community—but Rose didn't really reflect or expand on Stephen's work at all, and I didn't ask.

We wandered on foot for a while. There were bright orange chanterelles growing everywhere in the surrounding woods, and we passed a couple of young men foraging them, and then, a minute later, we stepped over a dead armadillo steaming hot in the road.

She walked us to the community cemetery. Stephen Gaskin had a big headstone there. I asked about Ina May Gaskin, Stephen's spouse who'd started the Spiritual Midwifery movement and the Midwifery Center at The Farm in the 1970s, and she said that Ina May is currently living nearby the community with her son. She is old. "She's demented," Rose said. "Her head was going to strange places, so it's good she's not here anymore."

The Midwifery Center is still operational, and it functions not only as a place where women come to give birth, but also as a midwifery school and annual midwifery conference site. The buildings associated with the center are scattered throughout the two-square-mile property, some more centrally, others, like the A-frame dorms, off in the woods.

The Midwifery Center was totally revolutionary at the time it emerged, and it offered a corrective to the high infant and mother mortality rate in hospitals at the time. For its almost fifty years of existence, the Midwifery Center has been well known in the world of obstetrics for its low intervention and mortality rates. In *American Commune*, when asked about her educational background, Ina May said, "Well, some graduate literature courses, but that's it." She laughs about it in the film—a strange, gaunt, tall woman—speaking to a central tenet of her approach, which the Center was founded upon: that anyone can be a midwife, that the professionalization of midwifery has done a violence to birthing, has made women feel like they can't trust their own knowledge or the intuition of their bodies. The Midwifery Center created the premier model for birthing centers and midwifery education that proliferated for the next two decades across the United States.

There were, of course, some ethical issues with the two Gaskins' legacy: under Stephen's leadership, there were cultic elements, a way in which he had powerful influence over, say, the fate of people's relationships, marriages, and so forth. There were impositions on community members' reproductive lives; birth control and abortion were banned from use during the commune years. Something I've never quite understood was how Stephen and Ina May's different projects interacted or understood themselves in relation to each other—Ina May's outlasting Stephen's by nearly forty years, Ina May remaining hard at work on The Farm to run the Midwifery Center after Stephen had been asked to step down as leader in 1983.

•

I'd originally been drawn to the communal life of Middle Tennessee because of my awareness of a federation of communes just slightly west of The
Farm, in the region of Short Mountain—where today there are still something like a dozen encampments of Radical Faeries and queer communes.
Middle Tennessee saw a wave of communes emerge throughout the 1970s
and '80s, including two of the largest queer intentional communities in the
world: Short Mountain Sanctuary and IDA. These communities had formed
in the late seventies, a little after communities like The Farm and other back-
to-the-landers who had staked out territory in this region. Land was cheap
and property taxes were remarkably low. It is the tallest point in Tennessee,
and it was like many North American mountain regions, a place where the
social contract—even in the Bible Belt—was to leave each other alone.

The mountains are often a feature of people's efforts of radical removal—
the Appalachian chain in particular—and I can't help but drift to my soft
philosophies of geological meaning when the writer Alex Halberstadt writes
about this region in a *New York Times Magazine* article about the queer communes of Short Mountain a few years back:

> With its limestone striations and sandstone cap, the mountain is a
> remnant of the Cumberland Plateau and resembles nothing around
> it. What *is* around it looks downright strange. The ground erupts
> in perfectly hemispheric hills that the locals call knobs. They give
> the place the topography of cheese bubbling on a pizza, one reason
> neither industry nor large-scale farming ever prospered here. The
> knobs are fun to look at up close, especially in the summer, when
> the steep hillsides blaze up like billboards of neon green interrupted
> only by handfuls of biscuit-colored Hereford cattle. Sometimes,
> when a dog barks or a car backfires in Cannon County, the sound,
> bouncing off the hillsides, can travel for miles.

In his 2015 article, Halberstadt sets the stage of Short Mountain's story
with the gay rights activist and communist Harry Hay, a founder of the

neopagan Radical Faeries, who "urged gay men to 'throw off the ugly green frog skin of heteroimitation.' Instead of fighting for the rights that straights had, like marriage and adoption, the faeries believed that to be gay was to possess a unique nature and a special destiny apart from straight people, and that this destiny would reach its full flowering in the wilds of rural America."

For obvious reasons, the communities of Short Mountain are much more secretive and self-protective than The Farm. They had to form in even more culturally hostile decades than this hostile one we are living in now. In the 1980s and '90s, Short Mountain became an important sanctuary for HIV-positive gay men, who went there to be cared for or to provide care for others under the violent denial of the Reagan administration. I generally feel more wary showing up at separatist communes where I'm not among the ranks, and so while I did reach out to IDA to inquire after a visit, when I did not hear back, I didn't push further. Christian communes and hippie communes are easier to drop in on in part because they're conversion-oriented by nature.

The land parcels that the queer communes currently exist on were secured in the early seventies by a community of straight radicals from North Carolina who cooperatively bought the land from a retired couple. This group of hetero predecessors, Halberstadt says, was "committed to ending the war in Vietnam and to improving race relations; the group put out an underground newspaper and had spent time in Cuba. In Tennessee, they found pockets of sympathetic neighbors, back-to-the-land types who had come to the area after seeing an ad in a magazine called *Mother Earth News*." That group started to fray and disband over the next few years, seeking different kinds of lives than the ones they thought they wanted at the peak of their radicalization. One remaining member, committed to keeping the property under communal ownership, eventually connected up with the Radical Faerie community by chance on a trip to New Orleans. With them, he started to collectively devise a plan to bring them onto the land as owners. And so slowly the life of that original encampment changed to serve its new people.

But this wasn't unusual, or specific to Middle Tennessee. At the time of

The Farm's inception, there were hundreds—in some counts, up to a thousand—communes emerging all over the United States, in virtual simultaneity, between 1966 and 1971. This is a more familiar story to our collective cultural consciousness than some of the other eras I've been thinking about. In the years leading up to and during the Vietnam War, that generation of Americans coming of age began to question the values that had been bequeathed to them following the war most of them were born on the tail of: consumerism and sexual mores, the nuclear family, and the virtues of globalism. And they, like many utopians all over the world before them, and for similar reasons, began to drop out. Of course, those kids, the Baby Boomers, were standing on the shoulders of a generation's long critique of individual wealth acquisition and capitalism—even a robust and nearly spiritual American communist movement, the last vestiges of which had crumbled apart right before the hippies came of age, such that a sense of political or cultural genealogy did not seem to endure for the hippies. These kids by and large were from the suburbs, and not from the inner cities or industrial exurbs or communist midwestern farms which had been the hotbeds of leftist radicalism that Vivian Gornick is singing the swan song of in *The Romance of American Communism*. So as far as they understood themselves, they were stumbling upon an entirely new thing.

There were things that made each community and movement unique, and certainly a diversity of aims: "getting back to the land," saving the environment, getting free from sexual repression, leaving waged labor, unlearning sexism and racism, expanding one's or the collective's consciousness through the use of various drugs, and the revision (and appropriation) of various religious teachings.

The challenges, the things that would lead to their unbraiding, were also diverse, but often had some common themes: On the one hand, it was the same as the kids at Brook Farm, one hundred fifty years earlier: a lot of artists and soft-handed suburbanites who didn't know how to farm, just showing up hoping that they'd either learn fast enough to keep the project solvent, or that the novelty would give them enough energy to get through the grueling period. Eventually, though, the chickens come home to roost—no pun intended. They ran out of patience and energy, or they ran out of money, or they got just a little bit older and grew tired of being cold, muddy, tired.

In 1970, journalist William Hedgepeth described gender relations at the famous early-seventies commune New Buffalo, in Taos, thus: "Without becoming bogged-down in sexual identity crises and the 'feminine mystique' type trauma that idle females flagellate themselves with back in Suburbia, the New Buffalo girls fulfill themselves naturally not only in sewing, cooking, cleaning, and child-tending, but also in freely voicing their views and mystical visions, and then acting upon them." But Fred Turner, author of *From Counterculture to Cyberculture*, which effectively charts how the people from the hippie movement, and their utopian philosophies, architected what would later become Silicon Valley, reframes this report, saying that "[New Buffalo] did not so much leave suburban gender relations behind as recreate them within a frontier fantasy. One man who lived at New Buffalo could have been speaking for many at other communes when he told Hedgepeth, 'A girl just becomes so . . . *womanly* when she's doing something like baking her own bread in a wood stove. I can't explain it. It just turns me on.'" It's creepy—it gives me the creeps, and is the kind of thing that frequently leaves a slimy taste in the mouth regarding the hippies. So many of those communes reinstated the already prescribed hegemony and gender roles existing out in the world. It's what Joan Didion, as early as 1967, is already jaded about in "Slouching Towards Bethlehem" when she encounters a woman named Barbara in the Haight-Ashbury scene baking a macrobiotic apple pie for her kids and boyfriend, while talking about finding a renewed happiness in "the woman's thing," and realizing that "that's where the trip was," the woman trip of baking, cleaning, caring, tending. Didion's depiction is an eye roll in itself. "Whenever I hear about the woman's trip, which is often, I think a lot about nothin'-says-lovin'-like-something-from-the-oven and the *Feminine Mystique* and how it is possible for people to be the unconscious instruments of values they would strenuously reject on a conscious level, but I do not mention this to Barbara."

The feeling of jaded-ness comes from what Turner describes of how the "New Communalists recreated the conservative gender, class, and race relations of cold war America." He observes that where women were joining

the body politic through radical interventions on the "outside," in communes, "women often pursued authority by asserting a neotraditional fem-
ininity in the domestic sphere." But this critique isn't new. Most people of
my generation who are reflecting on the veritable failure of that decade have
that dismissal on lock. It's easy for my peers and me to dismiss—I suppose
because it was so much a Baby Boomer movement, and that the individualism, hedonism, lack of long-term vision or analysis of power showed its
hand more clearly as the Boomers came of age, became our parents, and
revealed themselves to be the Worst Generation: the most extractive, oppor-
tunistic, and corrosive consumers the world had ever seen.

But then what of the fact that many of these communities still exist, and
so many folks hung on to the things they believed in when they started the
project of trying to build a new world? It required sustained planning and
work. The persistence of The Farm seems largely due to the way it operates
like a small town. Twin Oaks in Virginia maintained a vigilant practice
around vetting membership with a focus on adherence to common principles. Short Mountain's longevity was formed so deeply by its becoming
a sanctuary for folks diagnosed with AIDS and those who were caring for
them, even though its purposes changed over time. For a 1960s commune to
survive, there had to be some force that pushed it beyond whatever fantasy
it started from.

It was a sweltering afternoon, now at one o'clock on The Farm. We paused
at the community's blueberry bushes, walking the rows and eating them.

"Who takes care of them?" I asked Rose.

She shrugged. "We just let them grow," she said. "Some people come
in from the outside for a U-Pick situation, ten dollars a bucket. We have to
really figure out all the ways to make money in the community—all the
ways we can."

We continued on through different enclaves, different clusters of homes
in different parts of the woods—arranged like unofficial neighborhoods.
We drove along what Rose called "millionaire row," which was just larger,
more elaborate manufactured homes or multifamily kit houses. "No one

actually owns their homes here," she said, "or the land it sits on. And every-thing's gotta be built with cash. So sometimes people retire and take their pensions to build something, and that's who's on millionaire row."

It turns out, at The Farm, you can't get a mortgage for building any-thing. The entire property belongs to a land trust, into which community members pay dues. It's a similar situation to something like an HOA, with a particular focus on environmental conservation and stewardship. The com-munity's median age falling somewhere in the sixties, there is a way that it feels, in part, like a low-overhead, members' club retirement community today. "And it's a majority woman community," Rose added. "I like that."

Despite the ways it has changed, there's a residual level of communality at The Farm that's quite remarkable. Even though the commune ended in 1983, with everyone dirt poor and basically bankrupt, many of the original buildings remain or were repurposed, as well as the social structure. There's still, for instance, a conflict resolution committee, a holdover from the com-mune days.

"Who's on it?" I asked Rose.

"Well, me for one," she said.

Community members rely on or try to rely on mostly internal forms of money-making—nursing, teaching, building, cleaning, cooking, making plant medicine, working for one or more of the cottage industries—but many people have to seek employment on the outside. Rose moved here in 2011 to retire, and a lot of people live with their elderly parents here, too. There are some second-gen Farmies, young adults, most of whom live in the community's closest approximation of a dorm.

Rose remembers the original caravan—Stephen Gaskin's wild band of school busses chock-full of seekers and freaks—coming through Nashville in 1971 when she was getting ready to graduate from high school. She was excited. But also, even then at eighteen, she knew what she was looking at: "Ya know, most of those people were coming from upper-middle-class backgrounds, and I was working class. My mama had ten kids, and I helped her raise them. I didn't want to be barefoot and pregnant on a commune—I was trying to get away from that. So I didn't follow them. I went to college." She tells us, more than once, that a lot of the money that went into buying and building the original commune was from individual inheritances of community members.

The last stop Rose took us to was the eco-village, which was built in the early 1980s as a way to bring in more money to the community once the commune had dissolved. It is now managed exclusively for eco-tourism. Girding the path down to the eco-village are five of the original caravan school busses, covered in murals and bright slashes of paint. A court of cob houses with green roofs greet us at the village entrance, each dry as a bone inside. A Farm resident and her teenage daughter manage the village these days, including the shop where she sells stones, various titles from the Publishing Company, and homemade CBD salves. We bought a couple of things, and thanked her, and then Rose drove us to the welcome cottage, back to our car.

"You girls have a good day," she said. Then she looked at me. "By the way, I can't remember: Did you pay me already?"

This final interaction highlighted the undercurrent of precarity that runs through the remains of the hippie commune movement, a utopia of individuals. While a place like The Farm has in the twenty-first century provided a way for some Baby Boomers to retire in a friendly community, it has left those people in the same fiscal security lurch as those on the outside.

We got back into Amber's hot little Ford and tottered back down the country roads toward the interstate. It was the three of us, once again, in Tennessee, driving down those winding leafy roads, listening to Belinda Carlisle as we had been the year before. We stopped at a Sonic for grilled cheese and milkshakes, then I napped in the backseat as we hurtled back to the city, listening to Amber and Laura talk about what lay ahead in the coming weeks, and about heaven and *Heaven*, about where their lives were headed. Laura had just broken up with her boyfriend of eight years and finished graduate school. She was working for the Poetry Project at St. Mark's Church in Manhattan. What she thought would be a year of applying for teaching jobs turned into a new role for her at the Project as director of learning and community engagement, a nearly utopian job that allowed her to show up to work at noon and hang out with or support poets all day. She developed her own programming, innovated new public pedagogy models, one of which was a series called Dis/Courses, free readings, and discussion groups hosted by beloved poets, across such subjects as ghosts and romanticism. Amber, on the other hand, was about to move in with her girlfriend, which was a big deal because Amber had decidedly not shared living space with anyone in her adult life, but here she was about to fuse her home and pets and deep Scorpio privacy with Jamie, the love of her life she never thought she'd meet. She had also, in the last year, slowly started to build a queer reading group and literary community in Nashville, which now had upwards of one hundred members. And I—where was I?

I was about to move to a pre-fab on a hilltop in the Catskills with Sweeney, for what was going to be the summer, but we were realizing was turning into a longer stay, and I had decided to begin in earnest the process of figuring out how to not have as much of a job.

utopianotes
earthships

I'm in graduate school. I wake up one morning in an "earthship" half-submerged into the ground outside of Taos. The structure, made mostly of tires and cob, belongs to an eighty-year-old German woman named Zena, who'd invited my friends and me to stay the night during a week we'd spent road-tripping and camping around the lower Rocky Mountains. The earthship she lives in is wedged into a big stretch of desert populated by dozens of other earthships—off-the-grid, passive energy homes extending for three miles all the way to the edge of an old airplane hangar which has recently been converted into a brewery. Towering over all of this in the distance are the peaks of the Sangre de Cristo mountains, still snowcapped in spring. Zena's kitchen, sunken one floor into the hot earth, is full of big, happy plants soaking up geothermal heat by the east-facing window which takes up most of the front of her house. Her living room is lined with books about the Holocaust, Jewish mysticism, and Christian apologetics, and big panoramic photographs of Jerusalem. This morning, she bakes eggs on bagels and brings a pot of coffee in a knit cozy to the guest quarters, and then waits until we are fully awake before handing out scrolls printed with biblical passages. "I started giving these out after 9/11," she says without further explanation. Then she seats us in a circle around her, tells us about the blitz at Hamburg, the insidious evils of consumerism versus the visible evil of the Nazis. She moves on to stories of raising her six children in the suburbs of Cleveland, and says that while she believes that the Lord Jesus Christ is her savior, she is not part of the "cult of church-ianity," and then she prays over us.

THE FLESH FAILURES
(LET THE SUNSHINE IN)

Pareesa told me about an anarchist collective in Ridgewood, Queens, called Woodbine, where she'd just seen Silvia Federici give a talk. When I looked Woodbine up, I realized one of the founding members was an old friend of Sweeney's, back from the Westchester punk scene days. The next event on the calendar was titled "Anarchist Communes in the 1960s" and would be given by Virgil Addison, a scholar of North American insurrectionist history.

The description of the talk highlighted Addison's angle:

It is sometimes forgotten that, while many of these new communards were hippie pacifists or religious seekers, many others were anarchists seeking a new road to revolution. For the most part, the anarchist communes grew from the urban projects of groups like Up Against the Wall Motherfucker and the Diggers, who left behind their free stores, crash pads, newspapers, and other anarchist projects to try their hand at farming and rural living. But contrary to the popular narrative, these anarchists did not abandon their hopes for an insurrection or sever their ties to urban rebellion, at least not immediately.

The description ended with this admission, which I appreciated:

Like many would-be communards, Virgil Addison has no lived experience on rural communes.

Woodbine, the space that was hosting the talk, started in 2013, after the wind-down of New York's Occupy movement, by ten or so people who were bonded by their sustained participation in the demonstrations at Zuccotti Park, and who wanted to find a way to afford to live in New York City in a less isolated way from one another. So they all moved to this neighborhood, within a couple of blocks from this storefront that they collectively pitched into to form Woodbine.

It was a plain white brick storefront underneath the rattling M track, and butting up against a triangular empty lot of weeds and stone. Sweeney and I passed into a cool unlit room, with cold cement floors and natural light trickling in the windows, and a few people sitting quietly in freestanding chairs, facing the presenter who looked plaintively at us from the front of the room. But soon the room was full of people. Sweeney's old friend spotted us in the back row of folding chairs, greeted us, and immediately handed me a sheaf of papers he'd just freshly xeroxed of a narrative essay by M. C. Richards about her first ten years at the Gate Hill Cooperative in Rockland County. Then Addison began the talk.

A classic 1960s hippie graphic was projected on the wall above the scholar's head: a crowd of young people gathered inside of and around a geodesic dome somewhere out in the American West. He started by stressing that he understood this history differently than most scholars, that "the communes movement *made* the hippies" and not the other way around. He also had a taxonomy of different types of people found at communes, both in the 1960s and now:

Dropouts: Escaping consumerist culture; escaping nine-to-five job
Utopians: Have a plan, big project, or vision that they want to
   carry out
Renegades: Outlaws, criminals, militants, and guerillas

The renegades, he said, get forgotten about often, as a significant and necessary part of this particular revolutionary moment of commune building in the 1960s. They came with skills to keep the bad guys out. Not infrequently, they came with the ability to provide arms training. Addison talked about how the Boomers were back-to-the-landers because that's in a sense what the generation before them had migrated from, so maybe, he suggested, we're now in "a movement of, like, taking-back-the-suburbs?"

Then he prodded the audience: "Every anarchist has an ideal commune in mind, right? I mean, mine is, like, a bunch of trailers on a piece of land, all arranged in a circle facing each other—but that's just me."

I looked around the room at all of the people asking themselves this question. Through the window above the front door was a strip of powder blue sky, the hazy orange sunlight of summer. I stayed very still and thought about it. What is my ideal commune? I thought about this group of friends who run Woodbine, renters one and all, who moved to Ridgewood within a few blocks of each other and started a community space, just so they could hang out and have some more leisure time. Why hadn't I done that? Why wasn't that happening now? While all my attempts at trying to imagine or forge a more communal life have been geared toward looking outside of urban centers, toward para-rural-suburban regions outside of large cities, is that actually where my ideal commune exists? Honestly, in spite of my tendencies, my idea is not a collection of cottages, nor land stewardship, nor a farm or even a residency or open-door arts organization. It doesn't need a view, or a mountain, or access to "nature." My ideal commune is a cooperatively owned apartment building on a dense city block in the Bronx or in Brooklyn, stocked full of friends. But I don't have the money for that, nor do any of my most interested friends—at least not in New York City. And even if we did align our timelines, find the right place, coordinate our finances and lease-breakings, we'd be gentrifying a neighborhood, or we'd be setting in motion a basic life expense so steep that, even in communal ownership, we'd all have to work waged labor all the time just to make our commune run.

Something that I could hear in Addison's talk, something he wanted to push against or rethink, was the idea that hippie and especially anarchist communities were made up only of these apolitical dumb hippie kids, white people with stupid philosophies and a trust fund and some "grass"— the way that this history had been metabolized, in retrospect, by our generation. He impressed that communes absolutely and consciously emerge from within social struggle and political insurrection. And further, that the "anarchist communes of the sixties were consciously building relationships with each other" the whole time. Different communities and communes communicated with each other through posters and newspapers and other networks. Many shifted from one commune to another at different times, notably, say, the American Situationists who eventually moved to Cold Mountain Farm; the Diggers who ended up at Black Bear Ranch; Defectors of Hog Farm to the Reality Construction Company.

Pushing against the escapism narrative as a totalizing story for what that period and that movement were like was the most important thing I took away from this talk. That many of the communes actively understood themselves as working within liberation struggles was revelatory for me, as well as the fact that, while a lot of communities did not initially understand themselves as part of a utopian lineage, they often did retroactively. Whether or not they actually succeeded in their aims, insurrection or utopia-wise, or carried out further damage in their attempts, is another question. It always is.

I asked Addison, during the Q & A, if he knew of any "purposefully multiracial" communes from this era, and he said that the Diggers remained directly connected to the Oakland-based Black Panthers and other Black revolutionary movements located in cities, even as they began to build communities in Mountain West deserts. But that was not what I was asking. In fact, as I asked the question, I thought of Jim Jones's Peoples Temple, perhaps the largest purposefully multiracial commune from that decade, and I felt queasy.

Because the more my own search for commune building continues, the anxiety persists, for me, about how communes reproduce or often worsen the same kinds of stratifications and exclusions that exist on "the outside"— and that if communal life isn't in some way responding to that problem, or trying to, then it's not worth much.

Who in the twentieth century was actually trying to create multiracial community—other than the largest suicide cult in the Americas?

Well, cities were. The Bronx was—but not as a utopian aspiration. When poor people of all races live in the same dense city block, they work together, not because they are living out a shared devotional spiritual life or an experience of communally articulated enlightenment, but because they are people trying to survive in time and space together, against the powers that be. Father Divine's Peace Mission Movement did this, in part because it was the Depression and people needed to eat and sleep somewhere safe, and give their kids a place to live.

After the talk, I was having a cigarette outside, and a man started chatting with me about his work on Fourier and mine, more broadly, on "American utopian experiments."

"Have you found any examples in your research," he asked, "of a *really* successful commune?"

I thought about this. The Farm, in its durability, is what some people refer to as a successful commune, in terms of its having lasted as long as it has. But what is a successful commune? Just lasting—or is lasting actually indicating an opposite, a failed utopia which has become a rather staid institution? Gate Hill Cooperative has lasted for more than fifty years, as has Twin Oaks. The Family Divine, which emerged in 1921, still exists as a small monastic community of twelve or so in a mansion outside Philadelphia. Are they successful? Is that a success?

There is no shortage of personal or informal records of the lives of different 1960s and early '70s communes, either through reporting at the time or exhaustive logs kept by members themselves. The thing I keep noticing about these '60s commune accounts, we could call them "taking stock" narratives, which is what they are, three to ten years after the beginning of the experiment, is that it's sometimes hard to tell when the author is narrating about a difficult period or a good period in the life of the commune.

It's also distinctive how familiar the issues are, the needs, the questions, that are raised in the throes of commune conflict. The challenges of community building remain more or less the same, or categorically the same: compromising aims, getting bogged down by maintenance labor, figuring out how to decide if so-and-so can keep their shed rotting or isn't helping to clean up the kitchen, and how to talk to them about it, the split between people who have big mythic or mystic aims for the community versus those whose orientation is more about practicality or unlearning sexism/racism/classism.

In Joyce Gardner's lively and detailed account of her time at Cold Mountain Farm, from 1967 to 1968, in the Adirondack region of New York,

she encapsulates a lot of this. Addison had shared a PDF scan of the text before his talk. Her account is a study in these contrasts, and is mimeographed
into a red, stapled booklet, with a woodblock print of mountains and the
title: *Cold Mountain Farm: An Attempt at Community*. She divides the account
up by season over her year-and-a-half-long tenure. About halfway into her
time there, she writes:

> We had that good feeling now, of warmth, of family. We were
> becoming a tribe. There were long, good discussions around the
> fire, into the night . . . Slowly, things were beginning to move and
> take shape. With all its imperfections. I never felt so all together
> and good about any group of people. Everything that I did here felt
> good and meaningful—in the context of this place and these people
> whom I loved. Until now, I knew what it was like to feel free as
> an individual with a few people, but now, finally, I felt free to be
> myself without the horrible fear of being ostracized for making a
> slip here, doing something wrong there.

So things seem not just good, but even ideal. She seems soothed. I'm soothed.
But this declaration is immediately followed by

> But unfortunately, the ideal is almost always very far from the real,
> and with living so close to one another we probably made love
> with each other even less than when we lived in separate apartments
> in the city.

Then, while she discusses how each person brought their own ideas of what
the totalizing vision of life on Cold Mountain Farm was, she admits that they
were all "remarkably unreceptive" to competing ideas.

And then, right as the long winter is coming to an end, and it's warming
up, and they're in the throes of planting season and can lie naked in the sun,
things begin to fray. She describes all of their planting activities, their good
relationships with the local farmers for exchange of services, all of them
building their beautiful summer shelters. It sounds great to me. But then,

It was getting warmer now, and there were more of us, but we were not so close. There was no real sense of community between us. There was good feeling. A good sense of living and working together. But there was no "center." There was no clear-cut purpose behind what we were doing. Some of the men felt an unfulfilled need to fight, to participate in the struggle. The women felt an unfulfilled need to love. The men complained that it was a "love" community and that they wanted a guerilla farm. They reproached themselves and each other for not being more militant. It felt peculiar for "revolutionaries" to be living such a peaceful life. It was difficult to think about fighting the enemy while you planted peas. And the enemy was certainly not as clear-cut here as it had been in the city.

She describes other goings-on of the summer, including "the great chicken dispute," new people coming up from New York, conflicts regarding the standard of living, issues with their dissenting expectations coming to the fore—but nothing in the narrative sounds like a deal breaker until suddenly she says:

We seemed to have reached an all-time low.

This admission seems to come out of nowhere, after an exhaustive description of their daily subsistence activities. Then again, I think the big question that comes up in the life of a lot of American communes is how they end up working themselves to death. Life on a commune is, in one sense, all about work: every person participates in keeping everyone fed, clean, the food growing, the house repaired, the new houses being built, birthing the babies, caring for the babies, the animals, harvesting the vegetables, the eggs, maintaining whatever cottage industry they need to keep afloat. But then, the whole life—the spirit of life that brought them to this place or project—begins to get squashed by the vagaries of work.

Gardner gets fed up, tired of the infighting, tired from mothering, breaks up with her partner and skips town, to another famous commune in Vermont's Northeast Kingdom called Bryn Athyn. There's a shorter part of the pamphlet dedicated to Bryn Athyn, as though Cold Mountain Farm is really where most lessons about communal living at the end of the world were digested for her.

During a section titled "Reflections," before the narrative moves on to her experiences at the Bryn Athyn, Gardner discloses that she's recently been reading about the Hopi (the chapbook itself was written in 1970, just a couple of years after she left New York), and that it's helped her bring some things together about her time at Cold Mountain Farm:

> For Americans, the "greater family" is replaced by the State; the clan and tribal ceremonies are replaced by the Church, television, and sports. Now if community is going to be independent of Church and State and TV, then we have to find new ways of fulfilling these needs. At the farm, I think we were trying to be a kind of "greater family" for one another, trying to consider one another brothers and sisters, with the children belonging, in some sense, to all of us . . . But even if we had completely succeeded in establishing such relationships, it wouldn't have been enough. For two reasons.
>
> First, there was no tribe and no tradition. Second, we had no access to the present-day technology, which might at least have given us the leisure time to create our own traditions . . . We had rejected the American answer of Church and State, but we had put nothing in their place. And so, we soon discovered that our lives seemed empty and unfulfilled, that there was division amongst us, that we were unable to work in peace together to meet our needs. We had been so anxious to work together, but we never learned, and seldom had time, to relax and play and grow together.

What she's describing is in part just the spoils of the colonial project, and that she draws her lessons directly from her readings on the Hopi is even more disturbing, in its lack of self-consciousness. But I can hold it in tension with the fact that she was twenty-five years old at the time, writing her reflections on what was a very recent experience in 1970. It does get at the heart of a blind spot in settler ideology, though, which perhaps explains the centuries of fallout: settlers are lonely-ass people. They never figured out how to not be lonely. Most utopian experiments that follow a settler-colonial model are about recouping in a very limited way the means by which to not be lonely, and in the twentieth century they were often grabbing at or appropriating models of North American Indigenous people, whom their settling effectively wiped out.

There's a lot of this type of record available—in the tone, style, and immediacy of Gardner's account—in an old magazine called *The Modern Utopian*. *The Modern Utopian* was an independently published magazine that ran from 1966 to 1972, gathering reports from and articles on different communes from all over the country, which were emerging (and folding) in real time. The magazine's run was basically simultaneous to the lives of the communities it was covering. In 2010, Process Media published a compilation of highlights, actual reprints from the original magazine, into a full-length book—a commemorative anthology by the same name, with a beautiful neon blue cover featuring three kids leaping in a meadow in front of a geodesic dome.

The collected articles in this anthology are written largely by non-professionals: college students, dropouts in their twenties, loners who want in on the fun, the Underground Press Syndicate, academics using the opportunity to write about a community as the way to get as close as they'll ever get to dropping out—garden variety utopian groupies. For the most part, the authors can already see the fault lines in the communities they're writing about, the ways in which they are going to fall apart: ideological disagreements, a generally shaky command of the skills necessary to carry out communal labor, the presence of unexamined racism and sexism. The interview subjects themselves are often describing what they already see as a fading project.

At one point, a contributor writing in 1968 opines about what was the brand-new Broadway production of *Hair*. He is actually discussing the play in earnest. He loves it. I was surprised by this because I'd always assumed that *Hair* was regarded by the hippies in its own time as appropriative counterculture pap, sorority girls playing dropouts, a Disney-fication of the earnest movement. But this writer felt taken seriously by the play, felt like it was changing people's worldviews, and this grabs something in me because I love *Hair*, and I will take any opportunity to love it even more. I've never been sure whether it's parody or totally sincere, and maybe that tension is why I love it so, because that tension is always, also, the utopian tension.

I still remember watching the 1979 film version for the first time at a sleepover when I was thirteen, on a small TV in my friend Caitlin's bedroom in the attic of her old Victorian house. I loved every second of it. It was funny, nuanced, psychedelic, so sad, so campy. I burrowed in the cozy nylon pile of my sleeping bag laid out on her brown shag carpet. I thought about the film's final scene for days afterward: There is Berger, played by a young, strapping Treat Williams, at the Army base. He's mischievously swapped himself in for his buddy Bukowski, the actual soldier, so that Bukowski can have one more romantic afternoon with his girl, Sheila, before he gets shipped off to Vietnam. And just like that the sergeant bursts into the barracks and starts calling off soldiers' names, and they all start loading into a giant Globemaster. The Globemaster parked on the base's tarmac looks like a monster, and a shadow falls across Berger's face and he gets in marching order and starts singing this weird song: "We starve, look at one another short of breath, walking proudly in our winter coats."

Then some women's voices start singing, in unison, disembodied from somewhere outside the camera's frame, because we are still on the tarmac with Berger, and all the other men, marching toward the plane—

Somewhere, inside something, there is a rush of greatness
Who knows what stands in front of our lives

and you realize he, Berger, the nice Italian-Jewish boy from Queens whose parents lent him bread to get his friends out of jail just a few days earlier, and who has been living and leading this multiracial, multi-class band of draft dodgers around in a jolly dropout life in Central Park, really is going to get shipped off to Vietnam. It's happening. He's going to war. And he disappears into the dark mouth of the Globemaster. And then there's a jump cut to his friends, all singing together now, singing that final cryptically devastating line of the last verse before the famous refrain begins: "'Life is around you and in you' / Answer for Timothy Leary, deary." Time has passed. You realize they're standing around Berger's grave at Arlington.

They're gathered there, mourning, holding each other's babies and each other's arms. And then they start singing that manic, desperate refrain, pleading, in a harmony that has broken into what sounds like a hundred parts: "Let the sunshine in / Let the sunshine in / The sunshine in."

And then it cuts to the increasingly weird, dreamlike scene of all these anonymous hippies, thousands now, racing and leaping across the National Mall's lawn, dancing and protesting both, and everyone still singing, begging, that same refrain—but you know that somehow it's already over, it's already crushed. Or at least that's what I knew, as the thirteen-year-old viewer in 2001, regarding a relic of what was already a relic in 1979: I was watching something that was both climax and death rattle.

The final scene in the film version of *Hair* gives me a similar feeling that I get at the eight-minute mark in "Alice's Restaurant," which also came out in 1967, the same year of the original Broadway play. Arlo Guthrie, after lots of comic deferral about his and his friends' hijinks in the Berkshires, says in his daft, rhythmic way, "But that's not what I came to tell you about. Came to talk about the draft." A balloon of joy rises in my chest at that sly revelation as he pivots into his slow protest, every time, every dumb Thanksgiving time, because, why? Because it's like we've all gathered around the fire to talk about how war is evil and friends are good and cops are dumb and the value system we've inherited is absurd, but our friends will remind us of this, and so will the guys on the Group W bench. Together, maybe, we will resist the death machine with goofy forms of agitation, noncompliance, interruption, and song. But maybe we won't, because we didn't. It is the twenty-first century now and we have paused our Thanksgiving dinners to remember this. We have paused for a moment to touch the good—the good has been held at bay, and we are touching it now, but it's already ruined or gone anyhow.

In the several months following the 1967 Broadway debut of *Hair*, MLK and RFK were assassinated. The year after the 1979 film's release, Reagan was elected.

utopianotes
Portland Night High School

I'm a junior in high school, but I want to graduate early. My academic counselor, Judy Large, directs me to a program called Portland Night High School, which runs four evenings a week in the windowless basement of Grant High School, after all of the day-students and staff have packed out. I call and make an appointment to speak with the program coordinator, a middle-aged woman on the other end of the line who tells me "come on by." I take the bus across town. The coordinator listens to my situation: I'm trying to figure out a way to bypass some upper-level math and science courses so I can get my diploma that June and focus on my writing. I can't read her reaction to my plan through the blond bob, glasses, and sensible slacks. Finally, she says, "OK, Adrian, I'm going to level with you. It would be really beneficial to us if you enrolled in our program. You're college-bound. It'll help with our funding and our numbers in general. So, we'd love to help you."

Portland Night High School had been a fugitive operation from the beginning, losing its headquarters and funding every couple of years, and then reconstituting itself elsewhere. It started in 1980, with permanently skeptical support from the district, with a simple mission: to create a way for students to earn a diploma who otherwise had work or childcare commitments that prevented them from attending conventional class-time hours. Because it took for granted that its student body attendance would be discontinuous, academic credits were earned on a tally system: Four days a week, two "blocks" of classes were offered, one after another (e.g., biology, English, social studies, 5:00–6:30 p.m., and then advanced algebra, physics, visual arts, 6:30–8:00 p.m.). Students could pick whichever two classes they wanted to go to, and for each class attended, the student was conferred a number of points. The classes were non-graded, each session being a self-contained learning experience. Once a certain number of points were accrued, students put together a portfolio that demonstrated new competencies and progress, and received a course credit in whatever subject their audit needed.

I start showing up a couple of times a week to a band of high-school-aged students who are full-time workers, parents, weirdos, druggies, artists, and dropouts, to engage in this odd way of finishing high school on our own terms, free of stigma. Every night we gather in a common space at the beginning of the evening where each student present is called by their name, before choosing which classes they want to take this evening.

The man who started it was named Dave Mesirow, and in 2006 when I enrolled for a semester, he had retired years before but was still very involved in its running, more or less on site every night, maintaining re-lationships with staff and students, and running a scholarship fund for any college-bound students coming out of that program. He was a wily, men-schy, white-haired old radical, probably in his late sixties. And he stayed in touch with me when I went to college, and we had an ongoing plan to meet up, though we never did. A year later, funding was yanked again, and the program was in limbo, eventually forced to operate with a lot more oversight from the district, robbing it of many of the features that had made it so radical. Years later I find an obituary. Mesirow had died somewhat suddenly in 2014. "When he wasn't fishing the Lower Deschutes, he did his best to irritate those who couldn't think—or allow students to thrive—outside the box."

THREE

HEAVEN

utopianotes
Garden of Happiness

Lisa and I have been trying to get together for several months, but our lives and schedules keep getting in the way. By the skin of my teeth in late July I take a forty-five-minute bus ride that encircles the entire Woodlawn Cemetery to the neighborhood of Norwood to meet her at a bakery. We drink old-tasting ice coffees, and I tell her about some recent visits to the Bruderhof community in the Catskills, the Marshes' life in the Bonhoeffer House, my time at the old hippie commune situation at The Farm in Tennessee. Light filters in the dirty window. She asks if I want to walk with her to a community garden about a mile away where she's been tending a plot. The Garden of Happiness, started by Karen Washington. She has to water the beds. We walk through the weird winding cut-outs caused by the Parkways, along Southern Boulevard against rushing oncoming traffic, sweating. We talk about starting a womyn's group at New Day. Eventually we find ourselves on a quiet residential street among a number of multi-family freestanding homes, some small apartment complexes, and then at a locked chain-link gate. "I was told to ask Robert across the street for a key." So we go to the apartment across the street and knock on the door. A man answers. We identify ourselves, but he says someone else has the key—an elderly woman next door. So we knock on the next door, and she opens the door. She doesn't speak English, but is very friendly and accommodating and seems to know what we're looking for, but she doesn't have the key either. Her daughter does. And her daughter is at her boyfriend's house down the street. So we all walk out on the sidewalk together in the sun, communicating in broken Spanish and hand gestures, to a small apartment building. We stand below a window and she yells up. Other people walk by, greet her, chat. Eventually her daughter opens a second-story window and throws down the key. We walk back to the Garden of Happiness, and she unlocks it for us and goes in. We water the tomatoes; she feeds the chickens. Neighbors talk to us over the fence. The old woman pantomimes a story to us about how many of the chickens were eaten by racoons recently. We end up back in her house across the street. It's cool inside. Her granddaughter is coloring at the kitchen table. She offers us water. We gulp it down. As we leave through the front door, her daughter has resurfaced from her boyfriend's place down the block and chats with us on the front steps. It occurs to me as we walk back toward our own neighborhoods that, in this moment, we have found ourselves in a utopian Venn: the garden and the city, both at the same time.

LIVING

The day we left Woodlawn for good, Sweeney and I drove up to Frank's Place in two separate cars, our belongings winnowed down to clothes and summer reading. We'd gotten rid of most of our furniture, the vast majority of which had been cheaply salvaged from roadsides and Goodwill anyway, and we stored our surplus books in my mother-in-law's garage. We had no plan come September when our temporary lease was up, save a vague faith that our agenda might become clear by then. I got to Frank's Place first—a long pull up the quarter-mile driveway into a clearing that skirted the house. The wind rippled the fields, and the sun glimmered beyond the saddle curve of the mountain. Sweeney arrived an hour later, and then we sat on the deck and watched the sunset.

A weird thing is that, in the weeks before we moved up to Frank's Place, a man from Sweeney's hometown of Pleasantville told us about a dude in his eighties who owned an old hunting cabin in the Catskills that he was currently trying to off-load onto a willing young outdoorsman. The old man had bought the cabin with his buddies, collectively, decades earlier. But of the twelve original buyers, most were dead now or had otherwise transferred their share to this survivor—and the property was too ragged, the cabin too dilapidated, to sell. Sweeney met up with the old man for dinner. The cabin, he told him, sat on a small parcel at the edge of a ten-thousand-acre state forest heavily used by hunters, and so there was no way to build significantly more than what was there, and demolition would be a long and expensive project that would outstrip any potential profit. He sent Sweeney away that night with a quit deed and a handwritten notarized contract saying that the cabin had been given to us, as well as a property tax bill for $1,676 that we were going to have to pay sometime soon.

The following weekend, we saw it for the first time: a small, janky lean-to, coated in dark brown aluminum siding and a fading American flag. It looked a little serial killer-y and reeked of mold, but it had basic structural integrity (electric, water, heat). Inside, it was supremely warped and grimy as hell, and packed with rotting taxidermized bears and a framed photograph of Reagan above the furnace and piles and piles of waterlogged pornography. There was a particular unnerving residue of fetid Republican male energy. But we figured—as we pushed through the trash and collapsing wall—that with a series of dump runs, a serious smudging session, some repairs, and a couple of hundred dollars from ten willing friends who might like having a share of a shack in the woods, we might be able to do something with it. It was ours now anyway.

When we moved to Frank's Place a month later, we realized that the hunting cabin was only fifteen minutes away, and so it became an ongoing summer project: tearing down the siding to reveal a covered porch, unsticking the linoleum to paint the plywood gray, burning slash piles of scrap wood, refinishing the loft, throwing out endless bags of VHS porn and crusted-over hand-held urinals. We chipped away at the tax bill with our friends' financial contributions, and those friends came up on the weekends to contribute to the repair of the "Commie Cabin," which might or might not get used since now we were ending every night by a bonfire in the back of Frank's Place.

On the road that connected Frank's Place to the hunting cabin was the Zone—an orthodox Jewish girls' summer camp on a large man-made lake. There were zip lines and an alpine slide and horse stalls and big beige bunkhouses that looked like office park condos. The entrance sign to the Zone was spelled partially in Yiddish and sported a friendly cartoon camel. Later that summer, a real camel was kept in the animal pen near the road, chewing cud alongside a few cows. The Zone's lime-green vans zipped back and forth between the camp and village for supplies. During their family weekends, I'd often run into women buying bags of flour tortillas at the local Tops franchise in Stamford, their heads wrapped in scarves.

The Zone had formerly been a multigenerational Jewish summer retreat during the Catskills' "Borscht Belt" era, which saw its peak from the early 1930s through the 1960s. Bungalow colonies, summer camps, and hotels for exclusive Jewish patronage popped up by the dozens throughout Sullivan, Ulster, and Delaware Counties, providing a way for the high density of American Jews in the Northeast to invest in and explore an American idea of leisure without having to make themselves vulnerable to the violent whims of antisemitism. All of this changed with the advent of common air travel and the tide of late-century assimilation. So while there were some towns at the Borscht Belt's height that were host to over twenty of these kinds of resorts at a time, there is little visual evidence left that this time ever happened. Those same towns are now virtually empty, abandoned, bearing no evidence at all that this had once been a Jewish leisure utopia, excepting where a few of the old resorts, like the Zone, were bought, eventually, by more orthodox sects.

I watched *Dirty Dancing* for the first time that summer. I hadn't ever really thought of this bygone era when middle-class and upper-middle-class Jews went to multigenerational summer camps, big estates in the Catskills, closed-circuit pleasure and leisure centers, to dance and eat fine dining and do activities like archery and pottery and swimming and Simon Says. The "Borscht Belt" years were before, during, and after the Holocaust—and included survivors, and families of survivors, and those who had just barely made it out of Europe under the gun. And here was the celebration of that survival in these havens, protected from the common threats of mixed society and yet accessible from the city by train—the safety and plainness that those places guaranteed is so striking to me. They were their own kinds of utopias, families staying for a month at a time, a sort of hangover from the nineteenth-century WASPy tradition of health retreats in better climates. What's so moving about Baby, I guess, is that she wants what is complex, mixed, the utopia within the utopia—something beyond the safety and security that has been offered her for six weeks at a time in the Catskills in 1963.

The crickets were out. I heard deer shrieking at each other in warning once they crossed into the dark tree line. I sat in the grass, lost in work as I had been for weeks, while Sweeney was inside at the long kitchen table, lonely for friends, which in a way was an odd blessing—his want or need of it, my lack of need. Things had changed. I joined a writing group on Wednesdays at the Bushel Collective space, converted out of an old Masonic lodge on Main Street in the town of Delhi.

A year earlier, my friend Rachel had looked at me while we were sitting at the kitchen table one night at a rented cabin and said, "I think you guys are going to just have to do something first, and let people follow." I knew she was right then, but I didn't know how we were going to do it. Now I was sitting in the grass on this hill, a bit nauseated, watching lightning flash silently in the distance over the green, dark hills.

It felt lucky and useful to have Frank's Place—this temporary space to test out our ideas on and invite other people temporarily into, every weekend. And every weekend they came, in twos or threes or fours. By the end of those visits, friends had plans, lots of ideas, as we'd burn to the bottom of a nightly bonfire under the stars: pop up a yurt, build a cottage, start a school, buy a neighboring property down the road.

Within a few weeks, I thought, *Oh my God, this is our home.* I wasn't sure what "this" was, except for maybe Delaware County. Regardless, the words flashed through my mind in red. I didn't want to mention it to Sweeney because for years anything north of Putnam County was too far from his father for him to consider as a possible home for us, but here we were—home—in a way I both felt certain of and deeply skeptical of, simultaneously, because had we actually just been living out a joint manic episode for the past year? I watched Sweeney every night, learning guitar on the porch in the evening, looking out over those glistening green hills, calmer than I'd ever seen him, and awake at dawn, naked with his coffee and his computer on the deck.

The thing is, I had had a dream of this land. Or not exactly a dream, but a vision that came to me nightly as a habitual self-soothing meditation during some of the worst anxiety in my early twenties. When I was feeling particularly doomed, I'd close my eyes, lie back on the futon mattress I shared with Sweeney in our room at Gates, and picture vast green meadows, fully exposed to the sun, sloping gently upward toward the deep-green-and-brown tree line. Walking through the meadow, in the vision, were me, my daughter, and Chanelle, trekking toward the tree line on some sunny, peaceful afternoon. It was an image that I telegraphed into the future, like a grappling hook to help get me there—to give myself some certainty that I would not always feel like I was slipping into the abyss. Or maybe I hadn't conjured the image at all, but had been called by *it*. I don't know which. I just knew I'd seen this land before.

I didn't want to tell Sweeney about my desire to remain in Delaware County, or how the intensity of that desire was buttressed by my ancient and inexplicable anxiety vision. I wanted things, above all, to stay on the up and up, as they had been for months now, and to avoid making this another hill for our relationship to do battle on.

But then, sooner than I meant to, I blurted it one night as we were driving in the dark back to Frank's Place from dinner. I said, "I keep thinking I could stay here forever." And Sweeney, his profile in shadow, said back to me, "Yeah, pretty much after five days here—I thought—well, I thought, I don't know if I could ever live anywhere else."

I found myself looking forward to this drift into the next season, with the intention to continue conducting life experiments, whilst writing a book about people life-experimenting together. Putting it that way is an understatement, actually, so here's another way: I lay down in a mowed circle on the hilltop at sunset, getting chewed on by blackflies, having just communed with a milkweed plant, as Pareesa and Alyssa lay in the oak grove downslope by the house, talking, and I literally said to the land (or God, or the truly tenacious biting flies, or all three), "Thank you for giving me my life back." I am not exactly sure what I meant at the time, because the feeling wasn't as literal as that phrase suggests, and nothing is ever over anyway; it was just harvest season, I guess.

How do you write about joy? It's hard because when you write about past joy, it's only ever under the present knowledge that the past has *passed*, that the joy was finite, and now that experience of joy has been bent into a new shape on the emotional continuum of the *now*, and the joy's once-clear edges have bled into some other murkier feeling, dulling the once-clear borders of the joy so firmly felt when it was happening. I woke up every morning and sat on the warm wood planks of that deck and listened to the birds. I lay in the grass and did Sun Salutation and followed plants around like a cat. Then I'd write in one of the big, light rooms, look out the window at the hot summer blue-green sky, and go skinny-dipping down in Anna's clear cool pond or the opening in the Schoharie Creek near the hunting cabin. Or we'd go down the hill to the only pub in town—a spot in an old farmhouse called the Bull & Garland—and sit next to the pretty gully of the West Branch Delaware at a picnic table outside, talking for hours and hours as the sky purpled, drinking sour beers and smoking rolled cigarettes until it got dark.

Every day that summer was this fresh gift. We ate on the porch, made pesto from things we found on the land. I woke up in the morning, surrounded by these huge picture windows that took up most of each wall: one looking into an ancient maple grove, and the other looking onto the mountain across the little water gap. I was literally thrilled to wake up every morning and drink coffee on the porch, watercolor, read, or see Sweeney when he walked into the door from early-morning fishing—smiling, clattering, tawny, happy, glowing, slim. He looked like a young man again, wide-faced and excited, and we talked every night next to the bonfire, and made love in the afternoons.

But maybe we were already running out of things to say to each other, now that we'd established this provisional outpost for our long-deferred dream. That's the part I can't quite wrap my mind around. Were we already beginning to reckon with dissipated intent? Or was it just the way I think I remember, the two of us feeling preternaturally connected and carefree?

Summer turned into late summer and we decided to stay on longer. Pareesa gave up her apartment in Crown Heights and moved up to Anna's house at the bottom of the hill. Sweeney started hunting wild turkey every misty morning in an all-camo outfit, and one day he shot one. He made an altar in the woods for its remains, and defeathered the rest of the body on the deck in the early fall rain. Pareesa came over that night for the turkey feast with cornbread and mashed potatoes and garlicky greens and gravy and stuffing from a box.

I started giving myself monthly tarot readings on the New Moon, after a long hiatus of reading for myself: Ten of Pentacles reversed was the outcome for the end of August. A card of abundance and great yield. In the card, the Pentacles are arranged so that they're available to anyone, encircling the man and woman who are symbolic keepers of the hearth, standing under an arbor looking at their spoils—a verdant hilltop, a garden, a small palace. There's a story of generosity and community in this card, but as Jessa Crispin says in *Creative Tarot*, in the case of a reversal, "note that there is a wall, so there is a strict boundary. Only certain people can gain admittance and take part in the wealth." I closed her book and put away my cards.

utopianotes
Woman Town

In Kansas City, Jessa and I try looking for the former site of Woman Town, a lesbian separatist neighborhood she'd heard had once existed for a decade in the 1990s. We have no other information beyond that, including the coordinates. We walk for a while down Troost Avenue, then hop on a bus, rushing past blown-out businesses and collapsing four-square houses that dot this weird old city. We stop in a plant nursery and a botanica. We decide on a neighborhood of small houses near the state college. "Maybe this is where it was?" We stand silent in big winter coats under that flat midwestern sunlight.

Half of the little flat ranch homes look abandoned. Two have trees growing through windows and rooftops. What was Woman Town like? Did they all move in at once? Did they squat or buy the properties conventionally? Did they plant this berm of trees and bushes buffering them from the traffic and men of Troost Avenue? Some of the backyard fences have been removed, creating the appearance of a long, continuous shared backyard. We find an abandoned high school and circle it on foot, talking about Jessa's idea of starting a secular convent.

We have a book reading that night at the Uptown Arts Bar. Neither of us have ever been there before, and we are nervous. We are met by a cheerful staff of queer women or nonbinary punks behind the big old bar. "You must be our guests tonight! Welcome!"

Then we are swept into a big, dim cabaret space, already set up for the audience and mic'd for us, and we are handed free drinks as they show us around. We can't believe our luck. We start yammering, nervous with our whiskey drinks, about our fieldtrip to the imaginary site of Woman Town that afternoon. One of the bartenders says, "Woman Town? I used to give bike tours of the old Woman Town site when I was in college."

She begins to tell us about the actual coordinates of the Woman Town occupation, which it turns out is the neighborhood where Jessa is currently living, a once upscale but now dilapidated enclave of grand four-level homes. "There's actually tons of information about Woman Town in the archives at K State, if you actually want to know anything."

In the early 1990s, a small group of lesbian activists in Kansas City advertised the effort to create a lesbian-only neighborhood in nationally circulating lesbian publications. Their proposal was to acquire and rehab these properties in what was the deeply disinvested center of the city, and create a community of abundance and care in a region hostile to queer life. Many women joined the effort, including dozens who moved from other parts of the country to join in. At its peak, there were one hundred women involved. Beyond that, there is very little known about what happened to the movement, excepting a couple of undergraduate research projects from the last couple of years that undertook some oral history collecting, much of which revealed the pretty ordinary interpersonal conflicts and economic fallout that led to a movement becoming what it is today: a neighborhood in Kansas City that has a high number of lesbian homeowners.

We finish the night at Jessa's house drinking cava, feeling lonely and depressed, and then we watch Isaac Mizrahi's *Unzipped* ("It's actually all about the creative process," Jessa says) and videos of George Michael, who has just passed away, including one of a rehearsal where David Bowie is watching, standing on the sidelines, and after George gives it his all, David is nodding, like, *Damn, that was a fucking serious rehearsal, George.*

WHAT'S HEAVEN GOT TO DO WITH IT?

I've gotten pretty far along on a problematic premise. I'm conflating heaven and utopia, paradise and communal life, without much theoretical or etymological underpinning. I'm just going for it—in part because these things are regularly conflated in ordinary conversations, and, at least till now, I thought I could get away with it, the way Belinda Carlisle could when she declared, "We'll make heaven a place on earth," and immediately followed with "Heaven *is* a place on earth." While I'm using the word "heaven" as a metaphor, for it to be a useful metaphor I've had to think about what it actually means—to me, to America.

A great deal of the utopians and utopian experiments we've been thinking about have believed in God, and believed in an afterlife, but many of them have not. Some have been religious; some have been secular. But everyone had some idea of a better life that they were commonly pursuing—everyone had some kind of investment in the idea of what felt at least colloquially "heavenly" to them, and everyone had a basic agreement that the world as is cannot be the end of the story. If heaven has any equal meaning for spiritual and secular utopians, it's that a belief in heaven is also a refusal to accept the world as it is right now.

More often than not, the utopian groups were modeled after their ideas of paradise, Eden, or, in a lot of cases, heaven, or the preparation for a heaven to come. But even those ones seemed to believe that if there is a heaven to come, we still must strive to live well, with some measure of pleasure and rest and love and care on earth. Heaven has meaning to me, especially in relationship to utopian experimentation on earth, because that's what it seems like—spiritually or materially—utopians are trying to bring into being in their comic and failed attempts.

As we all know, this line of thinking has led to dangerous places. Let's say, at best, it has led to a few really great ideas, more than a little mediocre and short-lived pablum, and a fair share of terrible tyrants and nightmarish tragedies. This breakdown has been true for organized religion, too: a few gems, a lot of mediocrity, and a lot of nightmare. But the horrors wrought by capitalistic societies and capitalism in general, and indeed a lot of nuclear families, share these same outcomes.

The 2016 TV show *The Good Place* specifically challenges an American notion of "heaven," in either its secular or religious dimension. The show's vision is entirely nonsectarian. Its opening episodes present the newly dead people arriving upon a scene of suburban street life and froyo and their very own dream homes, in a neighborhood populated by other dead people's dream homes. They are told they've arrived in the "Good Place" and even the canniest inhabitants believe it, only to have script flipped several episodes later, when they find out they've been had by a social experiment architected by demons. You fucking idiots, it says. This is the best you could think of? This is hell!

The twist reveals an impoverished imagination when it comes to being able to imagine what a good life looks like, what *heaven* forgodssakes looks like. It speaks to the ways that the garbage of the American Dream and manifest destiny and the spirit of individualism supplanted the dreams of millennial optimism and communal experimentation of yore. Regardless of anyone's beliefs about the afterlife, I think considering even our own crappy ideas of the metaphorical heaven can improve the ways we dream about life on earth.

My earliest idea of heaven came straight from the mouth of a Lincoln Street Baptist Sunday school teacher in Portland, Oregon, 1995: In heaven, where God lives, the streets are paved with gold, and the angels are always singing. You live forever, but you'll never get tired. It's warm and sunny, and everyone wears white.

This is a pretty ordinary Protestant description of the afterlife. Why always gold? Why always ceaseless music? What kind of fools are convinced that a child has anything but fear and contempt for this terrible existence they describe? It sounded to me, then and now, like a place of deep and awful boredom, a numb, empty, though possibly sunny void you get vacuumed into at the end of your life. The vast, silent universe continues to stand by, unexplained and unaffected by this white-on-gold affair, still terrifying, even as you, citizen of heaven, stride along your golden street. It is as a place where essentially *nothing* happens.

Believing in God, for me, had nothing to do with heaven. From the first days I went to Lincoln Street Baptist as a little kid with my best friend's family, God was very close—God was right *here*, a benevolent, even compassionate, if dense and mute presence. At night, I gathered my bedding around me and in the felted cocoon of my comforter before I fell asleep, I prayed into that planet-speckled black hole—which was where I still pictured God to live, not some weird-ass shiny town—for blessings to be conferred upon every single person I could think of, on whom I might have an effect or responsibility to.

And when I heard the Sunday school teacher talking about heaven as the place where God lives and where—if we're good—we'll get to go someday, heaven struck me mostly like this weird waiting room, a holding pen, and not having that much to do with God. At least in the Protestant imagination, heaven is not primarily about being close to God, or being with God, it's about hanging out as a reward for all of your good behavior and hard work on earth. (Catholic and Orthodox Christians have rituals for penance that make their conception of heaven much more mystical, and less about an individual's sense of their goodness.) Maybe this is because the whole thrust of the Protestant movement is so specifically defined by a belief in having a direct connection to God all the time while you're alive, on earth.

As a somewhat meaningless concept to me, I didn't think much about heaven until I was in sixth grade, beginning to distance myself from a childhood of self-selecting church attendance, and saw Kevin Smith's *Dogma*, where heaven had not so much to do with God, and is presented more as a clearinghouse for outlaws and freedom-fighters.

Dogma was hilarious: two angels, Loki and Bartleby, have been stuck in Milwaukee, Wisconsin, since Lucifer fell from heaven; they weren't condemned, just sort of demoted for eternity for not having picked sides. When the film opens, Loki has just read an article in *USA Today* about a hacky Catholic cardinal in Red Bank, New Jersey, played by George

Carlin, who's going to have a reconsecration ceremony for his cathedral in honor of the church's "Catholicism WOW!" campaign and its new avatar which will replace the usual representation of the crucifix, Buddy Christ (a life-sized statue of a big, healthy, wavy-haired Jesus, winking and giving a thumbs-up). Loki and Bartleby realize together that a loophole in Catholic dogma would allow them to pass through this newly blessed church and—schwoop—go straight back to heaven, all forgiven. Cut to suburban Illinois: A woman is tapped to stop the angels from doing this; because were they successful in violating a God-given decree, the act would blow the universe to smithereens. The woman is the last in Christ's bloodline, the last scion, and she's barren and works at an abortion clinic with Janeane Garofalo. She still goes to church, but she's lost her faith. Her destiny is revealed to her by a grumpy angel, God's spokesperson, played by Alan Rickman—and of course the rest of the story has all the Smith usuals: Jay and Silent Bob as the prophets, Chris Rock as the thirteenth apostle Rufus, who was never named in the bible because he's Black, Salma Hayek as the muse. Meanwhile, God's on an earth vacation playing Skee-Ball in Asbury Park, but gets beaten up by teenage demons on assignment from hell, and then stuck in a hospital in a mortal body. So the motley crew, headed by the last scion, goes on a cross-country adventure to stop the rogue angels, fighting demons along the way and delivering blunt, foul-mouthed critiques of the racist, patriarchal way Christianity has been controlled and disseminated here on earth. When the crew finally gets to the cathedral in Red Bank to stop the rogue angels from getting through, God—who has been incapacitated in a hospital nearby and is liberated from life support by the last scion—transcends the hospital bed and appears before the cathedral as Alanis Morissette, in a tulle tutu. The last scion walks right up to her and asks, "I'm sure you get this a lot, but . . . what's it all for?" God nods, thinks about this, and then touches her nose and says, "Merrpp," then walks into the sanctuary back to heaven. Like all those Old Testament barren women, the angel (Alan Rickman) reveals to the last scion that she's pregnant, and the forgotten thirteenth apostle Rufus (Chris Rock) looks at her and says, "Now do you believe?" And she smiles and says: "No, but I have *a good idea*." He smiles back at her like *That's the spirit, kid*, then ascends.

When the film finished, I felt transformed. It was a watershed moment for me. For one, heaven, it turns out, was populated by all kinds of wonderfully gnarly and unsavory characters, and God plays Skee-Ball. There was some porousness between here and there, and people seemed to be having an OK time.

I didn't think much about heaven in a religious context at all after those early Sunday school days. From that point on, most of my consideration of heaven between then and early adulthood stemmed from pop culture: *Touched by an Angel*, *What Dreams May Come*, *All Dogs Go to Heaven*, *Six Feet Under*, to name a few.

Something landed in particular when I saw *Angels in America*. I watched the six-part HBO production with my mom the summer before moving to New York for college. For one, it offers a divine politics of liberation, a long-game vision of time that is ultimately hopeful, though full of constant setbacks. It points to a future that is much deeper—looks at time as a deep material. What the character of Harper calls "a sort of painful progress" is the sensibility in the play I am drawn to, and the sensibility I am drawn to in other thinkers, an idea which does not stultify or freeze resistance action in the present, but also which does not rely or hang its hopes on shallow "wins" or "fixes," because time is long and jagged, and progress does not look like what you think it does if your vision is millennial; in fact, progress does not exactly exist, only the eschaton, so do not stop fighting for justice.

One character in the story actually goes to heaven—Prior. He climbs a cosmic, fiery ladder from his hospital room, where he's being treated for complications related to AIDS, and finds himself in an overcast city, a sort of Grecian ruin meets the trash-strewn streets of 1980s New York City. The colors of the landscape are dull, stone, concrete. It's full of trash, floating bits of paper, crumbling stone, and a tribunal of crabby angels who've been abandoned by God sit in a makeshift boardroom among the rubble. The heat's been shut off. They're in scarves, knit caps, turtlenecks, smoking cigarettes and shuffling papers around on a long board table, squabbling. Behind them is an endless bureaucracy of angels, sitting at desks, stretching beyond the puffy-clouded horizon. A lot happens, but basically, Prior tells the angels that he wants to live, in spite of the suffering that living in the world guarantees, in spite of what a thin and failing little thing life is, in spite of it being maybe only an animal habit, he wants to live and he demands his blessing, like Jacob.

What does heaven have to do with it if, a trillion years from now, the universe annihilates itself and becomes nothing but antimatter, formless and unformable? In the spiritual idea of heaven, as well as the zenith of a hoped-for secular heaven on earth, it seems like there would also be no markers, nothing for time to inscribe itself on because the idea is that, if successful, the heaven is a stasis. Utopianism tries to create a world also of dark matter in a way, a form of life or a way of life that will be so perfect as to not need changing over the course of its existence, for the rest of time, where the passage of time will become moot. Whether the spiritual world-builders of the Oneida or the Shakers or the hippie communes of the 1960s and '70s, labor toward these alternative models of living was carried out, however outrageously, in the sincere belief that once perfected, they wouldn't need changing later. They would, eventually, offer a way of life that does not wound the world, and so which does not need to end. It seems that timelessness is in fact what's being sought.

But whether our ideas of paradise come from God or physics or humanity, whether it is something that lives in each of us or somewhere *out there*, it can be at the very least useful to understand paradise as a particular place—whether metaphorical or metaphysical—because place is where things happen, and where people gather.

And if metaphors or metaphysics be damned, then what is it we want if, finally, the utopian society we've created has, at last, met all our needs? What happens if we finally are not governed by a state of living in constant scarcity? If the egalitarian government is in place, if the commune is running, if wage work has been abolished, what is it we're looking forward to? How might those things be different than the success of certain progressive policies or politicians in power? Medicare for all is a means to an end—the end being that Americans will no longer be punished for having mortal bodies, will not be held interminably in the snare of systemic inequity, will be able to live happy and healthy lives. White people reckoning with white supremacy is a means to an end—the end being that we can stop replicating the same violence over and over again, and allow for everyone to live happy and healthy lives. But under capitalism?

In their early critique, *The German Ideology*, Marx and Engels bemoaned the way that capitalism creates a division of labor that conscripts humans into certain kinds of work for the rest of their lives if they do not want to "lose their means of livelihood." But they proposed that in a communist society, it's possible "for me to do one thing today and another tomorrow, to hunt in the morning, fish in the afternoon, rear cattle in the evening, criticise after dinner, just as I have a mind, without ever becoming hunter, fisherman, herdsman or critic. This fixation of social activity, this consolidation of what we ourselves produce into an objective power above us, growing out of our control, thwarting our expectations, bringing to naught our calculations, is one of the chief factors in historical development up till now." So that's a kind of answer, I guess, even if it's tongue-in-cheek. Life would be full of variety. Life would be lived by the steam of your various pleasures and vocations, in collaboration with whatever work needs to be done or shared.

Generally, when we're talking about heaven, it seems like we're primarily talking about an ideal, that which makes everything worth it—all the hard work of the commune, all the struggle of renunciation, all the pain of resistance fighting, all the tiny fissures and negotiations and smaller fights of cooperation, all the senseless suffering of life. The idea of utopianism, I think, is not just to make the thing, not just to make the heaven, the farm, the commune, the home, for its own sake. It's not simply to make sure that everyone is watered, fed, loved, and cared for, though those are things that the projects take for granted. It's what happens after we are watered, fed, loved, and cared for—what we expect to happen after that—that's embedded in those projects, and what still feels most mysterious to me.

The "what now?" question of the successful commune has ancient and modern echoes. In *Paradise Now*, Chris Jennings writes about the nineteenth-century suspicion of people on the "outside" observing communal movements and worrying over the boredom that might be a product of such perfect symbiosis. Today, a similar conservative reaction emerges around socialized services and stimulus checks: if provided for, won't the people stop working, check out, and destroy everything?

After all is said and done here, what do I believe—given that belief is a living process anyway? I believe that heaven is the beginning and the end. Heaven is where all that was not possible on earth is made possible, or was, had always been, possible. Heaven is where it was all happening already, where everything has come to pass, and where every seemingly impossible good thing witnessed in life issued from. Heaven is the great reconciliation. It's where we'll learn the joke, and who's in on it. I remember backpacking with my friend and her parents when I was fifteen in Northern California's Trinity Alps, thinking over and over again as I walked the hot ridges about a quote I'd seen on a greeting card, attributed to no one: "In the end, everything will be OK; if it's not OK, it's not the end," while the opening riff to Led Zeppelin's "Over the Hills and Far Away" played ceaselessly in my head. Heaven is the Golden Gospel Singers singing "Oh, Freedom," that other place beyond bondage. Heaven is the new world that requires that we live in this one, fully—the two being intimately bound. In fact, heaven and earth are constantly imagining one another. They depend on each other's imagination to come into being, so much so that there are times where they are, like Belinda sang, nearly indistinguishable from one another, but only in glimpses. A gesture, a dinner, a conversation, an orgasm, communion, a mushroom trip, the way someone says something or looks at you, in birth and in death. Utopianism, and all utopian experimentation, is the hunt for heaven on earth in a literal way, perhaps. It's a really drawn-out process for establishing that proximity, trying to pin that occasional way where earth and heaven collide on a colony that will sustain the feeling, that collision, but that collision is only ever a moment, accidental, essentially un-pinnable. I suppose I imagine heaven as a process by which we get threaded back into something else, animals and plants and everything, a coming together, a communion. Anything less than a total communion of all organisms and all beloved objects, all specks and pieces, is worthless to me.

In Marilynne Robinson's novel *Housekeeping*, the twelve-year-old protagonist, orphan Ruth, finds a box in the bottom drawer of an old dresser in her house in Fingerbone, Idaho. It contains ephemera from her aunt's missionary travels in China decades before. As Ruth sifts through the box's contents, she finds a photograph of a girl and a "thin pig," with a note written on the bottom that says "I will make you fishers of men." She imagines her aunt's erstwhile missionary work to have been just that, a kind of fishing trip spent "leaning from the low side of some small boat, dropping her net through the spumy billows of the upper air," and gathering all of the people and things she imagined she was saving along the way. Ruth thinks,

> Such a net, such a harvesting, would put an end to all anomaly. If it swept the whole floor of heaven, it must, finally, sweep the black floor of Fingerbone, too . . . There would be a general reclaiming of fallen buttons and misplaced spectacles, of neighbors and kin, till time and error and accident were undone, and the world became comprehensible and whole . . . For why do our thoughts turn to some gesture of a hand, the fall of a sleeve, some corner of a room on a particular anonymous afternoon, even when we are asleep, and even when we are so old that our thoughts have abandoned other business? What are all these fragments for, if not to be knit up finally?

utopianotes
Northeast Association of Education and Industry

Outside the old mill building, I float on my back in the river that powers the turbine. Sojourner Truth and a few friends of hers that history won't remember used to aid in the production of silk and beet sugar, here, at this plant, where they also possessed the dual aims of a well-rounded liberal arts education and racially integrated living, while they battled what was still the tyranny of slave labor–produced cane and cotton. Today, there is a threadbare couch on the loading dock, outside what appears to be a record store run by teenagers.

ODD FELLOWS AT THE
ROCKLAND PALACE

You're at the Rockland Palace, sitting fifty feet above ground in a gilded mezzanine. You're looking down at two long tables each set for one hundred fifty guests. It's the Depression in Harlem. You're starving. Surrounding the table are three tiers of balconies soaring straight up to the ceiling and packed to capacity. The ceiling is painted like the heavens, giving those, like you, who are furthest away from the table the illusion of paradise. The table below is so full of food it's nearly collapsing. Waiters rush around producing limitless trays, serving bells, bowls of hot corn and corn bread so fresh you can see the steam rising. And the guests at the table, it's a rainbow coalition: Black people, white people, Jews, Catholics, praise the Lord—and the Lord is *in* the house. Father Divine stands and welcomes everyone to the banquet. He is a short, merry man in a gabardine suit, smiling under a tidy mustache. You feel warm. Soon, you, too, will be invited to the table. And while you are watching, too rapt by the scene below to notice, your foot knocks a tube of dusty old lipstick under your seat; and under your neighbor's seat is a generous but withered brassiere insert; and down the row, under another seat, are fragments of a golden wig, each of these objects left over from some other time and forgotten. Beneath the floors upon which the banquet tables sit is an old basketball court, dull from age, but you cannot see that, either. And somewhere in Kansas City, a teenaged Charlie Parker is practicing his sax, hoping to one day bask in the glow of stage lights, which will be *these* stage lights, though much later and long after you have eaten and left.

The Rockland Palace sat on the street that divides Harlem from Washington Heights—155th—at Frederick Douglass Boulevard. During the course of its life, this Romanesque-style theater served as a community center, a sports stadium, a drag ballroom, a utopian banquet hall, a bebop and blues stage, a roller rink, and probably uncountable other things, mini-phases of use in a continually shifting space. The histories of Prohibition, the Depression, and the Harlem Renaissance run through the Rockland Palace, though it is now a giant parking lot. Of course, this kind of palimpsest is everywhere. Neither is it unique that the Rockland Palace was once the site of many paradoxical things—queer people and celibate Christians not least among them. I mean, what building which survives for more than a couple of decades does not contain multitudes?

This becomes most obvious to me in New York—though I have lived other places, flirted with other buildings, wandered many neighborhoods and towns and places where humans dwell. In New York, the histories of buildings are more stark. One man's house of God is another drag queen's ballroom. In *Delirious New York*, Rem Koolhaas proposes that it is the city's grid which provides the pressure-cooker quality for such distinct phases. Each block, he says, becomes an impenetrable "urban unit" which is "immune to totalitarian invasion." The block is thus the street design of *le peuple*, and the city changes only through a "mosaic of episodes." In this way, New York City finds a way to evolve without conquest, even under conditions that mimic conquest—like urban renewal or parking lots. The buildings shift the way the blocks do: mosaics are lateral—they do not represent forward or backward movement, but rather a whole world on a single surface which you must be moved *into*.

According to the 1939 *New York Times* article "It's Not All Swing in Harlem," at Father Divine's New York City Peace Mission Movement "heavens"—including the banquets at Rockland Palace—you could get "food and lodging to thousands more cheaply than any other place in Harlem. A full meal (chicken dinner) costs 15 cents. Shoes are shined for 3 cents in Peace shops. Laundries, dress shops, barber shops, groceries and fruit stands have almost unbelievably low rates. The Krum Elbow estate up on the Hudson provides work for hundreds, as do the other farms, and fresh eggs, milk and vegetables pour into New York City daily on Peace trucks." Divine was against the social safety nets of the New Deal; the safety would come through joining his movement, and through him. One of his Peace Mission buildings on 126th Street displayed a sign that read: NO TRUE DIVINE FOLLOWER ON RELIEF! SAVED THE CITY $20,000,000 SINCE 1932!

The banquets were huge. Elaborate spreads—like those cookbook pictures from the 1960s, all red/pink light and pineapple towers pinned to sweaty meats. There's some video footage of one of the Rockland Palace banquets from 1939: the hall is packed. Packed! At one point, for three minutes straight, the camera is trained on Father Divine and he is passing out tureen after tureen after tureen, plate after plate, almost as though on a conveyor belt, sending piles of chicken and greens and bread down the table.

The Rockland Palace begins for me with Father Divine, not because his was the first or most important use of the building, but simply because it is through Father Divine that the building became visible to me at all.

Father Divine came to me, as many things have, by accident while walking through the library stacks. I was in graduate school at the University of Wyoming, looking for a book about Pentecostal celebrity preacher Aimee Semple McPherson, and across the aisle was this irresistible name on a variety of books: *Father Divine and the Struggle for Racial Equality* and *God Comes to America: Father Divine and the Peace Mission Movement*. I grabbed a couple of titles off the shelf and then never got around to much more than flipping through them: Divine was the leader of the International Peace Mission Movement, a utopian Christian religious community more or less established in 1919 and still going today, which hinges its practice on racial integration and communal socialism as a way to build heaven on earth. Also, Father Divine claimed to be the second coming of Christ.

Divine required his followers to cooperatively invest in businesses and divide profits among themselves. In the mid-1920s, he started his first interracial commune in a big house in Brooklyn, where everyone lived under strict rules to abstain from substances, gambling, and sex. When the surrounding community eventually had him arrested for public disturbance, and then the judge overseeing his arraignment died suddenly from a heart attack ("Divine retribution!" papers tittered), Divine's movement was thrust into the limelight and he moved his ministry to Harlem in 1931. In the blocks between 125th and 155th Streets, he bought up buildings—apartments, churches, hotels—and turned them into Peace Houses or "heavens," inexpensive, racially integrated living spaces, which were part of the communal trust. Within months, he was a celebrity, delivering a sermon to ten thousand people at Rockland Palace, followed by a banquet there, and another, and another.

An article about Gladys Bentley pops up on my Facebook feed. I follow the article to a Gladys Bentley digital archive. I keep the tab open in my browser in the way you do with things you don't want to forget but have no immediate use for. Bentley was a Harlem drag king in the 1920s, and I read about her life, her marriage to a woman, her performance routine in white tuxedo and top hat, who later in life renounced her queerness, found religion.

While I am looking for images of Rockland Palace a week later, I find one from the 1970s right before the structure was burned in a fire. It looks shabby with a sagging awning stretched to the street, like a sad hotel, stamped in block letters. Next to this image is another one with a common tag, though this image is of Gladys Bentley.

In the early 1920s, Harlem was home to a robust drag scene. A Black queer fraternal organization called the Hamilton Lodge held drag balls—the biggest and best of their kind—at a number of venues, though the biggest of these were at the Rockland Palace.

The full chapter name of the group was Hamilton Lodge No. 710 of the Grand United Order of Odd Fellows in Harlem. They had been hosting balls since the nineteenth century, but by the 1920s they were hot shit—and everyone came to see, even quivering white people from downtown. Inside the baroque cavernous ballroom were dancing, competitions, music, feathers, lipstick, golden wigs. Celebrities came. The aristocracy came. Langston Hughes wrote, "During the height of the New Negro era and the tourist invasion of Harlem, it was fashionable for the intelligentsia and the social leaders of both Harlem and the downtown area to occupy boxes at this ball and look down from above at the queerly assorted throng on the dancing floor."

Neighborhood organizations sought police sponsorship on the Lodge's behalf, so the police did not come often. This was not only pre-Stonewall, but prewar. Patterns of conservatism do not run in a straight line upward. Of course, when the police did occasionally show up, what freaked them out was how mixed everything was, gender, class, color. An official police report from a Rockland raid, circa 1928, focuses not on illegal alcohol sales, but the crowd: "About 12:30am we visited this place and found approximately 5,000 people, coloured and white, men attired in women's clothes, and vice versa."

Gladys Bentley was among the common performers at the Rockland Palace, "a bulky piano player and singer of low-down ditties" (says a bygone listing in the *Niagara Falls Gazette*). She sang at other venues, too—the Clam House, Connie's Inn—but especially the Rockland Palace, singing dirty songs and dressing in her signature tuxedo. She'd sing and parody blues standards of the time, obscenely—songs written mostly by men.

Of course, things changed in the fifties—there is a feature about Bentley in *Ebony* headlined "I Am a Woman Again," and in it she claims to be married to a man (though the man in question denies this later), and she wears dresses, is still recording, becomes deeply involved in the Temple of Love in Christ, Inc., and is even in the process of seeking ordination when she dies in the early sixties. Though when I look for the roots of the Temple of Love in Christ, Inc., now, literally the only mention of this church I can find is in connection to her name.

For Father Divine, real estate was central to the creation of heaven on earth. Real estate had metaphysical implications. Rockland Palace was the site of the paschal feast, the Eucharist, the Last Supper, everyone on the same level.

At Rockland Palace, Father Divine didn't take up a collection—though members offered donations. He endorsed the Communist Party of the USA in the thirties. (Later, of course, he changed his mind.) But Rockland Palace, the sermons and the banquets, were a vision of a kind of American communism in action.

During the video of his 1939 banquet, a voiceover of his sermon overlays the scene—the packed palace, the feasting followers. In the sermon he says, "Now I would like to say once again, as I said yesterday, it has long since been declared that the MESHIACH—the MESSIAH, the CHRIST—was to come, and when HE comes you will get your money that the people owe you. Isn't that true? You know they told you that! Now aren't you all getting your money from everyone who is converted to ME?"

They were surviving the Depression. What could they say?

Things get more and more conservative after the war. The drag balls go underground, Bentley moves to California, Divine moves to Philly, and the Rockland Palace gets used as a musical performance space. Ray Charles plays. B. B. King and John Lee Hooker play. Many others play, though no one in drag, and the audiences are not mixed, not really. Rockland Palace starts hosting the big annual "Down Home Ball," which is quite different than the balls from before.

In 1952, Charlie Parker plays there. He is fucked up on smack. He will die in three years, a ravaged old man in a thirty-four-year-old's body. Here he is, doing his thing—changing music forever. He doesn't believe in God, but he believes in bebop. McCarthy witch hunts are on. The night Parker plays at the Rockland Palace, it's allegedly one of his best performances. It's part of a benefit for communist city councilman Benjamin Davis, who at this moment is serving time.

That Parker and Divine have ties to communism, though opposite theological positions, is interesting. That Bentley pressed the boundaries of sex in this place, where later Divine would espouse a sexless utopia, is interesting. That the heteronormative Harlem of Parker's tenure did not realize they were bumping up against the Prohibition-era gender-bending Harlem of Bentley's time is interesting. Rockland Palace provides a common, a surface for all of that, though they are not in conversation with one another. Rather, their histories in that space are like the Last Supper, though they were all present for the supper at different times, missing each other, specters at the table. Weren't they all invited? The sexual outlaw, the addict, the charlatan?

•

Today, the parking lot where the Rockland Palace once stood advertises long-term Yankee Stadium passes—the stadium gleaming out of eyeshot over the Harlem River. I walk along the sidewalk. Overhead are the kingly white rails of the Macombs Dam Bridge.

It's not just Rockland Palace that was demolished in the 1970s, but the whole street of buildings: the stretch of 155th Street between Frederick Douglass Boulevard and Macombs Avenue is all pavement, and all behind chain-link. The lot, as well as the fact that it is set against a cliff, a ledge, gives the impression of a ghost of a once very tall building. Today, men are working in the lot. Cement trucks. City workers? At the far edge of the lot is a white curlicue railing against a staircase that brings you up to street level with the bridge. It's bright blue today—and, ah, there is the stadium! The sky! I walk and take pictures. Pass Colonel Charles Young park, Thurgood Marshall school, BLACK LIVES MATTER on the small marquee of St. Matthew's Baptist Church. Delis, beauty shops, laundry—no ballrooms.

In 2012 there was a successful "reoccupation" of the old grounds of the Rockland Palace—a tent was put up, a Kiki ball was thrown—mostly Black and Latinx LGBTQ youth. They pulled it off, reoccupied the space as it was once used, and then it was gone.

You're in Harlem and it's the Recession. You're a spectator on the sidelines in a folding chair, watching a genderfluid teenager in leopard-print lamé sashay down a stage before a panel of judges. It is a hot, muggy summer night—the bodies on the stage are stamping and pounding, athletically dancing, voguing, whipping their arms with serpentine precision. Everyone around you is whooping and hollering. Someone's arm clips your ear as they pump their fist. The drag queens are sweaty and exhausted, and dancing on anyway. It is so hot outside you feel you might collapse. Around you is the crowd, and beyond the edges of the crowd is a parking lot, the asphalt ringing with the day's heat. There are some cars. There is some garbage. There is a sense that even this is not the end.

utopianotes
Eleanor's Farm

Sweeney and I visit a small farm my cousin Eleanor is living on as a tenant "intern" with her two-year-old son. The farm is in a rural rainforest valley at the foot of the Cascades outside of Corvallis, Oregon. Eleanor and her son's father have recently split up, but he is also there for the night, roasting a whole chicken on a grate over a bonfire. Eleanor, who looks bright and lean and tanned, tells me that the farm's landowner reminds her of my grandmother Gale, who was her great-aunt, and who she grew up across the street from in Seattle. She tells me that her grandmother Mary Jane, *my* great-aunt, is dying of pancreatic cancer, which I did not know. She asks how I felt after my grandmother died and I just start crying over the outdoor chicken dinner, choking on the squash, as I finally say, "It was really hard—it still is. I'm not over it." Later, she shows us a pen of peacocks, three vegetable gardens, a rabbit shed, and beyond that a goat shed, with a mean goat named Betsy. Her son runs around, offering us sticks and rocks and assistance with the milking, and he leads us through the bamboo forest and past the chickens, like some kind of dream. There is a futon on a frame that Eleanor has set up in the middle of the vegetable garden, with two down comforters and pillows for Sweeney and me to sleep on, open air. She is currently living in an apartment above a stilted garage. When we get back to the stilted apartment, Sweeney is smoking, and the dog is being bothered by the child. It is very quiet and chilly and blue in the valley tonight. Leaves bow down from every angle; the trees are heavy with wet green. We sit by the bonfire where the chicken and squash were roasted earlier, and the dog takes refuge in my lap. Eleanor puts her son to sleep and brings down a samovar from the house and gives us some herbal tea from a blend she made, and the light from the fire grows up around us. This is the first time we've hung out since we were kids. We talk about what we've been up to for the last twenty years, our weird families, the way motherhood has radicalized her. I remember suddenly, though I do not say, reading her Facebook posts from around the time her son was born—these very long, white-hot, kind of prophetic, spiritual-political revolution clarion calls, and at that time I even thought, *Seems like Eleanor is on the verge of a breakdown, but goddammit she's fucking right.* I talk about the Bruderhof. I talk about the utopia book I am working on. I see the faces of the two men listening on either side of me, and then Eleanor looking at me over the fire and laughing, asking if this is a utopia, and I say, yes, why not, yes, I mean yes, anything that offers something other than capital and death. Sweeney's head is in my lap and when I look up the stars are bright blue. Sweeney has gone remarkably silent, but partly because the baby daddy, Eleanor's son's father, this hippie kid who grew up off the grid, has been talking nonstop all night long. Because even in utopia it is often the case that men still talk so much and say so much stupid shit, like "there is no truth" or "your truth is my truth," on and on and on.

DIVINE UPSTATE

Before I moved to the Catskills, I'd known that Father Divine's Peace Mission Movement had outposts up there, but I hadn't realized how many: between 1930 and 1942, the movement built a total of thirty-one "heavens" in Ulster and Sullivan Counties. Unlike those "heavens" in the city, those racially integrated apartment buildings buttressing mercantile and communally run charities, the "heavens" in the Catskills were developed around farms. There were lots of reasons for this: land in the Catskills was cheap; affordable food systems needed to be put in place to augment Depression-era retrenchment and provide goods for the Harlem-based enterprises; the movement had a lot of people to house, some figures of that period attesting to upwards of two million followers worldwide; and a great deal of Peace Mission Movement people in the northeast were part of the Great Migration, including Divine himself, and deeply uncomfortable in the dense urban areas they had sought refuge in, longing for the rural life. Plus, Father Divine liked to drive, and those beautiful scenic parkways that led to the Catskills had just been developed as WPA projects all over the region. And the Catskills were diversifying accordingly. This was the same era as the "Borscht Belt," when many Jews were heading into the Catskills as well, now accessible from the city by train, for safe sites of summer vacations.

The Peace Mission Movement's biggest and most well-known upstate outpost was the Krum Elbow Estate, a five-hundred-acre farm and inter-racial housing compound directly across the Hudson River from Eleanor Roosevelt's house in Hyde Park. Evidently, Father Divine moved to the very visible Krum Elbow intentionally, to put pressure on the Roosevelt administration to put into effect anti-lynching laws that were on the table. He knew FDR was ambivalent about the policy, but that Eleanor was not. Looking out across the river at her new neighbors, she wrote in her regular newspaper column, it "must be pleasant to feel that in the future this place will be 'heaven' to some people." The anti-lynching laws were not passed.

I'm particularly interested in the Peace Mission Movement because while there might have been a number of movements and communities in the United States over the years, secular or religious, which were multiracial, most of them were not, and if they were, it was often so only incidentally, not as a central tenet of their existence. Even W. E. B. Du Bois at the time, however skeptical he was of the odor of Divine's charlatanism, couldn't help but highlight this most distinctive feature of the movement in a *New York Amsterdam News* article, noting that the Peace Mission Movement "is (and this is the most curious of all) interracial among people of the laboring and middle class." I have never heard of a racially integrated communitarian movement of this scale, though unfortunately a smaller and more famous one is the Peoples Temple, Jim Jones's community in Guyana, which was multiracial as a central part of its project and theology. Jim Jones and Father Divine had actually met and been in contact during the years Jones's church was still in Indianapolis and not yet a death commune. In the late sixties, after Divine had passed away and as the Peoples Temple was growing, Jones publicly claimed to be Father Divine reincarnate and after that the Family Divine distanced themselves from him.

In my search for more on-the-ground information about Divine upstate, I came across the writings of an old white man, Rik Rydant, a retired Ulster County high school history teacher, who regularly gave talks on Father Divine's Ulster County days at local historical societies, as well as tours of all the sites and buildings where the "heavens" once existed, particularly in the town of High Falls, where he's lived for most of his adult life. I asked if he'd meet me for coffee.

He was very tall, white-haired, and had an old-school Massachusetts accent. We shook hands and sat outside at a table by the parking lot. He had brought a pile of literature. Among it was an illustrated children's book from the 1980s about Father Divine, with an introduction by Coretta Scott King, reminding me that the Peace Mission Movement has not always been regarded as an insane fringe event; a book called *Promised Land: Father Divine's Interracial Communities in Ulster County, New York* by Carleton Mabee; an old newspaper. He told me that he had first heard about Father Divine and the

Peace Mission Movement accidentally, at a flea market years ago when he found an old 1936 copy of the movement's magazine.

"Yeah," he said, searching through the pile of books and pulling it out. "It was called *New Day*." He handed it to me.

I felt a zap. "New Day? That's wild," I said. "I, uh, in the Bronx, see—"

Rydant continued, though; he was telling his story now. "I recognized all the images of the properties printed in the magazine, including Mother Divine's house, which was on the main drag in High Falls, right there." He pointed next door. "They owned a lot of the real estate in High Falls at the time. A small department store, the apartments above it. They made and sold candy from there," he said, pointing to a USPS building, "and had a doctor's office—as well as all the farms." Rydant told me that the Klan was active in the Catskills then, too, but didn't have enough power to boycott the Peace Mission Movement's cottage industries.

There was so much property available at the time, Rik told me, as landowners were liquidating their assets to buoy against debt. "Everything was for sale in the Depression," he said, "and Father Divine and his Family had cash." Buildings and farms in Ulster County were run-down and taxes were low—though the Family Divine had always paid their taxes on time. Rik told me that the International Peace Mission Movement, with their extensive, unprecedented number of real estate holdings, never did file for religious exemption, and perhaps because they behaved on paper like a business, they did not receive much regulatory opposition.

Rydant continued to walk me through his process of unearthing the other Ulster County "heavens," which of course by his lifetime had all been bought and reconstituted by other people.

"I mean," he said, shuffling the stack of literature back together, "they were amazing, really. They changed people's worldview, in all their hoping to get to heaven here on earth." He sipped his coffee and marveled that Father Divine "gave people hope during a period where there was no hope. He could have been ambassador to the United Nations!"

As he was talking, I found myself thinking as I often do both about the utopian movement in question and also about people like Rik and me, stuck in these histories, hoping against hope that it will all matter in the end. Seeing that he was a utopian groupie in his own right, I found myself wanting to make meaning of Rik's interest in the Peace Mission Movement, as a way to make meaning of my own. The thing is, we all start somewhere, and without my even having to ask pointed questions, Rik launched into the ways in which his own biography embedded him in the American utopian tradition: he told me he was born in Harvard, Massachusetts, between an old Shaker village and an abandoned Transcendentalist utopian agrarian commune from the nineteenth century called Fruitlands. I looked up Fruitlands on my phone, and it turns out it was started by Amos Bronson Alcott, an account of its "less-than-successful activities" apparently available in his daughter Louisa May Alcott's book *Transcendental Wild Oats*.

At the turn of the twentieth century, Rik told me, the old Fruitlands compound was bought and developed into a museum by Clara Endicott Sears, a wealthy Yankee who he said effectively "started the American preservationist movement." One of Sears's other preservation projects was the home of writer Sarah Orne Jewett. Rydant loved Jewett. So do I. Her exquisite novel *The Country of the Pointed Firs* is a beautiful local history of rural Maine at the turn of the twentieth century, masquerading as a series of fictional vignettes from the point of view of a local woman doctor and herbalist.

I looked up Sears, the utopian preservationist. Here is an incomplete list of books that Sears published in her lifetime, as they appear on her Wikipedia page. It strikes me like the bibliography of a utopian groupie, if I ever saw one:

> *The Power Within*, writings of various New Thought authors
>   (compiled) (1911)
> *Bronson Alcott's Fruitlands* (Houghton Mifflin, 1915)
> *Gleanings from Old Shaker Journals* (Houghton Mifflin, 1916)
> *The Bell-Ringer: an old-time village tale* (Houghton Mifflin, 1918)
> *Peace Anthem* (1919)
> *Days of Delusions, a history of the Millerites* (1924)
> *Whispering Pines: A Romance on a New England Hillside* (1930)
> *The Great Powwow* (1934)
> etc.

As Rydant thought about the way his own biography predisposed him to utopianism, he speculated about the way Divine's biography might have predisposed him to the ministry of the Peace Mission Movement: Divine was, reportedly—though his earthly biography was rejected whole cloth by his followers—born and raised in rural Maryland as George Baker Jr., the son of former slaves. George Baker Sr., Divine's father, was himself among the earliest Black landowners in Maryland, and had developed a rich matrix of cooperative relationships with other Black farmers in the region. So this was the context in which Father Divine came of age: among Black farm cooperatives, with the first generation of Black landowners, in a region with the most Black landholders at the time, which included Prince George's County, an area that today is home to the largest population of middle- and upper-middle-class Black families in the country.

Divine's early life produced a body of knowledge that, Rydant implied, may have uniquely equipped him for the vision of the Peace Mission Movement and its network of "heavens," both upstate and in the city: the logistics of cooperative enterprise, defection from empire's message of scarcity by creating your own systems of abundance—and it is obvious to me how Divine's particular witness would have taken on a spiritual dimension for him. This is admittedly one of my weak points as a narrator, my (to borrow a phrase from Dennis Covington) "tender regard for con artists and voices in the wilderness, no matter how odd or suspicious their messages might be."

Rydant wondered: "What if Father Divine had stayed in the Catskills—after the Depression?"

Divine's upstate "heavens" began to thin out in the 1940s, as people left the movement—during wartime and the postwar boom, the Peace Mission's once-staggering numbers plummeted. The urgency of communitarianism had dissipated. There was no longer an immediate need for people to make the sacrifices or commitments—celibacy, for one—the movement required in order to maintain room and board. The country was flush again, with cash and jobs. The Family Divine started to sell off the Catskill properties to a new generation of farmers and homeowners and vacationers and developers. Many of the properties don't actually look that different now, though, than during the Depression. It's a lot of the same nineteenth-century buildings they'd briefly repurposed, now vacation houses or real estate offices or bed-and-breakfasts or gentleman farms or post offices, like the one next door to the coffee shop where Rik and I sat.

Lenny Feinberg's documentary about the Family Divine, *Father's Kingdom*, had just been released on Amazon. Rydant told me he'd actually taken Feinberg on the full tour of every former Peace Mission Movement "heaven" in Ulster County, negotiating admittance to the private properties, but that Feinberg used almost none of the footage in his film. I had seen this documentary. It was good. It told most of Divine's history the way you can find it most places. But it was the front story of the documentary that I found most riveting, and which added something new to the sometimes calcified narrative of the Peace Mission Movement's legacy as some wacky and tragic utopian artifact locked in the past: he chronicles the twelve elderly present-day remaining members of the Family Divine living in the Woodmont mansion outside of Philadelphia, talking about their lives and their theology and their celibacy as monastics, and the relationship they'd formed with a middle-aged gay man from West Virginia, a remote devotee of Divine's, who is wrestling with his belief in a life of all things in common while also not wanting to leave his long-term boyfriend. He never makes the leap, but he does eventually marshal his skill as a computer engineer to develop the Father Divine Library, a public archive, at Woodmont.

I guess what I found riveting was how the story never ends, even after Divine has left this plane and there are only twelve old people left and someone as horrifying as Jim Jones tried to usurp the legacy.

I asked Rydant if he knew that story about Jim Jones claiming to be the reincarnation of Father Divine.

"Sure, I know that story," he said, smiling. "I'm the reincarnation of Sarah Orne Jewett."

utopianotes
"Heaven Is a Place on Earth,"
music video dir. by Diane Keaton

It begins with a dozen illuminated globes—those novelty lamps from the 1980s—splashing into a dark pool of water. The globes break the surface in slow motion. Then, a line of adolescent girls in gray smocks and black masks marching into a dim triangle-shaped room, each holding their own globe lamp and singing the choral refrain: "Oooh, baby, do you know what that's worth? / We'll make heaven a place on earth / They say in heaven, love comes first / Oooh, heaven is a place on earth." Meanwhile, Belinda Carlisle is writhing around stage left, pressed into a corner, her pink sweater falling off one shoulder. The camera cuts between her, the girls marching in with the globes, the globes splashing in the water, and a slowly expanding view of the triangle-shaped room, in the middle of which is now a cultic pyramid formation of globe lamps. When Belinda starts singing the verse, a man enters the visual narrative: cut to her and the man, in the dark pool of water, embracing and spinning around. Then to the cadre of adolescent girls, who are now on a Zero Gravity carnival ride, still masked, still globe-holding. Then cut to Belinda, clawing the rungs behind a metal grate! Then to the cadre of globe-holding cultist middle schoolers, who are now lying supine on their backs in a line, swishing the globes above their bodies in imperfectly timed rhythm! Belinda gets a long minute then on screen, dashing coquettishly around her weird little corner, but she's skipping, happy, cresting with the admittedly and genuinely powerful, "In this world we're just beginning / To understand the miracle of living / Baby, I was afraid before / But I'm not afraid anymore." Cut to the adolescent cultists craning their necks upward and singing "Heaaaaven," into the bird's-eye-view camera. And then it's everything that's already happened, but quick now, staggered: The man! The triangle of glowing globes! The creepy slow-motion cult kids! Belinda smiling! The pink sweater! The Zero Gravity ride! The globe splashing into the water, over and over again—SPLASH!

FOUR

THE GARDEN &

THE CITY

utopianotes
Woodbine

Peter Linebaugh is reading from his newest book, *Red Round Globe Hot Burning* (titled from a William Blake poem), about the eighteenth-century marriage of Kate and Ned Despard and their shared lives of resistance to enclosure. Ned Despard, a poor Irish guy, is sent to the Caribbean for ballistics support, to stop the counter-rebellion, and Kate is a Black Jamaican freedom fighter. Ned and Kate meet in Honduras right in time for the French Revolution of 1789, July 14, the day the women storm the Bastille.

Peter Linebaugh looks a lot like Ted Danson—a lot like Ted Danson now, in his late sixties, as he appears in the NBC metaphysical comedy *The Good Place*, lithe and white-haired and elfin. He is wearing a black t-shirt that says TO HELL OR UTOPIA.

Ned gets kicked out of Honduras—and then in 1791, two years later, is the Haitian revolution. There are revolts everywhere at that moment, not just in Haiti: India, Ireland, Germany (and these are all the places that Kate and Ned go). They join together in the struggle everywhere, until Ned is executed in 1803. Kate by this point has become a diplomat and courier for the United Irish, during a time of repeated public hangings (tens of thousands of public hangings by the state to instill fear). At this point in the talk, Peter hands out business-card-sized pieces of paper: on one side is an eighteenth-century engraving of a bunch of people gathered in the cleft of a mansard roof, onlookers, soldiers with bayonets, and men hanging from the gallows.

On the other side of the card is an address that Ned Despard wrote and delivered to a crowd at his execution. Linebaugh reads the whole thing aloud:

Fellow Citizens,
I come here, as you see, after having served my country faithfully, honourably, and usefully served it, for thirty years and upwards, to

suffer death upon a scaffold for a crime of which I protest I am not guilty. I solemnly declare that I am no more guilty of it than any of you who may be now hearing me. But though his Majesty's Ministers know as well as I do that I am not guilty, yet they avail themselves of a legal pretext to destroy a man, because he has been a friend to truth, to liberty, and to justice.

(Applause from the people)

Because he has been a friend to the poor and to the oppressed. But Citizens, I hope and trust, notwithstanding my fate, and the fate of many who no doubt will soon follow me, that the principles of freedom, of humanity, and of justice, will finally triumph over falsehood, tyranny and delusion, and every principle hostile to the interests of the human race. I have little more to add, except to wish you all health, happiness and freedom, which I have endeavoured, as far as was in my power, to procure for you, and for mankind in general.

Sweeney asks a question from his seat at the back of the room. "Do you think of these histories of resistance as, like, histories that definitively ended and then evil prevailed?"

Linebaugh struggles to answer this question. He thinks about it. He answers it twice, three times. Finally he says:

"I don't mean to tell a story of dreary sadness . . . Is enclosure the end of the story? Of course not! People escape from prison. Every day! People rob banks every day. People malinger. People take naps."

THE CATSKILLS

There is some speculation that the Catskills—the Appalachian chain in New York State—are among the oldest mountains on earth. Their waterfalls and rivers have been cutting through the granite and bluestone for ten million years. As a landscape, the inscription of time gives these ancient hills an odd mix of gravitas and humility: they are very worn down, low and rolling, like a wide inland sea. They are not at all like the soaring volcanic peaks of my Pacific Northwest youth, peaks whose tops were still sharp and smoldering well into the twenty-first century. By contrast, the Catskills are quiet, nonchalant, with a cool, plain-faced beauty that, as one of the countless *New York Times* Catskills features puts it, "enfolds you rather than inspiring you with awe." In the spring, their gently blunted peaks and valleys are silvery wet and brown, then a deep, shimmery green in the summer, and then electric red and yellow in the fall, and then crusted in snow all winter long, which lasts, in some parts of the region, from November clear into April.

Despite their ancientness, the Catskills have the distinct feeling of being very man-made, or man-mediated, both as a physical landscape and as an idea. Because of their surreal proximity (just a couple of hours' drive) from the largest city in the country, the Catskills have been continuously under gentry speculation in lifestyle and travel rags from the nineteenth century to today. They are always being "rediscovered," or "dying out," under threat of development or in recovery from said development after the tides of leisure and industry have once again changed. For as long as there have been northeastern newspapers in circulation, there have been annual poetic odes on the Catskills printed in them, of one kind or another, including the summer of 2019 when Sweeney and I moved up to Delaware County: the *Times* had just published an article about the Catskills' "comeback" for aging millennial hipsters, among whom, I suppose, we were counted.

Delaware County spans the more remote northwest corner of the

Catskills, and as such is less used as a tourist destination than Ulster or Sullivan Counties—though no less man-mediated. When I first inched into Delaware County en route to Frank's Place, the landscape blasted open, up out
of the forested valleys I'd been snaking through. It was full of sun-drenched
fields and meadows straight out of a children's book, or a Dutch Renaissance
painting. There were ribbons of hardwood forests, encircling lots of deliber-
ately cleared farmland, and the hills dipped and swooped in such a way as to
leave me constantly cresting into a new view, a new vista, that was at once
marvelous and also obviously produced by human intervention: the county
had at one time been one of the major dairy producers in America, and
though the intensity of that use had died out, the pastoral visual spectacle it
created had not. The pastures have either become edgewoods or have been
maintained as anarchic wildflower meadows, brush hogged every five years
to prevent what would otherwise be the natural creep of the forest.

But dairy was the least of these human interventions. In the southern
counties of the Catskills, it was logging, granite quarrying, railroads, cement
mining—the vestiges of the giant old kilns still pock the mountainsides,
like airplane hangars built into the soft rock. Massive aqueducts were dug
and dams were flooded to bring fresh water to the city. Today, the Catskills
are lousy with a thick coating of softwoods and hardwoods, and though the
deciduous foliage is famously dazzling in the fall, these forests are relatively
young: a lot of the trees, maples and pines and birches and ashes and locusts,
are forty to sixty years old, sort of timid and fragile-looking, and in some
cases are hypnotically symmetrical because they were all planted or otherwise
went to seed at about the same time. At the end of the nineteenth century,
a big chunk of the region was made into state-protected parkland, and over
the next few decades the state subsumed more and more land, putting hard
limits on logging and other industrial activity, ushering it into another phase
of bucolic domestication, as a stage of shifting pastoral fantasies for wealthy
urbanites, as well as the full-time homes for people who had lived here, or
whose families had lived here, for a long time. Now, the old industrial rail
lines are being converted, transmuted even, into hiking and biking trails. As
second homes and pleasure farms cropped up, the memory of the Catskills
as an industrial wasteland, flattened, gray, smoking and flaming, snuffed out.

•

By the time the painter Thomas Cole was reaching the end of his Catskill tenure, he knew his beloved landscape was about to be wrecked by industry—forever, he openly figured, and as far as his own lifetime was concerned, that was true. But what's eerie is that when I look at Thomas Cole paintings of the Catskills in the early nineteenth century, before the era of quarrying and mining and logging and other extractive activities, I do see a landscape similar to what I see now. Or perhaps I see the land, most disturbingly, the *way* that Thomas Cole and the other painters of the Hudson River School saw it. Only now do I realize that my feelings about the Catskills had been telegraphed to me, long before I'd ever seen them in person, in these famous, ever-circulating images that captured the ideal of white supremacy, depicting the emotional experience of manifest destiny with those ever-glowing horizons, and those landscapes, completely empty of people and ready to be populated by whites.

Because what undergirds all of this is of course the fact that the Catskills had been man-mediated long before settler colonialism. The Indigenous people of the region—the Esopus, Haudenosaunee, Delaware, Oneida, Mohawk—had long used the Catskills as a seasonal hunting, fishing, and medicine wood, for thousands of years, during its gentle and fecund summer months. They used the rivers that ran through the mountains as thoroughfares, as a means to get *to* places. They tended and took care of the Catskills as one might a massive garden. There is limited research confirming that communities lived in the snowy bowels of the mountains long-term, or at least year-round, though that doesn't mean it's not possible. The land is rocky and cold and hard to cultivate. Their more well-documented permanent settlements were wisely nestled in the temperate valleys and river shores at the base of the mountains, where the land is more yielding and the temperature is consistently twenty degrees warmer. The microclimate of Catskill winters is so harsh and damp and freezing and long that year-round living might be a poor strategy, especially if a gentler climate is so nearby. But eventually such an existence is insisted upon by brittle white people, who came and occupied and pushed the Indigenous people further upstate and west. They cut them off from their ancestral medicine wood and plundered to make milk and cement and timber and money, and a couple hundred years later, after all of that, to make beautiful views for aging millennial hipsters seeking a new life outside the city. The Big Ag monopolies sent so many of the farming operations into bankruptcy that by the 1980s many of those old dairies were bought by the state and turned into jails, and in the absence of old industries and robust town centers, would become among the largest employers of rural New York. Since the 1980s, the New York State prison system population has tripled, an astronomically high proportion of which is made up of Black and brown people from New York City cast into facilities operated by poor white minimum-wage employees in places like the Catskills. The organization Milk Not Jails does organizing in areas like the Catskills today toward diminishing the region's economic reliance on the carceral system, as well as revitalizing its agricultural operations in hopes that this generation and the next can build an economy on literally anything other than death and despair.

The Catskills are a palimpsest, and so a site of sorrow and hope and dreaming, all at once. Is it surprising, then, that the Catskill region has long been full of utopian experimentation? Between its proximity to the largest metro area in the county, its weird combination of accessibility and remoteness, its layers of contested use, and its being a highland and so hard to tame, it was positioned well to become a utopian laboratory.

Today, the Catskills and their foothills are home to six of the North American Bruderhof communities, each populated by two to three hundred people: Fox Hill, Woodcrest, the Mount, Ulster Park, Rondout, and Platte Clove, the last of which was developed in the 1990s on the site of a former police training camp. On the western slope ebbing toward Troy, there's Soul Fire Farm, an Afro-Indigenous centered farming cooperative and school, and on the river slope there's East Brook intentional community. In the central peaks there are two massive Buddhist monasteries, where people retreat for short stays or live year-round in long-term monastic commitments, eating daily communal meals and carrying out communal meditation in the Zendo.

In the mid-twentieth century, there was Camp Woodland, an interracial folk music retreat started in part with the help of Pete Seeger. He and a few others bought an old church compound near the town of Phoenicia and created Camp Woodland as a site to develop a "democratic spirit" in young people by inviting participants from of a variety of racial, ethnic, and religious backgrounds from the tri-state area to come make folk music together. Then there is of course the Woodstock festival, which didn't happen near the town of Woodstock at all but in the foothills of Sullivan County, and which itself—in all of its mud and chaos and folly and eventual sublimated spirit of a new age—was itself a utopian gesture, in that it was about action, making an action, however ephemeral, that illuminates the edge of a different world. And there were dozens of small hippie communes dotting the landscape, before and after, which had mostly disappeared by the 1980s.

In the late nineteenth and early twentieth centuries, artist communes and colonies cropped up in the craggy mountainsides: Cragsmoor, Pakatakan, Palenville. At the turn of the twentieth century, in the actual town of Woodstock, there was Byrdcliffe, the artists' colony that was supposed to save the world with arts and crafts. The Arts and Crafts movement was a reaction to industrialization—based on the belief that if we made more beautiful things, by hand, at a handmade pace, in a communitarian context, the world would change along with it, one lovely shingle or rocking chair or hand-loomed wool garment at a time. But the world, it turns out every time, can never be reduced to a single element—not even beauty. In recent years, Byrdcliffe was made into a nonprofit organization and artists' residency down closer to town, but the original colony is still up in the hills, and it has some architectural suggestions of its vision of a better life on earth. It's a cluster of cabins and single-story motel-style dorms on the top of a hill, with one big central house. All brown, all rooftops covered in moss.

There were all manner of things that might fit into a broad definition of utopia: during the Borscht Belt, the Catskills were often referred to as a "Jewish utopia," and later in the twentieth century the (erroneously named) "Spanish Alps," as it became the vacation haven for burgeoning Puerto Rican, Cuban, and Latin American communities in New York City. The town of Woodridge openly understood itself as a kind of socialist utopia in a feature article from 1947, when the author—a resident—described its five worker-owned co-ops, communist sympathies, and its multiracial population (refugees from Europe, Colonial India, the American South).

I'm not sure what all of this means or amounts to except that there's a particular kind of palimpsest at work.

And now I was here, adding to the palimpsest.

At exactly the point when the human history of the Catskills became so congested with contradictory meaning, the flowers started to change my life.

First was the mountain phlox, which sprang up suddenly in late May, sprawling across shady groves and roadsides in fragrant purple colonies. Then the dame's rocket, with its smoother, stringier stem, bouncing out of ditches. I got lost in fields of four-foot-tall milkweed, when its sweet, drooping fiberoptic blossoms burst open. Later I picked its fresh, firm pods and poisoned myself slightly when I ate them with garlic and olive oil. I picked ripe raspberries and their freshly dew-dried leaves for tea. Then the time of the day lilies came—all at once, the kind people cultivate for ornamental gardens, but growing everywhere, wild: orange and yellow and speckled and red, flanked by waxy, sword-like wings. Chicory bloomed baby blue, light as tissue paper, and the tall, thumping mullein shot six feet up, like a torch, popping open just a few tiny yellow flowers each day. Prunella pushed up in the grass like many-headed Martians, their little purple flowers coiled up a cone and their stringy stems tangled in a fist. And the oyster plants and oxeye daisies. And the violet cow vetch that lay so gorgeously, weightless, in the hay field, but if I picked it to put in a vase looked like a bunch of sad leftover rumpled party décor left out in the rain. The St. John's wort, poking up here and there in groups of two or three—and which the bees loved so much. I hadn't seen so many bees in years. I let those starfish yellow flowers rest in jojoba oil for two weeks until the oil turned deep red—because way back when I was recovering from shingles, an acupuncturist said I should use this oil for the ghostly residual nerve pain in my face. The goldenrod emerged in August, swaying in the wind like Sideshow Bob from *The Simpsons*, sometimes as tall as me. Bright red clover like a carpet out my door.

The tangy smell of yarrow and the royal purple aster flowers in the fall. I roasted plantain leaves with spices until they became brittle as chips. One day, I bent down to inspect a low, thick carpet of tiny pink flowers blanketing the humus. I pressed my face into their softness, and realized it was all wild thyme.

My methods of flower engagement and inquiry and harvesting were so haphazard and unmethodical, and happened at all different times of day. All the things I gathered and processed from the land that summer I used as medicine for the following year. The land that Frank's Place sat on was just an old grazing pasture probably, now hay grass populated by a generation of new wildflowers that no one planted, no one needs to intervene on, are too plentiful to ever be over-harvested, and will be here long after we are gone. I made such large amounts of everything by accident, teas and tinctures, with such tiny fractions of what grew around me. The abundance was staggering to me, and kind of life-changing, in a very plain way, that lots of other humans already knew. All of my ideas about prudent use of time and effort and intent were subsumed by the way this ecosystem worked, and only because for the first time in my entire adult life my days were wide open, so I could pay attention to the kinds of forces in nature that made me question how much intention really matters, if the world is so old and has gone on without us for much of that time. Instead of intent, the land and my own life seemed to be asking for presence.

It was getting on in the season. An unexpected windfall came through to us when Dan settled out of court on a medical malpractice case from four years earlier—from when he was still in the coma—and suddenly we had enough cash to pay off a significant portion of our student loans, making our debt-to-income ratio, for the first time since we were each eighteen, such that we could apply for a mortgage on my adjunct income alone. We decided to try to buy a house up in Delaware County, though we had not yet begun looking.

The night we decided we would do it, we sat by the woodstove scrolling Zillow. Pareesa came by with two friends of hers, a couple, both goat farmers and cheese makers who lived on the other side of the Hudson. They came into the house and just started cooking: spreading artisanal cheese, breaking out the bread, searing hand-packed sausage, unearthing puffball mushrooms in the fields outside. While they cooked, they talked about their work on biodynamic farms, and about their relationships to the local Waldorf schools and Camphill communities in Columbia County, both major developers of biodynamic methods.

There are three different Camphill communities in the Hudson Valley, and dozens worldwide. Camphill is an international communitarian movement. It was started in 1939 by a German pediatrician and educator who fled the Nazis. Each of their secular intentional communities is home to a mixture of about one hundred adults with developmental and intellectual differences living and working, in an ethic of mutual aid, alongside one hundred neurotypical adults—and, I believe, some children, too. The neurotypical adults do not understand themselves as charity workers, but as part of a community of equals in a non-hierarchical system of life in something that resembles a nonbiological family structure. For the most part, the Camphill communities also collectively run biodynamic farms, an organic farming practice that includes additional esoteric practices as a means to emphasize the spiritual interconnectedness of the ecosystem, the land, and the farmers. I'd read about them before, and I had heard folks at the Bruderhof talk about cross-community exchanges, but I was surprised to find this overlap, learning more as the goat farmer couple jetted around the kitchen preparing meatballs, vegetable sauté, glugging wine from the bottle.

After dinner, they made a viscous tea from a pile of psilocybin mushrooms they'd brought along, which we all drank in the living room next to the woodstove, and then I dropped rapidly into my first trip, which had almost entirely to do with flowers, fields of flowers undulating like water, effortlessly irrigating and irrigated, while silhouettes of women danced, hopped, and canoed between the rows. The message that kept coming through that night, like a cool cloth to the forehead, was *This is how to use your erotic energy.*

utopianotes
Yellow Springs, Ohio

I stop in Yellow Springs with my mother on a cross-country drive. Neither of us know anything about Yellow Springs—we just happen to have a family friend whose son lives there, and whose house is empty for us to crash in. We arrive in the middle of the night, emerging from roads along rustling cornfields. We turn off the tape deck playing Ann Patchett's *State of Wonder*. We struggle to find the key under the mat in the dark. We share the queen-sized futon. It's an empty house, huge for just one young man. The next morning, we are so road-weary, eating breakfast in a café in town, which, in the light of day, is unbelievably charming. My mom says, *Why don't we stay another day?* And I immediately feel light and say yes. I spend the afternoon copyediting, dicking around, while my mom wanders to shops. I hear the brand new Sia album overhead in a coffee shop. I walk around the neighborhood, cry on the phone to Sweeney. It is warm and balmy. There is just one movie at the movie theater. It's about a stand-up comic who decides to get an abortion. We eat dinner. We see *Obvious Child*. We drink wine later at another little café. We feel fresh and new as we wander this tiny and bright Victorian village, free for a moment, outside of time, together. Later, I realize that Yellow Springs started as an offshoot of New Harmony defectors. For years afterward, I whisper to myself before I go to sleep, "Meet me in Yellow Springs . . ." the way Kate Winslet whispers it to Jim Carrey during their dreamplane encounter in *Eternal Sunshine of the Spotless Mind*.

AT LEAST I WILL DIE FREE

Sunlight poured in through the curtains. I'd slept on the couch because every room in the Adjunct Flophouse was unexpectedly booked. I listened to the birds begin to chirp at the dawn, and then to the other "floppers" wake up and make their coffee in the kitchen, while I hovered in and out of sleep from a flickering dream where I made out with my friend Gabriel in every bedroom, Donald Trump following us around the apartment talking about Iran.

When I was finally fully awake, Jen sat down on the edge of the couch in her bathrobe. "You look pretty," she said in this quiet, astonished way. My makeup was smeared under my eyes and I was wearing the same beige leotard I'd worn the night before, smelling of cigarettes. How could I explain what had happened? With Sweeney's blessing I'd met up with Gabriel, a new flame, for a date at a dog bar in Williamsburg. Immediately on the barstools, I kissed the side of his neck, and he put his cheek and jaw next to mine, and then we were making out, and then we were laughing as the dogs of the bar rallied around our stools. I'd taken off items of clothing right before I'd arrived at the bar—a seventies-style secretary blouse I'd worn to class that evening, literally ripped it off in the school bathroom like a sex ninja and underneath was this beige ribbed leotard, sleeveless and hugging my breasts, and then I'd gone on this multi-bar odyssey, and then I'd jumped into a cab back to the Flophouse, and it was what I was wearing, still now.

I didn't say any of this, though. Jen cozied up on the couch and we talked about the classes we'd be teaching that day. She was also in the process of finishing her own book about modernist design as a kind of utopianism, through the lens of her lefty parents' legacy of building rural utility cooperatives. I had an internship course to run, and then a flight to catch. Candice walked by in her jammies with a plate of toast and smiled. Anna emerged from her room, her hair long and loose. The cool fall breeze came in through the window screen and ruffled the crepe curtains.

On the plane to North Carolina, I sat staring in a reverie with very little sleep, feeling like I was in high school again, the way images of Gabriel approaching me on the sidewalk the night before kept playing in my mind like a movie, the loose, flirty way he looked at me, his dark hair pushed to the side, his eyes like frying pans, and then just the small gestures or moves throughout the night, the tiny line of kisses up the side of my neck, the common language our bodies spoke. It was funny. He noticed and named things about me no one ever had. We drank Miller-and-shot specials in the dark of the window-edged bar at Clem's, one after the other, staring into each other's eyes, and didn't eat dinner. I was falling in love. I was open about this with Sweeney. We were curious about it together. It felt thrilling, rather than threatening, like life was getting bigger than I ever thought it could. *Someone should arrest me*, I thought, a phrase that occurred to me whenever I felt like I was having too much fun.

Arriving in Raleigh was good, though I was tired. I needed a change of perspective. I had some research to do. My sister, Olivia, had recently moved there from Portland, into a big apartment complex with a pool and a screened-in porch. She'd stopped smoking and her sweet boyfriend, she told me over text, was making us stuffed zucchini for dinner.

I got a tiny silver rental sedan at the airport and set out on the never-ending loops of beltways. I cursed when I couldn't get my seat to sit upright, and so I drove stooped over like a granny until I got to my sister's place. Maybe I am squandering my relationship with Sweeney by sending all of this crazy energy hither and thither, to this other person? Where is this all going?

The next morning, Olivia and I took 401 out of Raleigh, north to Soul City. We stopped at a Waffle House for breakfast, and then as we crossed out of the metro area, the landscape immediately gave way to narrow two-lane roads, the dense pine forests loud with bugs.

Soul City, North Carolina, first proposed in 1969, was (and in some ways still is) a Black-led multiracial community, envisioned to become a totally self-sustaining city in the middle of the mountains north of Raleigh, when the region was still a major KKK stronghold. In fact, when Soul

City was putting up highway signage for their new town—after they broke ground on building in 1971—there were still billboards cheerfully welcoming people to "Klan Country!" Founded by a cadre of activists, including civil rights leader Floyd McKissick, Soul City flowered for one brief bit of the 1970s, as affordable houses and a clinic and a school, and the only post–Jim Crow public swimming pool outside of the Triangle area, were constructed in what would be the largest federally funded development project helmed by a minority.

Soul City was a direct response, even a corrective to, the fact that federally backed mortgages had been almost exclusively available to whites after World War II. McKissick was also responding to the further inequities caused by the rural drain of southern Black people to northern cities and exurbs where labor had been so consolidated. The Department of Housing and Urban Development conferred a great deal of grant monies to the project, though a lot of the momentum was got through grassroots organizing and fundraising strategies developed during the civil rights movement. Now that it was the seventies, McKissick did find himself in conversation with the politics of the Black Power movement, but they did not believe that mutual aid-based armed defense—like that of the Black Panther Party—was enough to empower Black Americans, and that the next move, beyond pacifism or survival militarism, was for Black people to make concerted strategic use of capitalism's financial instruments en masse.

While Soul City invited white people to become residents, the city's government and its industries would remain decidedly Black-led. And while Soul City's aims were deeply informed by Black liberation, they were also formed by a critique of how mid-twentieth-century city and suburb designs had deformed our lives, in more ways than just racial stratification. For instance, early ads described Soul City as "the only freestanding new town in the making," which is to say not reliant on a major city for economic support. McKissick himself liked to emphasize that it was a city designed "to fit into people's plans," not a city in which people's plans must fit. And because it's not a commuter suburb, the ads also promised that living in Soul City would "add an hour to your life." What is an hour worth? A lot. Brochures and full-page ads circulated to prospective homeowners all over the country, asking them to imagine "a city without prejudice. A city without poverty. A city without slums. A city tailor-made for industry. A city with a booming economy. A brand new shining city."

The community broke ground in 1971 on 5,180 acres of land that had formerly been farmed by slaves, making explicit the failed promises of the Reconstruction era's "forty acres and a mule" and inviting the politicians in power to own up to this in a direct way. The creators of Soul City wanted to face the terror of the past directly, and build something new from it. They started with a few trailers, mobile homes, and building sites for inexpensive town houses and the first phase of the industrial park (dubbed Soultech1). Sitting centrally and intact was the original nineteenth-century Satterwhite family plantation house, the "big house," in which they immediately fashioned a Head Start program and daycare center.

In his article "Soul City, North Carolina: Black Power, Utopia, and the African American Dream," scholar Christopher Strain offers readers an image of perhaps the community's public zenith, during its official ribbon cutting ceremony in 1973, after years of building. Then Republican governor James E. Holshouser—whose administration had contributed $1.7 million to Soul City's construction, and who, according to Strain, had a public and private record of remarkably enthusiastic support for the endeavor—said some things that perhaps no white Republican has ever said since:

> This land we stand on today was once the site of a plantation that depended on the labor of slaves. It is significant of how far we have come that Soul City is being built here as a "freestanding" community with its own industrial base to be developed by black-controlled corporations, but to be open to people of all races.

> Perhaps some of the men and women who will make their homes, who will build their lives in Soul City will be descendants of some of the very men and women who toiled on the old Satterwhite plantation. Many of Soul City's citizens are certain to feel a spiritual kinship with those slaves.

On top of being a site of multiracial community and Black industry, Soul City planners specifically did not want it to be a commuter suburb, but rather a self-contained city for work, leisure, healthcare, and play. McKissick was a proponent of "Black control of institutions" as a necessity for Black American independence. And through this, he changed parties—became a Republican in a bid for HUD money from the Nixon administration in exchange for helping to invigorate a Black voting base for Nixon's reelection (a president whose "law and order" policies McKissick had previously publicly called "fascist"). People started to move into the modestly priced homes from all over the country—New York, Michigan, Texas, Georgia.

By the mid-seventies, though, when it became clear that this wasn't just going to be a feather in the Nixon administration's cap, but an actual and actionable plan, a real place coming into being, Soul City started to be targeted for audits and suspicion for misuse of taxpayer dollars and nepotism (because McKissick named the pool after his mother and father). It was all just racist backlash in new forms, marking the end of that glimmering weird moment in the 1970s when national (fiscal, moral) desperation resulted in imaginative coalition-building, even between utopians and the government, and the inky cloud of neoliberalism moved in like a violent weather front that we are still in.

In 1975, Soul City was marred by allegations of corruption and misappropriation of tax money. HUD froze funds until an audit was complete—and Jesse Helms got involved, at the crest of his burgeoning career as a monster. All of this slowed down building and chilled community morale, as well as the interest of would-be investors. Even though Soul City was ultimately absolved of any wrongdoing (with the exception of the swimming pool "nepotism"), the frankly strategic effort of bad press had made it energetically icky. Instead of marveling at its innovation, the public discourse started to center around Soul City's supposed scandals and suspicion. Some former supporters began to back away due to concerns about "racial separatism," which is outrageous when you consider the racial stratification of basically every American city, town, and suburb, then and now. And during this time, HUD was scrambling to come up with reasons to pull out of its contract, and eventually, by 1978, it did. Soul

City went bankrupt, with a few houses and an unfinished industrial park to its name.

But stories of its death were greatly exaggerated—in the press and now. People remained. Assets existed. For about eight years, thirty families lived there in multiracial suburban harmony—and though that number plateaued and dropped, Soul City is still here.

We turned off of 401, into a circuit of country thoroughfares, but got confused, briefly frantic and turned around when the GPS told us we'd arrived but all we could see before us was the parking lot of an abandoned health clinic. We got out of the car. This clinic had been one of the main sources from which Jesse Helms had extracted the most blood and focused his efforts of press smearing through repeated unfounded allegations of misuse of public funds. Olivia and I walked around the building in the hot breeze, peering in the darkened windows drawn over with cracked venetian blinds. Through some slits, we could see pulled-up carpet, desks, some rolling chairs, empty shelving.

We got back onto the small highway and eventually turned left onto Freedom Road. To the side of the road were clusters of tract housing and beige single-story manufactured homes, with clipped summer-burnt lawns. We passed by the gleaming white Soul City Baptist Church building, as sturdy-looking as the day it was built in 1974. Eventually we turned onto Liberation Drive, where the big concrete monolith of the sign marking an entrance to the community had been moved—off the main drag—in the 1990s.

The groovy triptych of Ss seemed in a weird way to offer a direct challenge to the presence of the KKK, whose own signs this one was directly contesting when it was erected in the seventies. Beyond the sign were single-story apartments, and straight ahead was the large cream-colored "big house" that had been formerly occupied by slave owners, and later used as Soul City community programming headquarters. It now looked all but boarded up. There was a sign on the lawn announcing the tenets of a Soul City historic landmark project supported by the state of North Carolina. There were some small single-story apartment units kitty-corner to this, where one person stood, getting a grill going. Otherwise, we didn't see anyone around.

We parked and lurked around the house a bit, peering up and down the empty roads. Eventually a man pulled up to us in a big silver SUV, Tyrone Melton, who got out and introduced himself as the spouse of McKissick's granddaughter. She had grown up in Soul City, and the two of them still lived there. He invited us to look around—at the public pool, the park down by the lake—and advised us about who to talk to, including his wife, whose phone number he gave me. He called her "Dr. Mac," because that's what everyone calls her—the associate professor of media studies at UNC and the department's internship program coordinator. "She'd love to hear from you," he said, "she loves to talk about this place." Above all, he told us about all the current projects, including turning the old plantation house standing before us into a museum. "There is so much we are still doing, we have so many plans," he said. "But we are still really not happy about *that*." He waved his hand northwest, referring to the medium-security prison that the state built a quarter mile down the fucking road in 1997.

It was late September. Before I'd left on this trip, my father had come to visit us at our rental house in the Catskills. I picked him up at the Albany airport in the middle of the night and drove down Shaker Road as we headed south on I-90 back to my house. (The Albany airport is built on top of one of the oldest Shaker villages, Watervliet, where Mother Ann actually lived.)

The next morning, we had coffee on the porch. When we'd run out of things to talk about, I gave my dad a jar, and I took one, too, and we ventured to the upper meadow to go gather black raspberries. They were still exploding off of their thorny mauve bushes. I had been surprised to find them that late in the season, and I led my dad to the biggest patches I'd seen. We picked and fumbled around the dense waist-high meadows of goldenrod. The monarchs were still feeding placidly on their stalks.

I was telling him about Soul City, and we started talking about Lyndon Johnson's Great Society policy initiatives. "No one really talks about it," my dad said, "the way they talk about the Depression-era programs under FDR—but they were just as big." Johnson's Great Society was an expansion of social safety nets he cleared in the mid-sixties and which lasted until the late seventies that made possible things like HUD-funded projects such as

Soul City—backed, of course, by the momentum of all the preceding and concurrent social movements. It was, however, a mechanism I hadn't fully understood until that moment—my dad was right.

My father had three volumes of Robert Caro's four-part biography of Lyndon Johnson growing up. I have no idea why. I don't even think he bought them himself. I think someone gave them to him as a gift. But they dominated the bookshelf above the desktop computer for my whole childhood, and a good percentage of his cultural and political references and anecdotes seem to come from Johnson's life. After he brought up the Great Society policies in the berry bushes, my father and I had started arguing when he asserted that he thought overpopulation was the greatest threat facing the planet. I thought that that was not the way to think about it, because overpopulation wasn't addressable without addressing patriarchy and capitalism, without drifting into eugenics, and he thought I was saying overpopulation was not worth addressing because it was too big of an issue, too impossible to be worth thinking of it at all—because that's the kind of thing he was used to hearing people say, in his lifetime of work as a labor officer for the American Federation of Musicians. "But I'm a utopian," I shrieked. "Of course, I believe in talking seriously about impossible things, don't you know that?" We grew terse and never quite leveled, but eventually found an apple tree hidden at the edge of the meadow and helped each other pick the last of its fruit.

That conversation pushed me to think further about how the 1970s were so particularly weird because, yes, it was the end of the end, before hypercapitalism settled in. But in a Hail Mary pass, my God, the United States was briefly a place where a Republican government helped, albeit cynically, build interracial communities, not because the government was good, but because it still believed in a future that included the survival of more people than just a few billionaires living on Mars; a United States where a post–civil rights Democratic son of a peanut farmer could be elected the governor of Georgia (Georgia!) and then the president of the United States. Who has ever heard such a thing? A liberal evangelical? A liberal evangelical who would have a huge role in helping to expand Habitat for Humanity in the following decades, which I think we all now know finds its roots in Koinonia, a multiracial Christian utopian project on the outskirts of Americus.

We forget, I think, that the South was leading the country in a more progressive direction (in fact, in the 1970s, southern states were lousy with progressive governors), and that a lot of that changed direction during the Reagan revolution, what followers of Reagan genuinely experienced as a countercultural revolution against the failings of liberalism.

Olivia and I pulled out of Soul City and drove a mile around the bend to Warren County Correctional, a silent, haunting sandstone compound. This prison—privatized and yet paid for with taxpayer dollars, on land that once belonged to Soul City, and which before that was farmed by slaves—is now the largest employer in Warren County, holding a large majority of Black inmates, at a time when prisons are the third-largest employer in the nation.

The next day, Olivia and I drove from Raleigh to Asheville, tearing through the mystical haze of the Blue Ridge Mountains, alarming in their actual blueness. I wanted to visit Black Mountain College. It was warm and sunny. I didn't feel compelled, as I had in the past, to solve or fix a problem she was telling me about; the tyranny of my big sister-dom was relinquished. At lunch, we listened to the audible pleasure sounds both of us made while we ate, which were the sounds our mother makes, and our grandmother made when she was still alive, and we delighted briefly in that matrilineal continuity.

North Carolina is an odd cultural borderline state: partly conservative, partly progressive, lots of mountains, lots of coast, lots of flaxen flat farm-land, all of it. It's very beautiful. I don't really know what to say about the similarities between Soul City and Black Mountain College, other than the generally shared aim of innovating more humane, more democratic in-stitutions where the country failed to. Maybe what they had in common was me, using grant money to visit my sister in North Carolina, trusting I could make meaning out of whatever I came into contact with. Or maybe what these places have in common is geology, is Appalachia. As Olivia and I

continued cutting through and further up into the Blue Ridge Mountains, I
realized that if my sister did ever move to Ashville, she and I could look out
the windows of our respective homes every day—me in the Catskills, her
in the Blue Ridge Mountains—and we would both be looking at the same
basic landscape, the same flora and fauna. Whether in New York, Virginia,
Maine, North Carolina, when I found myself in the Appalachian chain, I'd
feel this homeward bound-ness, though I had no ancestry that I knew of in
these hills, but invariably in whatever state they ran through they were lousy
with utopian experiments.

It was a four-hour drive, and we'd driven there at my behest for basically one reason: to visit the Black Mountain College Museum & Arts
Center in downtown Asheville. The museum houses archival materials and
memorializes Black Mountain College—an experimental student-faculty-
artist-led liberal arts school that lived in the Blue Ridge Mountains from
1933 to 1956. The Center offers classes, lectures, and rotating exhibitions of
former faculty and students. The actual former campus is about ten miles
from Asheville itself, where it is now the site of a lavish Christian boys'
summer camp called Rockmont, and has been since the college shuttered
nearly seventy years ago.

But when Olivia and I arrived at the museum, we found a piece of paper
taped to the glass door: the museum was closed due to the annual conference
of Black Mountain College historians being held at a UNC campus down
the street.

As we stood there looking dejectedly through the door, a light flick-
ered on in the lower level, and a woman walked up and opened the door to
see if she could help. I told her our sob story, my scattered research intent
and our long drive, and then she let us join a private tour that happened to
be coming by right at that moment as part of a city-sponsored pub crawl.
Afterward, she invited us to come on the annual historic campus site tour
that accompanies the conference, happening first thing the next morning.
I couldn't believe our luck: the site of the old campus is largely off-limits
now. We did not tell our kind docent about our original plan, which had
been to just drive out there and find a way to break in. This was better. So
Olivia and I settled in for a lovely night in Asheville, where Olivia cried as

we walked its funny streets, because suddenly—except for the Blue Ridge Mountains—it felt like we were back home in Portland, a place which we had both been estranged from for a while.

We found a cheap room at a Holiday Inn near downtown. In the morning, I sat in the janky continental breakfast nook where the plastic floor tiles bent beneath my feet, sipping scalding coffee with an embarrassingly over-sized book—*Black Mountain College: Experiment in Art*, edited by Vincent Katz, checked out from the library—set next to me, unopened, while I struggled to spread cream cheese on a bag bagel. A man took an empty seat across from me, and I grew more self-conscious of my book, its ostentatious presence—What did I plan to do with it? Why did it take up so much space? I didn't open it, because I knew by doing that, I would reveal to both myself and this man that I didn't know where to start.

After a while, he asked: "Are you going to the Black Mountain College walk today?"

I laughed. "Oh, you mean, because of *this*?" Pointing to the book.

We talked about our relationships to BMC—and he asked if I'd read the Martin Duberman book. "No," I said, "I haven't," but then later that day I realized that I had, years ago, that it was in fact the very book that Robby had been hauling around with him when we'd lived together in college, the book that had been the original source of The Corresponding Society's interest in Black Mountain College to begin with.

"The Katz book is good," the man said. "But it also does this thing that a lot of books about Black Mountain do, where it's focused on the superstars the college nurtured, and the stories are told as though those people had always been great artists, or even that their becoming a great artist, individually, was the point of telling the story about the school at all."

When I asked him about his relationship to BMC he said, "I'm leading the walk!" I felt the highest order of dilettantism. "I'm David Silver," he said.

He told me about his interpretive point as a scholar, which is really that the spirit of collaboration and community at BMC can primarily be understood by the Work Program, and the school's farm in particular—which was also the basis for all of the school's alliances with the community at large. He approaches the women of BMC, and their maintenance of the Work Program, as the true north of BMC's existence, the bedrock of its community and collaborative alliances with the returning WWII veterans, farmers, and folks dispossessed by the Depression.

I told him a bit about my project.

"Tell me, in your time of studying this phenomenon of American utopianism, do you find that communities usually fall apart because of tensions around work, like who's doing all the work, who's not doing enough?"

"Ya know," I said, "yes—but also it's made me confront a lot of the assumptions I brought into this project with me. One of which was that communities fall apart because of dumb ideological disagreements and mundane things like squabbles over who's doing the most shit work, but for the most part, it's fiscal. It's just money. They go broke."

Which is, I think, largely Black Mountain College's story, too. They were broke for the entire twenty-three years of their existence. Because the thing that they, like all the other utopian experiments, are trying to do still exists within a paradigm that makes it impossible to not be affected by money, by going broke, even in as much as you are trying to build something that is impervious to that. The going broke, the sense of scarcity, spurs the other things—the factionalism, the drop in morale, the fights about who's lazy. "But, also," I said to David, "I find that they often don't end or fail in the ways we think they do, they often mutate and live on in some other form."

And then he said, "Yeah, that's kind of the case with Black Mountain. Have you heard of the Gate Hill Cooperative in New York?"

Olivia and I caravanned out of town with the group of BMC scholars. As we neared the turnoff onto Lake Eden Road, which encircles the old campus, there was—and this time I hadn't seen it coming—a prison, ensconced by layers of barbed wire: the Swannanoa Correctional Prison for Women.

Black Mountain College was like many early and mid-twentieth-century experimental colleges, not exclusively organized around the arts, but centering the arts as a matter of course, as worthy of making central to all courses of study because of the ways that an art practice nourishes self-discipline, collaboration, creative thinking, and problem solving. That the school actually and most famously ended up fostering the careers of some of the twentieth century's most famous artists was not its intention, but is not so surprising. The school was started in 1933 by a bunch of scholarly dropouts and rogue academics of the time—well-connected wild men with big egos and rich friends—and its growth was quickly buttressed by making itself a haven for many Bauhaus artists and scholars fleeing Nazi Germany. Josef and Anni Albers, M. C. Richards, and Heinrich Jalowetz, other famous folks joined the faculty. (Over the years, they'd be joined by Willem de Kooning, Robert Creeley, John Cage, and Buckminster Fuller, among others.) For the first several years, they ran the school out of a giant neoclassical conference center in the mountains called the Blue Ridge Assembly, which was owned by liberal Presbyterians who needed the building only for the summer months. Classes were experimental, free-form, discussion-based, lecture-based, studio-based. There was mixing of girls and boys, sex in the woods, hitchhiking, late-Victorian bohemianism. There was a shared sense of being on the edge of the world, at the edge of their own time. The school had to improvise programming and facilities at the last minute, every single year, because they never knew if there was going to be enough money to keep the thing going when fall came around.

Olivia and I roamed with the tour group around the grounds, the old milking sheds and former nut tree orchards, and then gathered around David Silver for his talk.

Black Mountain College finally moved to Lake Eden in 1937. In their first decade, they had to reinvent themselves every year. During that time, they were barely paying their professors, but were providing room and board. The Lake Eden property had most recently been used as a leisure resort, so there were some existing buildings to start with—cabins and tool sheds and such. But they needed to build more. As they awkwardly transitioned between the old campus and the new one, everyone was expected to collaborate on building its new existence—the school with no money trying to stay alive and build anew during Depression-era retrenchment—and it was then that the Work Program was born. Everyone was conscripted into the labor: students, faculty, staff, family members. They built and winterized the structures, laid ground for the farm.

The deliberation for how the Work Program would function, and how the farm would be maintained, included all of the same people named above. The meetings were lengthy and contentious and slow and methodical and centered the voices of the students in spite of the higher administration's efforts—and many of those meeting transcripts remain with us today. Silver argues that the style of deliberation undertaken to start the Work Program set a precedent for how debates and thinking through egalitarian consensus would ultimately take place at BMC for its entire existence—and that its operational model is, in fact, its most impressive legacy.

"Did you all see the prison as you were driving up?" Silver asked us.

People nodded.

"The prison used to be a model farm test site during the Depression," he said. "It was a government-funded facility built to *serve* the people of the region—to help develop and disseminate information about which practices or plants would work best for the area, or economically, and the Work Program collaborated with them often."

That prison, which I had seen as I drove in the caravan that day en route to the remains of Black Mountain College, sits like a monster at the terminus of Lake Eden Road. It's a site which has apparently been taxpayer-funded for the last century, and which, like Warren County Correctional down the street from the remains of Soul City, tells us a lot about what Americans value. Given the choice of utopian city or model farm or experimental school, we choose to spend our taxes on prison—prison is what we can agree on in this insane centuries-long debate about what we're all willing to spend our common wealth on. We should be ashamed. If I've learned anything, it's that wherever there is a utopia in America, there is probably also a prison—or wherever there is a utopia, it won't be there long, or wasn't there long, and will probably give way to a prison, and probably later will gave way to something else, maybe something better. Either way, all of this troubles my ideas of progress.

"My only point," says Martin Duberman in *Black Mountain: An Exploration in Community*, a book I return to after this trip, "is that mere durability (like mere transience) is not a sensitive barometer for measuring the quality of communal experience—though it's the one usually favored by historians of utopia."

It's one of the few times in Duberman's book that he uses the word "utopia" to characterize his subject, though I think it's clear all along that that's the critical framework we're in. And it's odd, particularly because we are mostly talking about a college, an institutional form that by design kind of works toward durability, dogma, in that institutions eventually become inevitably concerned primarily with maintaining their continued existence. But perhaps that is the most utopian thing about Black Mountain College— if we're reinterpreting utopia as I am, not as "no place" but as a place that, according to the laws of capital and conquest, was never supposed to be able to exist, but did anyway: a college that never became a college, an institution that spent its entire existence actively and consciously thwarting its own becoming an institution, or at least questioning that trajectory to such an extent, for so long and so thoroughly, that it could never really become one. As with all American utopian experiments, Black Mountain's chief virtue is that it didn't last.

Eventually, the tour group headed over to the original Studies building, which now sits on the actual Rockmont property, the Christian boys' camp, where there was—that day—a large father-daughter retreat. People zip-lined into Lake Eden, screaming, as the rest of us stood on the deck of the mammoth stilted modernist-style Studies building where all the studios, classrooms, and other common spaces of the college used to be housed, and which now house offices and guest rooms for the camp. The Studies building is long and rectangular, grayish brown, stilted above concrete pillars, looking out over the mountains and the lake. It was built in this crazy ragtag style by architecture students and faculty, and it is kind of a marvel—the virtue of transience be damned—that it's still standing sixty years later.

When we entered, there was a big flag on the wall screen-printed with a bald eagle, espousing the virtues held fast to by the Rockmont camp, and as we walked through the narrow hallways, I realized that each door opened into what used to be a small, spartan BMC student's studio—where the likes of Dorothea Rockburne and Merce Cunningham and Ruth Asawa and others worked. The BMC students lived and slept in really tight quarters elsewhere on the campus, in bunkhouses of no fewer than eight people, but everyone had a private studio and workspace of their own guaranteed.

As I continued moving down the narrow hallway, slowly, like a ghost, one of the guides gestured out the window, saying that Buckminster Fuller built one of his first geodesic domes just off to the side there, down in the grass. We looked out the window on to nothing, but could imagine it there, a great white polygon structure being gestured to by Fuller himself, that bespectacled, white-haired man in a three-piece suit who ended up so strangely providing the later hippie commune movement with its most enduring architectural symbol.

We passed by a couple of small, tidy apartment rooms, and then out to the porch; the whole tour crowded onto it, looking out at the mountains, shaped, as one BMC student described in his interview with Duberman, "like a woman's breasts." There was a palpable sense of nonprofessional excitement now, all of these scholars in the tour group seething with longing, maybe even something like jealousy. The people who are enthusiasts of Black Mountain College are also people who, I think, sort of wish that they could have been there, could have gone, could have made art and drunk wine with their friends in one of these studios—and being a legacy keeper is the closest thing you can be once that is accepted as no longer possible.

In his book, Duberman actually front-loads his history of Black Mountain with its (in my opinion) most unsavory characters and most questionable ethical behaviors: how cowardly they were about boarding Black visitors in the 1930s; their discipline and rejection of gay faculty and students before the war; John Andrew Rice's affairs with his students. (I was hoping in looking at the book's photo insert that I would at least find John Andrew Rice sort of hot, to complicate my contempt for him, but he really wasn't. Just this squatty stuffy pipe-smoking chubby pedantic dude with a mustache and tiny pinched eyes.) But there's a freedom in Duberman's decision to do that. Because it reveals immediately that the goal of this book is not to tell a history that positions the school as a model, as a city on a hill, nor as a den of dysfunction (because hundreds of pages remain), but fundamentally as a process.

It's interesting because Martin Duberman's approach to chronicling the school's history in *Black Mountain: An Exploration in Community* articulates a history-telling ethic of my own, which I did not remember. He inserts himself not just into the historical exposition as a first-person narrator, but also through his journal entries, which are more circumspect than the exposition, and he even inserts his voice into the old transcripts from the 1930s of their board meetings about best practices, about what constitutes intelligence or a "high-performing" student, about what teaching is, about whether they are a college or a community first. To be clear, he maintains the integrity of the transcripts, and he notes when he's entering it as a speculative voice, telegraphed from the future, wishing he could have been in that room, could have stopped them in their prewar homophobia from expelling gay students.

It's also silly for me to say Duberman does something that *I* do as a writer, because I've already admitted that I'd encountered this book years ago, but just forgotten about it—but there it sat somewhere, both as a body of historical knowledge and also as a formal model that had contributed unwittingly to how I've done my own work. It's weird, I guess, how one book just leads to the next; how one encounter becomes the interpretive medium through which the questions at hand will be developed, just because that's what happened to be there. In my case, I formalize incident as a writer. I work with an intentionally small set of tools and materials, restrict myself to the texts and experiences I accidentally accrue, and even though I doubt the process for nearly the entire time I am carrying it out, assuming it is insufficient and inefficient, it does always seem to work—or do a kind of work at least.

Olivia and I left Black Mountain. We got biscuits and gravy from a café. We got on the interstate. Somewhere along the way, barreling down the asphalt, we sang along to Prolly's version of "Wagon Wheel." Everyone knows this goddamn song. It's not special. It's only particularly special to us because—haven't I told this story before, somewhere? Sweeney and I went to New Mexico when we were twenty years old for no reason, except that we had been given free airfare to use in a short amount of time. We camped, we road-tripped, we backcountried into White Sands National Park, and on the last day we swung briefly through Santa Fe, which we found kind of demoralizing. We'd been listening for months, in our apartment in New York, to this teenager who recorded this sublime cover of "Wagon Wheel" on Bandcamp. We'd whipped up excitement in all of our friends about it, and anyone who came through Gates for a visit had to listen—we had to play it for them. It was this husky, guttural, white-knuckled, neo-screamo version of that already partially salvaged Americana tune. Anyway, as we were walking back to our rental car in Santa Fe, getting ready to leave after a short walk-through, we passed a seventeenth-century mission that had been made into Santa Fe's oldest park. It was dark now and there were a bunch of teenagers gathered around a fountain, playing guitars, and I heard a voice, a singing voice, I knew the voice. "That's fucking Prolly," I screamed. I broke away from Sweeney and ran into the dark park, Sweeney trailing behind me, unable to make out the figures of the teenagers by the fountain. By the time we got to her she was finished with a song, and her friend said, "Play 'Wagon Wheel,'" which I realize now, in retrospect, she must have at seventeen already been extremely tired of, her dancing monkey act where her own original music making had far outgrown this one measly cover. But of course, we were excited, nearly fainted at the coincidence. It made no sense. The timing. We couldn't believe it. We stood there watching, tears streaming down our faces. We tried to explain it to her afterward—that we had come in from New York, had been just about to leave, had been listening to her all summer. The recording eventually disappeared from Bandcamp, but later reappeared on YouTube which we had to rip an mp3 from, and that file passed between me and my friends and eventually my sister, who sat next to me now, singing at the top of her lungs along with the singer gone hoarse from exhaustion: "And if I die in Raleigh / at least I will die freeeeeeeee!"

We got back to Olivia's, and then I repacked and drove myself to my friend Chanelle's house on the other side of town. We hadn't seen each other in a year. She was running an herbal workshop in her garden shed that night, and as soon as she was finished I stole her partner's pack of cigarettes and the donated bottle of wine and resolved that we would stay up all night talking, and we did, right up until the exact hour and minute of the fall equinox, by accident, 3:56 a.m. Her hair was gathered in its dirty blond glory like a piece of cloth bundled on her head, a white sleeveless band tee tucked into a long gray skirt. I felt so much love for her. I told her all about Gabriel, what it was I was experiencing when I was with him, how electrified I felt, how much I craved his attention and his touch. She laughed at me. "Can you learn to touch yourself that way?"

utopianotes
Waffle House

I drive from New York to Nashville, then from Nashville to Raleigh, then from Raleigh back to New York for practically no reason at all except to be on the road for a very long time by myself. I'm hoping that will help me feel free, but it mostly makes me tired, the longer I go. I've packed too much driving in too few days, and bags are building under my eyes. It's a cold mid-March. I sleep in Elkins, West Virginia, in a cozy Super 8 with clean carpet. There is snow out the window in the morning. Later it turns to a gray, heavy rain. I drive great distances just talking to myself out loud. I pull into a Waffle House.

Inside, it's everyone: a seventy-year-old white woman, a nineteen-year-old queer Black man, two middle-aged women—one white, one Black—and an old Latino man at the grill flipping those hash browns I had just ordered smothered. I sit at the counter. It begins to sleet outside. I order more: a scrambled egg, a biscuit and gravy, coffee. It's so cheap. The rain beats against the windows, and other people come inside from the cold. All kinds of people, all ages, all classes, all races. Surely someone has told me this before—has sung the high praises of the Waffle House, but I didn't get it, I haven't gotten it till now. Someone should have told it to me differently, not about how much they love the Waffle House, but that going inside of a Waffle House feels like the eschaton, the end of time, when everything is finally knit up. "Race, taste, and gender finally overcome," Belize says about heaven in *Angels in America*. I can already feel how outrageous these thoughts are, but I'm elated, I can't help it. The Waffle House dissolves the firm boundaries of the country, and all of their locations are natural disaster relief sites.

GATE HILL COOPERATIVE

There's a weird lacuna in this story—perhaps the whole story of this book, and the way I tell stories about my life—which is that though I am an educator, an adjunct college professor by trade, I have always felt somewhat alienated by this role. I have never regarded it as my career or vocation, but as one of the things I ended up doing just to get by. Regardless, it is how I have ended up making a living since I was twenty-four. Eventually, I was able to consolidate my contingent teaching appointments at one school, my alma mater, Pratt Institute, where I taught writing workshops, creative nonfiction electives, freshman English, and a recurring women's studies course called Bad Girls in Music, Art & Lit. Eventually I absorbed a series of required courses for the BFA writing students who are carrying out their internships. The course sequence begins with Writer as Worker—which attempts to equip students with the skills to build material lives for themselves as artists through learning to compose resumes, cover letters, grant applications, artist statements, pitches, and research toward obtaining internships, jobs, grants, and fellowships, as well as weekly visits from other writer-artists who have made lives in various ways—and it follows with two possible courses called, simply, Internship I, and if you do another internship, then Internship II. Every course of study at every school that has any kind of fieldwork component in their curriculum has a course like this. You meet regularly, you read a text about labor or the politics of your field or whatever, and students talk about their experiences and troubleshoot issues they're having, share intel from "the field" as it were, develop the skills and experiences they're having into something usable, bankable for later, and maybe they do an assignment for next time—an informational interview, a budget based on entry-level income, etc.

The funny thing is that I hadn't done an internship in college—I had used this same exact course in the same exact program at Pratt to get credit for the "fieldwork" experience of running The Corresponding Society with my friends. At the time, Anna Moschovakis—current-day friend and facilitator of the Adjunct Flophouse, curator of Frank's Place, writer extraordinaire—oversaw that course, and helped my friends and me, before and after, build out our small press enterprise. Unexpectedly, years later I am teaching this course, year after year, as I myself become more and more circumspect about the virtues of waged work in general, already a lifetime of being dispositionally averse to a career trajectory.

The students these days, in a way, are already primed for my worldview. They're hardworking and articulating interests in different fields, but they—more than I was at their age—understand quite deeply, I think, that the current economy is built on speculation, that one multibillion-dollar media company might be upright one day and folded the next, that we have no idea what kinds of technologies are going to replace the ones we've become proficient in, that the death knell of publishing has been sounded many times, over and over again, and yet books do continue to come out, and so on.

Over the semester, I ask questions about the things they're learning. We have conversations. A lot of the conversations are about using their experiences and reactions to their experiences to uncover latent values, ethical practices, creative and community commitments that they already have—but that are showing up now, against the pressures of "real life," in starker relief. For a couple of years, I required each student to keep a weekly internship log, wherein they dutifully recorded some of the most wooden, nakedly pro forma writing I had ever read, in a way that shamed me, year after year, because *I* had asked them to do it—*and why*? I had no framework. Reading those logs was a weekly accusation of my superficial pedagogy. Finally, years in, it occurred to me to rename the assignment—Living Journal—and write a little treatise on how to use it. They could use it to write about anything happening outside of school, including but not limited to their internship. It had to be one entry per week, and they had to approach it seriously enough for it to form the basis of our class discussions. Admittedly, I just wanted to read better writing, while still having something to show that would satisfy the institution's stated learning objectives for their internship curriculums.

The course changed for me after that, unexpectedly, because of the way that students began to use that assignment. I realized that centering the Living Journal that way was effectively asking students to treat their lived experiences as texts, and to bring to those experiences the rigor, curiosity, delight, and analysis that they might bring to any other kind of text. Look at what is going on around you right now, outside of class, whether that's at work or at home: What are you doing? What are you thinking about? Where are you spending your time? What do you find you wish you were doing instead? Who are you talking to? What do you see or feel when you're at work, and what do you think about it? What other kinds of waged work are you doing, and how does that feel or seem to you by comparison? What are you reading or watching or listening to, in your own time? Formulate some of those things into a "required texts" list. Make some fieldtrips for yourself out of excursions you would already be taking, and bring to them the focus you might to something you were assigned. Chronicle your reactions and thoughts to the text of your life, as though you are an anthropologist or an explorer. Use these assignments to test your discoveries against. The end result of this is a mystery. You will be evaluated on your sheer willingness to engage in the process. Rather than the way an independent study at least supposes a subject around which one will gain mastery, we are arranging the raw material of our lives—ideally not even going out of our way or changing our course to do this—into a kind of reverse-engineered map, a backwards syllabus that, if we follow, might tell us something at the end of the semester about how all of the things in our lives that seem disparate at first might actually be conspiring in similar directions, might show us where we are actually pointing our lives toward versus what we think or hope we are.

There was a moment of thrill as I experienced this clarity around what it was this course could be, suddenly being able to articulate it to students in a way I hoped would make the course itself feel less arbitrary for them as they carried out what felt like the more central work of showing up for their internships and padding their resumes. But also, as with any thrill, any clarity, I snapped back: isn't the point of my discovery that the course has been doing this all along, without my having to articulate it? Haven't I only just caught up to what Anna was doing ten years earlier? And had the course simply molded itself around my own living and writing practice? Had I turned an internship course into a course where students are mostly just doing the kind of writing I do, the kind of writing that galvanizes into my books, my books being the process of treating my lived experiences like a text? Had I written myself out of the play, so to speak, spent years running the professional development curriculum of the BFA Writing Program only to find that I had been using it, the curriculum, my students' experiences, as a space to theorize my way out of a professional life in general—even as I became more savvy and effective at helping them learn how to get the things they wanted, or *think* they wanted, professionally? Or had my students, in their heightened Gen Z awareness, their casual inborn dismissal of society, or as my friend Robert says, their experience of having been *actually* born with a full awareness of the Matrix (whereas millennials had only kind of woken up into the Matrix in their twenties), done this to me, over time? Did we even believe in work or professional development, and if not, what should we be doing in these class meetings instead? Soon, mostly what we were doing was freewriting about our families, our anxieties, our novels and chapbooks, our ideas for communes and utopias, our pleasure and experiences of freedom. Did we believe in any of it anymore, and if not, should someone else come take my place—someone who did still believe that any of it matters that much?

The weird thing is that I wonder if I met Anna at this same moment in her own use of this role as internship coordinator at Pratt in 2009. She had, at the time, just moved to that big fixer-upper in the Catskills and was trying to build that out. She had, I think, just gotten married. She was over a decade into working closely with the publishing collective Ugly Duckling Presse. She had been an adjunct professor in a variety of programs for ten years. She'd had multiple books published to great acclaim. By the time I met her, when I was twenty and she was thirty-eight, she maybe didn't believe in any of it either, was en route to writing her own self out of the story of professional development. We met biweekly in the school's Pi Shop, and a small group of us shared our experiences from the field: I would report on the progress of our upcoming issue of *Correspondence*, our chapbook series and recent readings and events, tactics for promotional emails. She made herself an ongoing resource. A few years later, when I finished graduate school and moved back to New York, then up to Woodlawn so Sweeney could be closer to Fordham, she asked if I wanted to cover the role for her for one semester, and slowly it became my role—which I knew how to do only through my dim remembering of her modeling, but which it took me years of inhabiting to be able to theorize. Maybe she could have said all this to me then, at twenty-five, when I took over. Maybe she could have told me what would happen, or what was already happening when I was twenty and her student—or maybe it just had to be lived.

I suppose all courses of study, all classes, all teachers and students, are locked together in an embrace of perpetual transformation through exchange—which is time-based and extends beyond the classroom. It's never really clear who's teaching and who's learning, where one ends and the other begins. It's just that there's not often such an intimate case study, like Anna's and mine, like the continuum of this course I passed through, and then taught, and then possibly taught my way out of.

I'm thinking of this now because Black Mountain continually shuddered with this existential question, and was at its strongest when it could just live, liminally, in that flux—where the students and the faculty and the other resident workers were all subject to an indiscernible exchange, even where hierarchies attempted to consciously or unconsciously assert themselves. The relevance of this dynamic, the willingness to live in liminality, has meaning beyond educational spaces. That effect lived on, in fact, in a community that grew out of a group of Black Mountain defectors: the Gate Hill Cooperative.

I became aware of Gate Hill when an old friend of Sweeney's that we reconnected with at Woodbine xeroxed me a copy of an essay M. C. Richards wrote called "Taking Stock of Our First Decade," a reflection on the first ten years of Gate Hill's existence. He just handed it to me, casually, while I was walking by at a Woodbine Sunday lecture. I didn't know about Gate Hill, had only seen a few stray images of the community today that he had posted on Instagram, and which I'd asked him about. But I was drawn in when, early in the essay, Richards—a ceramic artist and poet—likens her experience of community building to being like the act of art creation: "We may aid these natural processes in the way that artists aid the natural processes of creation: by knowledge of materials, by imagination and vision, and by working to embody our visions in physical forms and acts." Here was a way of talking about community building that seemed utterly fresh to me—not religious, not political, not sentimental, not strictly practical, but embodied, aesthetic, and grounded in a process familiar to me, or perhaps just grounded *in process*.

The Gate Hill Cooperative in Rockland County, New York, was started in 1954 by a bunch of Black Mountain College faculty who left North Carolina as the school was going underwater. This group felt the "strength of Black Mountain ebbing," which smacks to me of the sense that when even a very cool and "successful" project loses the edge or the power or the prophetic force it once had by its ability to accommodate its liminality, then there's a feeling like you've got to move on, or rethink things radically, otherwise you're just pouring concrete over a dead thing onto which power can be exercised. Some of the more well-known Gate Hill people were M. C. Richards, the composers John Cage and David Weinrib, the choreographer Merce Cunningham, and the visual artists Paul and Vera Williams.

Richards recalls the first days of the cooperative's conception, when they had all just relocated from North Carolina back into small dirty apartments in New York City, considering some of their primary needs: "What did we want to do, asked Paul Williams as we sat around John's marble slab table in Manhattan. We wanted to be within commuting distance of New York, so that people who needed the city for employment could have it. John and David wanted a theater and electronic music research center. Merce decided he was not ready to commit himself. Neither Earle and Carole."

Richards writes that Paul Williams wanted, in starting a community, to experiment with inspiring architectural design after social forms and values, and that he wanted the land to "have the spirit of one of those hilltop towns along the Mediterranean coast. Thirty or forty families, heterogenous, maybe some small stores, small industries, a village economy." Richards describes him wanting to use "the architect's imagination as a humane force in social vision," which strikes me especially because during that era—the 1950s—the modernist city planner's vision was a force being wielded for evil and power very visibly in New York City.

They had lots of other questions, though. How would they begin? Where did they want to be? I was familiar with the crudeness of their methods for answering this question: "We got a map and drew a circle, within which we would search," but I was surprised with their method's swiftness, when she writes, "At the end of March, 1954, we made a trip out of New York in the Williams' Jeep Station Wagon to look at property at Hook Mountain near Nyack," which is exactly where they ended up settling.

Paul and Vera Williams ponied up a lot of the initial cash for the property, which had on it just one house that they would share at first, with the intention to eventually build other dwellings.

But once they had the land, they also needed help figuring out a fiscal and legal form to grant them each ownership, so they sought the counsel of a co-op lawyer. "The problem of agreeing: should we ask for unanimity? The feeling was yes, we should, wherever possible." Though Richards, in her essay, grants that "legal precedent often settled for less" virtue than what they hoped for themselves as a community.

As they established themselves, other friends and associates from the city became interested in Gate Hill, and so they started thinking about the terms they might use to accept new members. She writes, "What should we require? A reasonable human compatibility, a sympathetic relation to the tastes and purposes of the architect-designer-coordinator, financial solvency?" Of course, these were and are often the reigning set of questions for most utopias.

Still, as they forged ahead and moved onto the land, she remembers feeling vague about their collective vision, and that they were all "cowardly about making demands on each other," learning that "the pressure that is withheld is just as potent a force between people as that which is openly expressed. Feelings that are withheld are more tyrannical than open hysteria." This, too, feels like a fairly pat rule at work in any cooperative context; not just communes, but marriages or roommates or classrooms. So, through the tyranny of unexpressed grievances or the differing visions for the land, the Gate Hill Cooperative did lose some of its original people, then gained others, then lost some again. Multiple dwellings emerged so that they could all move out of the main house, and there was a new slate of resident projects now. Richards mentions John Cage and David Weinrib growing crabby as their music center and theater did not come to fruition, how they both began to turn their noses up at all the couples having babies now. She describes various architectural modes they tested, as a community, like having studios both inside of and outside of the houses. "Another principle, not to have maverick dwellings off by themselves in the woods was tested by the application of [the painter] Peter Ostuni, whom we turned down." Her thinking on the page about these things felt familiar and even comforting to me, the idea that all of these things, every new idea at Gate Hill, and all of life, is a continuous round of low-stakes testing, aiding "natural processes of creation," embodying "visions into physical forms and acts," neither of which imply finality.

Eventually, they all started to brainstorm ideas about how to generate more subsistence income from the land. M. C. Richards wanted to create "Gate Hill Weekends," creative workshops and retreats for adults from the city, but they also talked about creating a summer camp for kids, too. They thought of renting plots out for camping, or long-term shares for summer use, or single-use cabin stays, essentially something like Airbnb-ing in the 1950s. None of it had happened, though, by the time she was writing this essay. "The land is a problem to us," she says. The taxes were expensive. At times, they had conversations about selling it, or donating it to the state park. "It is difficult to act clearly because we are unclear in our attitudes toward money, toward accrued value, toward profit . . . It is my personal belief that what would help us would be some more thorough experience of money as an imaginative force. I think it would be worthwhile to study this subject in a community study course."

There's a lot I love about Richards's essay—but perhaps what I love the most is the way she moves easily between the concrete and theoretical considerations she and the community are making. She asks big, broad sets of guiding questions folded into more immediate and minute ones: "How do we act in this realm? By agreement and mutual responsibility? Separately, by individual initiative, doing what we feel like doing when we feel like doing it? Some sensitive combination of these?" And then: "What do we do about . . . the old rotting shed at the end of the corral? About our long post-poned car shelters?" And then: "The bridge is in serious trouble. Dan spoke to me about it last night."

Something about her use of "last night" stops me in my tracks, in the way it signals brute temporality in a consideration otherwise so timeless. When was "last night?" Was it 1965, when this essay was written? Yesterday, in my own kitchen? The daily problems and gripes of utopia perpetually live in the space of a conversation that happened just last night, and which as of now, as you read about it, have not yet been resolved.

As Richards continues to walk through all of these active questions and challenges that Gate Hill presented in its first ten years, out of nowhere she reveals that she was seriously considering leaving Gate Hill a few months back, and moving to a Camphill Village. She does go for a few months to a Camphill community in Pennsylvania, but she decides ultimately to come back to Gate Hill Cooperative at the end of that trial period—which seems to be not that long before the writing of this particular essay. She returns, however, with new insight that Camphill's stability comes from their clarity of purpose, their incredibly organized community design, and their shared daily habits. She comes back to Gate Hill with a message for her people: "I would say our purpose here is to bring in activity and physical embodiment of the imagination of the artist in the creation of environment, human re-lationships, perception of reality, prophetic sociology. What is prophetic sociology? I think it is acts of imagination and of love. That's how I get art and community together; or rather, that's how they keep coming together for me as a twofold reality. Acts of imagination are those in which we bring our dream into waking life. Acts of love are those in which we embrace the stranger and the enemy."

It's not that she returned from Camphill thinking that their com-munity's very specific mission—residential mutual aid for adults with dis-abilities, and those without—might be a model for Gate Hill Cooperative. It was, again, not one particular outcome or another, but rather their shared clarity of purpose.

I am not interested in so-called structured goals for the community any more than I am for an artist. Artists do not have structured goals. They have visions, high intuition, a feel for the true ring, a golden ear, balance if they are dancers, their souls pour into their senses . . . As artists we work through images. As a community of artists, I propose that we think of the way we use our land, ourselves, each other, as artistic images. That we solve our problems of money with the exactness and originality of artists. That we approach our meetings with the earnestness and attention we give to other performances. That we extend ourselves into the larger neighborhood as if we were extending an image: working big, architecturally, with the same care for quality, tone, freedom and wholeness.

Over the years, the Gate Hill Cooperative grew and changed and shrank. It's still here, people still live in their rotting structures, their hybrid geodesic domes, though all of the original members are long gone and it can hardly be called a commune, though I have heard more recent residents refer to it simply as the Land. And when I think about the drift, how one community gives way to another, grafting what wisdom it can from its past experiences before kind of dissolving itself, it speaks to something I think I've held fast to since I started this inquiry, which is that the permanence of a community or an experiment is not the point. The attempt to live in ways beyond the dominant culture's destructive influence, to live in community, is more like a spirit that works through us and not the spoils of any particular individual's or group's excellent idea, or ingenuity, or moral character, or goodness, or hard work. This makes me sound a little bit Calvinist. And— I'm already backtracking—this declaration I just made ignores the existence of the communities that *have* lasted, or fought to last, like Twin Oaks for fifty years, Bruderhof for a hundred years, and the Camphill communities for nearly one hundred as well.

    M. C. Richards did eventually leave Gate Hill permanently for that Camphill community in Pennsylvania she had tested out, and she lived there until she died.

    It's funny how much Richards's short reflection has stayed with me—a ten-page essay, handed to me on a whim. On the surface, especially compared to the other communities I've written about, her description of Gate Hill does come closest to the kind of communal life I'm moving toward, but more than that it's the way she *thinks* about communal life that has stuck—because it touches more than just communes. The same propositions could be made of marriages, households, collaborations, classrooms, "that we think of the way we use . . . ourselves, each other, as artistic images. That we solve our problems . . . with the exactness and originality of artists." Creativity and precision, in the context of art making, do not mean permanence and perfection, but presence, attention, constant revision, turning the painting upside down, changing the point of view, being able to follow the new thing that emerges, even if it is so different than what we hoped or thought it would be, and—well—knowing when to walk away, allow something to be finished, even if nothing is ever actually *done*.

What would it mean to turn Richards's proposition into a way of evaluating my own life, my own communities? Are all communities art projects? Are my classrooms an intentional community, where "we approach our meetings with the earnestness and attention we give to other performances" and where we extend ourselves to the world outside our classroom "as if we were extending an image . . . with the same care for quality, tone, freedom and wholeness"? Her proposition offers a way of creating non-hierarchical leadership without waxing about the virtues of "non-hierarchical leadership," a phrase that once used seems to almost always signal the presence of hierarchy, in the person, or institution, or teacher who is saying it.

At the end of the day, with or without a proposition like Richards's, the vectors of influence, in a community or a class, are impossible to pinpoint for very long before the lines blur. No single person's design or sense of power determines the final legacy of a community or a college course, which are both living things. When I think even of the more concrete tools I've given to my students to build their lives, they've made those tools their own to such an extent that their use of them in turn teaches me something I couldn't have taught myself, and anyway those tools were given to me by someone else long before, who couldn't have told me how it would all turn out, even if she'd wanted to, even if she knew.

utopianotes
the Sou'wester

The Sou'wester Lodge sits on a tract of land a quarter mile from the vast, tire-marked beaches of the Washington peninsula. Its flat, grassy grounds are populated by evergreens, guest cottages, and a dozen vintage travel trailers—the accommodations of my earliest and most enduring childhood vacation memories. Each trailer has a clever name and corresponding broadside mural: "The African Queen" features Humphrey Bogart's riverboat; "The Disoriented Express," a sixties-trip railway. My favorite was "The Potato Bug," a twelve-foot Airstream with a built-in bed at one end and a tartan sofa on the other, complete with kitchenette. The trailers have been stationary since Len and Miriam Atkins, South African Jewish émigrés, then recently retired, visited the peninsula in the early 1980s, ending up, unwittingly, with a deed.

My mother met the Atkinses when my older brother was still a baby. I imagine her twenty-nine years old, wearing black stirrup leggings and a Patagonia windbreaker, drinking tea in their cluttered kitchen and planning her first show. The Atkinses, once therapists and first-generation kibbutzniks in Israel, had intended to turn the Sou'wester into a treatment center. Instead, they ended up as innkeepers who hosted cultural events in their living room. My mother, a classical flutist, started putting together performances for the public of Seaview, Washington, in exchange for free lodging.

The Atkinses had thick, high-pitched accents and always seemed very old to me, though spry. I recall Len introducing my mother's performances in what looked like a nightshirt, his long white hair and beard radiating around his head. He'd give twenty-minute preambles, and when my mother played barefoot once, he announced to the audience that next time "she'll be playing in the nude." My mother and my stepfather were married on the grounds, my sister was born, and soon it was this new family of five in the old "Tramp Tower." Eventually, we upgraded to "The Imperial Spartan," furnished with bunks and a full bed. Len installed a small TV and some-times loaned us kids *Indiana Jones and the Last Crusade* on VHS.

The beach lies just over the dunes, which are always under the threat of commercial development and whose conservation efforts the Atkinses frequently saw to with the proceeds of my mother's concerts. During the day we'd go to town, visit Marsh's Free Museum, admire Jake the Alligator Man's mummy. Or the go-cart track, the horse stalls, a tiny amusement park that featured the Octopus. At night, it was 42nd Street Café, where my mother sat placid and quiet among the seated racket of her three children, over deep-fried fish and strawberry rhubarb pie.

My brother, sister, and I had all been children there, each of us so far apart in age and experience that our memories, of all the joys and miseries of our family, varied accordingly. Vacations are like that. Each party recalls them with such particular distortion, relying on photographs and years of pleading silently in a gathering of people that your spouse or child or whom-ever won't say how the whole thing went wrong one way or another, but will instead remember the sunny day on the seashore, the horse rides, the *Mad Libs*, until you believe the stories yourself.

When Len was diagnosed with Alzheimer's, they announced that they'd be putting the lodge up for sale. The trailers had always been musty, but they'd grown so beyond endearment. The koi pond was black with scum. The whole place seemed to be disintegrating into the sea, and all my memories started to be obscured along with it, though the lodge would eventually see its revival as an artist residency. I haven't been back since the Atkinses sold it.

LIVING

You think you're on the hero's journey, but you're not really. No one earns a life. Nothing is ever won. Did you think you were an exception? There's a weird point in the making of this book where I, the narrator, start to lose the thread, where the book becomes self-conscious because the story I am writing and the story I am living converge, and it is at that moment that—rather than feeling a surge of clarity or certainty or purpose—the future, its goals and possibilities, become less clear than ever.

The Mutual Aid Society began as a half-joking moniker we were giving to the idea of our future life and home, which did not yet exist. I started using the moniker as a label for the group text threads with Sweeney, Alyssa, Zach, and Pareesa: during the spring our friendship with them began, Sweeney and I were reading through our respective book stacks the way that Lady and the Tramp unknowingly slurped that final spaghetti string until their noses touched. Without realizing it, we both read Peter Kropotkin's 1901 anarchist biology treatise *Mutual Aid: A Factor of Evolution* in the same week. Sweeney had found his way to it from some Dark Ages commentary, and I had found my way to it from *Communal Luxury* by Kristin Ross, a book about the Paris Commune, and how what is commonly understood as the Commune's "failure" actually gave birth to another less-documented century of radical discourse and action in western Europe, which largely galvanized around Kropotkin's *Mutual Aid*, a collection of scientific essays on evolutionary biology as a process of fundamentally symbiotic and mutually beneficial relationships between all living organisms. (Kropotkin was the less popular of Darwin's two star protégés. His rival peer, Thomas Huxley, popularized the term "survival of the fittest" and got us into that bullshit.)

We knew where we wanted to be, finally—the finicky questions of perfect proximities to work, Dan, city, friends having been resolved or rather dissolved by Delaware County. We had some people we wanted to be around, and though no one was in alignment around a single plan of action, there was enough energy and will present that, we figured, if we just went ahead and bought some land and a house, over time, something would form.

Around this time, I read Amanda Kolson Hurley's *Radical Suburbs: Experimental Living on the Fringes of American Cities*, and found myself particularly interested in her chapter on Stelton, an anarchist community in what was then kind of countryside New Jersey in the 1910s. They existed on one hundred forty acres of agriculturally zoned fallow scrubland outside of New Brunswick, between a suite of shacks and a couple of shared buildings. The residents of Stelton were all politically active radicals, but their aims for migrating outside of New York City for a more cooperative life had to do with having a higher quality of life, a lower overhead, and a more robust education for their kids, through an independent school they created and put at the community's central raison d'être. They were all devotees of Kropotkin's work, contemporary at the time. They created a formal association through which they could cooperatively purchase the land for $100 an acre, upping the cost per acre to $150 for buyers so that the surplus covered the costs of shared goods, like the school and utilities. And, as anarchist as they were, they still had to go to work, so they bought a bright red bus and painted the words "Stelton Cooperative Bus Ass'n" on the side, and it shuttled them in to Manhattan factories during the weekdays. In *Radical Suburbs*, Hurley frames Stelton—like all the communities she profiles—as a proto-suburban development, even a hopeful revisioning of what a suburb could be and perhaps, in the twenty-first century, are currently, as they become rapidly more diverse, pluralistic, and affordable than the cities to which they owe their income. I loved reading about Stelton; I shuddered at my identification with Stelton as a suburb, because I'd be goddamned if I'm a suburbanite, if this whole journey had just led me to a suburban existence simply decorated with radical accessories. But what would we be other than suburban, if what chiefly defines suburban life is its ultimate economic reliance on the city from which it has removed itself in favor of the pleasures of pastoral life?

The further away we moved, geographically, from New Day Church, the more involved we became in the life of that community—and yet the more heightened the obvious paradoxes of distance became, too. Who were we, two white people, to think we could somehow be a robust and meaningful part of the struggle for liberation in the northwest Bronx, when we were so clearly apart from it, complicit, and able and desiring to leave? But also, what kinds of things might we all miss out on if we assumed those things were incommensurate, incommunicable, intractably opposed? Was there an opportunity to build coalitions, lines of transit and exchange, between the urban and the rural? During this time, Sweeney helped start the Mutual Aid Ministry in the church; I became a part of a base-building team. We lived in the country and drove down the beautiful summer roads almost every Sunday, three hours, listening to the news, to the Bronx for church, to see friends, to hang out with Dan. Dan had, reluctantly at first, started coming with us to services in the cafeteria of Mount St. Ursula, and soon everyone in that cafeteria on Sunday mornings knew him by name, hugging him, greeting him, celebrating his arrival like a prodigal son or a legend, women flirting with him. There was a major pastoral transition, where the pastors that had always helmed the church left and a yearlong process helped us determine his replacement—a twenty-five-year-old queer Black woman from just outside of Columbus, Georgia, who was almost finished with her MDiv at Union Theological Seminary. She became our pastor. She was prophetic. She gathered the church around Black liberation as the central tenet of our theology, which, like any prophecy, was not about introducing something new, but revealing what had been latent all along. Dan, at best, was skeptical of everything New Day stood for. *What's wrong with empire? Empire's great!* He'd sometimes heckle Tabatha from the back of the room, this Baby Boomer white man in a wheelchair, when she'd preach about white supremacy: "That's prejudiced!" Sweeney and I would turn purple. Tabatha would keep preaching. And Dan would still come with us the following Sunday, listening, occasionally grumbling, hugging, flirting, being seen and known, what else is church for? When, a few months later, he entered into a long period of endlessly repeating hospitalizations, Tabatha visited his bedside—Fox News blaring—over and over again, to talk with him, to pray with him, to laugh with him. After that, Sweeney fell in love with another woman, which in and of itself was not a bad thing—perhaps a beautiful thing, as I had been thinking for so many years in the abstract. But then everything took such a strange turn.

I cracked open my utopianotes notebook and read through my scratchings of the last two years, and then I scratched some more:

> It's weird—the prophetic undertones of those summer 2018 journal entries, and the total absence of anticipating the fallout of indiscriminate erotic desire. It's funny cuz I'm not sure what I'm so upset about right now . . . the longing for comfort, love, and attention. All of it is maybe just a cipher for other stuff I don't want to think about, one train covering another.

On the first weekend of October 2019, we went on our first and last appointment with a real estate agent in Delaware County: we looked at four properties for sale in one afternoon, and made an offer on one the next day: a five-bedroom 1860s farmhouse on sixty-four acres of hardwood forest and fallow dairy pasture and apple orchards, with an underground spring that fed two ponds and a cistern in the house's cellar that pumped the water into the house for residential use. There was also a two-story garage with the framing for an apartment. No zoning laws. And all the furniture in the house—a bed in every room. The house had been lovingly and expertly cared for as a second home of a retired Ford engineer and his wife for the last twenty-one years, including a new tin roof, paint, and a poured concrete basement. Two hundred eighty-two thousand dollars.

My mother had happened to arrive for a visit the day we headed out with the broker, so she came along. That night, my mom, Sweeney, and I sat at the bar at the Bull & Garland pub and started drawing our future on a napkin in the form of a map. On the back of our bar receipt, we crunched numbers.

The next morning, we got up early and headed over to the property to walk around it by ourselves. The sixty-four acres followed an odd hourglass shape, a mile long and a third of a mile wide, with a single mottled logging road running from one end to the other. It was a kind of wild meadow and forest land, left to do its own thing for what looked like about fifty years, based on the size of most of the trees—maples, ashes, aspens—flanked by cleared commercial hay fields on either side, belonging to other people. When we'd walked through the house with the owner the day before, he'd gestured to the land, saying, "My wife and I always saw ourselves as stewards of a kind of land preserve. We found, basically, that if you treat the land well, it'll be really sweet to you in return." So my mom, Sweeney, and I walked through the apple orchards, along the fields of goldenrod and blackberries, over creeks, through scrub brush, and into the forest, up a fern and log-strewn hill, and found ourselves at a ridge. The ridge looked out over the sprawling valley below and the rolling blue of the multi-layered Catskill foothills. The view really did something to me in that moment, as it burst open in front of us on the other side of the tree line and the rock wall property line: this endless, undulating view of the leafy hills and peaks turning to fall. We stayed there for a long time. "I'll build a writing tower here," I joked, "My own corner, looking out at this view."

My mother stood next to me, and laughed. "It's in your genes," she said.

For a moment, I thought she meant this in reference to herself—her desire for and deep appreciation of "views"—*Such a beautiful view* is often the first thing she'll say from within a house, or a hill, or a walk. It is the first thing I say, too. I privately, in that moment, thought of the email she sent me on my twenty-fifth birthday while I was living in Wyoming, which really stuck with me over the years:

> Can't believe it was 25 years ago, on a lovely Labor Day in NYC when you entered the world. I was in a hospital room with the most beautiful view of the "village" (rooftops, water towers, blue skies . . .) . . . and beside me was this beautiful bundle of baby girlie!

But what she meant, standing at this ridge and joking about my writing tower, I realized a moment later, was her father, my grandfather—Grandpa George, who rode his bicycle around every evening after classes at University of Washington, in 1956, looking for houses for sale in the area, while his wife was holed up on a houseboat on Lake Washington pregnant with her second child, antsy to get the fuck off that leaky death trap. But George was thorough, slow-going; he needed to find, in his own words, "the house with the best view." Finally, he found 7043, a sparkling, tidy white bungalow at the apex of the incline of the Ravenna neighborhood, the tallest point of the highest neighborhood. He went upstairs without a real estate agent, just knocked on the door—maybe the seller was moved and beguiled by his certainty—and he looked out the back windows of the second floor, and could see all the way out over the reservoir, all the way to the Olympics on that clear blue day. He went to the windows facing out the front of the house on the second floor: my God, there he could see all the way to the Cascades, going east, clear down over the University District and downtown, and straight out toward Mount Rainier, which on that evening was as clear and looming as an old spirit, a god. He already knew then he would build a tower on top of the house, and after he bought it and they moved in, he did.

That's what my mom meant, as we stood there looking at our new view. But it must go further back than this. It's maybe a little too obvious now, too on-the-nose, even—the way that apprehending and even idolizing a view relates to imperialism, manifest destiny, power, conquest. Embedded in the act of beholding the view, if you're a man, if you're white, is the belief that all you can see before you is yours, even if just to marvel at and enjoy. And yet, what a spectacular view it was, and deserving of awe. We stood there regarding the receding blues of those ancient hills, imagining our beautiful future, which was also our present, and neither were we free from a history of perspective riddled with evil, my ancestors of pillage and plunder.

Sweeney and I bought the house, the compound, really, and turned it immediately into a residency, a guest house, a misfit multi-use space, and spent a total of seven nights alone together over the course of the next seven months. All winter, it served as a clearinghouse of the American left, both its spiritual and secular factions crossing paths, our New Day world and art school world finally meeting each other, talking, staying up late.

That we had, like many utopians before us, bought a "ready-made" compound was not lost on me: an autonomous fresh water source; the old farmhouse itself retrofitted like a bed-and-breakfast, with a separate unit; a two-story garage poised to be turned into additional housing; enough furniture to outfit all five bedrooms with a bed, a mattress, a dresser, a desk, and a chair; a riding lawn mower; pots and pans; power tools; even lightbulbs, enough cleaning supplies, and hand soap to last a lifetime; three books about tarot and a giant groovy 1970s zodiac medallion, golden plastic, hanging above the kitchen table.

One of our new neighbors, who'd lived next door for fifty years, told us the entire and complete history of our house's human occupancy: the original family who had built the house and parceled out the land, the Pecks, had descendants living there continuously until the 1960s; after the last one died, a man bought the house and leased it to his son, who brought all of his friends up from the city and turned it into a hippie commune. "They were naked all the time," he said, "even when they answered the door for the postman, or when I hired them occasionally to hay for me." The naked hippie commune lasted ten years. Then, two couples bought it together: a gay couple, both stained glass artists, and a straight couple, both schoolteachers or maybe real estate agents. The straight couple had two children, and all six of them lived here for twenty years. Then the couple we bought it from took over. And now us.

Sweeney and I continued this experiment of each of us having one other lover, one of whom was shared, and we hit roadblocks. Sweeney quit drinking for a month, and then quit quitting. The winter lasted for six freezing, snowy months. Dan was in and out of the hospital, a pileup that became toxic. We shuttled ourselves back and forth to the city, to tend to him, to teach. I had spent years being critical of the purpose and structure of "the family life" under capitalism, which leads to privatization and atomization, and makes any kind of meaningful communal life impossible to sustain. The surety of my own critique made me arrogant, maybe lazy, maybe just laissez faire and devil-may-care. But now I had questions. We were not Harmonists or Shakers or Oneidans or Peace Mission Movement celibates; we were people who lived a life where relationships were in fact differentiated. A brother is not a mother is not a friend is not a lover, and—it turned out—a marriage still does require a distinct kind of care and attention, if it is to remain a marriage, if you'd like it to, if you still believe—having pushed the edges—that it matters in a particular way. There's a limit to every critique. There's a limit to everything.

Even though I had so much, I found myself feeling a great deal of need. I was hoarding tender-love-and-care. I hadn't even known what it looked like before. Having my hair or arm stroked. Having my reality affirmed—the less it feels affirmed, the crazier I feel, the more relentless I become seeking its affirmation. I wish I understood why. "Can't you touch yourself that way?" was the question Chanelle asked me about Gabriel when I visited her in Raleigh, but it's the same question therapy and other healing modalities ask me to figure out getting over the wounds I feel from my childhood, and I guess over time it has worked. What is it I am looking for from Sweeney? I see him giving it to others: Comfort. Affirmation. Presence. Attention. I found myself stewing. If you have three hours a day to sit in the woods looking for a turkey that never comes, and three hours a day to give to your father, and three hours a day to give to your girlfriend, and three hours a day to drink, could you devote a half hour a day to making sure there is not a lake of food and dishes in the sink, sweep the living room floor, wipe up the piss from under the toilet bowl, stroke my head, coo in my ear, tell me everything will be OK, assure me that you are in my corner? I knew these thoughts were unfair given the daily strain of his caretaking duties, but it makes me feel crazy coming home year after year to the image of someone doing exactly what they'd like to be doing, reading and writing in a small room, talking about freedom, while I still felt oppressed by work and his self-righteousness, driving back and forth to the city. I could make a different choice. The hot volcanic feeling was rising up through my stomach, through my throat, and I knew that if the temperature rose, I wouldn't be able to snuff it out. When I feed the fire, the fire grows.

•

During the never-ending winter, I found a spotted salamander on the cellar stairs—a species defined by mutual aid in its biological interrelations. I walked into and out of the basement to move things around, put away tools, straighten the leftover pipes and window glass inserts left over from the previous owner. On my third trip down the cellar stairs, I spotted a brown salamander with bright neon yellow spots. It looked fake, ornamental almost, against the browns and grays of that late winter. Later, a friend told me that it was a particularly remarkable kind of yellow-spotted salamander, which grows its own algae inside of its eggs, rendering it a phosphorescent green. I watched the neon egg sacs begin to appear at the edges of the pond, producing a rich photosynthesis for the nearby plants, nutrients produced symbiotically for the shared benefit of all the pond's organisms. I googled the salamander, clicked on only one link, an article in *Nautilus*. The ecological relationship that the yellow-spotted salamander models, unlike the "red in tooth and claw" survival of the fittest, is one of "cooperation, of mutual benefits, of the beautiful ways evolution has found to sustain life in alliance."

utopianotes
The Mutual Aid Society

date: Dec 10, 2019, 11:15 PM
subject: Welcome to the Mutual Aid Society

Dear friends,

We recently bought a huge farm house on sixty-four acres of meadow and hardwood forest in Delaware county in the western Catskills. On the one hand, this email is a general invitation to please visit whenever! On the other hand, we are also introducing our beta-residency program, for folks who want to be here working on a project for a longer period of time.

We bought this compound (now, the Mutual Aid Society), as many of you know, so that it could be used and shared by as many people and for as many projects as possible over the course of its lifetime. In the not-too-distant future, we genuinely hope and expect to turn the house and the property into a self-sustaining residency program for organizers/artists/scholars, as well as dedicate pieces of the land for friends and loved ones to build homes and studios on as they wish, or host retreats or workshops, all of it. We are 100% committed to an open-ended, cooperative vision of what kinds of things could happen here.

Beta-residency program:

In the meantime, we are trying to encourage as many people we know (or through referral) as possible to come up for two- to four-week periods (or longer)—for resting, working on projects, dreaming of the future.

The house is 3,700 sq. ft. It has four (large) bedrooms upstairs, and then a separate wing on the first floor with a fifth bedroom where we sleep. The four upstairs bedrooms—all big enough to double as studios/offices—have beds, desks, closets, and dressers. We've dedicated this entire floor to other people's use. The four bedrooms share two full bathrooms. By spring, we hope to have additional studio spaces elsewhere on the property (including in the lofted garage, which we just need to insulate). Accessibility note: you do have to climb a small set of stairs into the first floor of the house, and a larger flight of stairs to the second floor.

Friends are already beginning to plan their long-term/residency stays with us. We're really excited about this, and it's exactly what we wanted. But, until we figure out a way to support this land and space through grants, membership, collaborators, or whatever else, the practical reality is that we need financial contributions from our beta-residents. We're using this period to evaluate what the needs of residents are, and how much it will cost to house them (until we develop sustainable modes of support), so—

Here is what we are asking:

—for anyone who is coming just to hang out and visit for a weekend or whatever, you are always welcome to come up free any time (even if we're not here; just let us know you're coming)

—for anyone who wants to come here for a residency, retreat, or longer-term stay (about a week or more), we do want to ask for contributions to keeping the place financially sustainable

—as we can estimate, so far, it costs us about $150 a week (or $400 a month) to maintain each occupied room, with heat, electric, mortgage, taxes, cleaning, food, water, and so on. (When other people aren't here, for instance, we don't even have to run heat on the top floor.) We stand to make no profit from this arrangement whatsoever; we're just trying to keep this residency model alive and afloat until we secure other forms of support.

—the money would also include access to whatever food and drink is in the house; as well as occasional family-style meals, etc., when they happen. You would never be obligated to join if you didn't want to, but you'd always be welcome. For any special/additional food or provisions you may want, we can grab them for you from town at cost, or you can use one of our cars to go procure whatever you need.

—if you don't have the money to be a resident, don't worry about it; offer what you can or even come up for free; we really mean that

Other things to know:

—The Mutual Aid Society lives five minutes from the town of Stamford, NY (grocery store, hardware store, thrift store, Walgreens, etc.), as well as Hobart (five book stores & a lovely pub/restaurant called the Bull & Garland) and Delhi (natural foods store, bigger shops, SUNY)

—There are other artists and friends who live in the area, as well as a collective arts space in Bushel where we can plan or attend programming, and other things

—You can get to us by car (2.5 hrs from the Bronx; 3.5 hrs from Brooklyn), Trailways bus (to Delhi), or Amtrak (to Hudson)

—We have two cars between us, and can facilitate transit, food/materials acquisition as needed, or loan our cars for local use

😎 LET US KNOW IF YOU'RE INTERESTED 🕷

In love & solidarity,
Adrian and Sweeney

THE BEGINNING AND
THE END

There is a famous photograph of Jimmy Carter during his 1977 visit to the South Bronx, walking through the rubble of Charlotte Street. It's a black-and-white print, several figures silhouetted against an urban desert of brick and ash. A few apartment buildings emerge in the background against a bright plain sky. Carter looks mystified. During the two-block tour, he reportedly instructs one of his housing staffers to "see which areas can still be salvaged." Then he squints into the textureless landscape before him. "Maybe we can create a recreation area and turn it around." The *Times* reporter describes the area as looking like the "result of wartime bombing," ushering in language that will shape public discourse about the Bronx for the next three decades.

From this point on, Charlotte Street becomes visual political rhetoric. In 1980, Ronald Reagan campaigns at Charlotte Street, using it as evidence of Carter's failed promises. He stands on the same pile of trash, mobbed by protesters. One woman asks what he's going to do for them, and a visibly flustered Reagan screeches over the jeers, "I'm trying to tell ya! I can't do a damn thing for you if I don't get elected!" Four years later, Jesse Jackson visits Charlotte Street during his bid for the Democratic nomination. He walks down through the ruins, too, and stays the night in a housing project nearby. A decade passes. The rhetoric remains the same: Bombed-out. War-zone. Etc. But when Bill Clinton visits Charlotte Street in 1997, he finds himself, instead, in Charlotte Gardens.

Between Jackson's and Clinton's visits, something extraordinary has happened. Unlike the countless times the word "gardens" has been used to name public housing that all but warehouses and segregates the urban poor, this is exactly what it sounds like. In Clinton's Charlotte Street photo, he stands by a sidewalk lined with trees and grass. It's fall. You can tell because a small dogwood off to the side is changing colors. Behind him is a beige, sub-urban-looking split-ranch house with a front lawn and a tidy white fence.

•

The legend is that at a 1977 Yankees game, the announcer said, "Well, ladies and gentlemen—the Bronx is burning," and though there is no record of this, it is scorched in civic memory as the moment when the private crisis of the Bronx became public. Slumlords were hiring gang members to torch their depleted properties. And gangs controlled most borough resources. The destruction was swift and unyielding. City workers were abandoning firehouses and police precincts. Trash collection ceased. And a lot of people—a lot—still lived there. There were 1.2 million Bronx residents in 1977.

The Bronx had been under siege since the 1950s, when the Cross-Bronx Expressway was blasted through the borough by Robert Moses, tearing up housing and neighborhoods, displacing entire communities. Then middleclass white flight followed by Nixon slashing urban renewal funds in the 1960s, part of the systemic racism and classism that engendered a total abandonment of those who were still in the Bronx, leaving the poor to carry on in the divested borough.

What often gets left out of the master narrative of late-century Bronx, though, is that by the early seventies, there were already restoration plans in place, mobilized almost entirely by local, grassroots operations. Among the prominent organizers was Genevieve Brooks, who would later become the first female deputy borough president of the Bronx. Early on, Brooks helped to secure the return of sanitation services, as well as neighborhood trash clean-ups, and she helped create a daycare under community control that still exists today. When the fires came, she quickly grew weary of "sleeping with her shoes by her bed" lest she had to flee flames in the middle of the night. So in a gesture that smacks of a benevolent version of *The Warriors*, Brooks started a coalition of community groups called the Mid-Bronx Desperadoes.

In an interview for the PBS series *Makers*, Brooks says, "When funders would come in, and they said 'How are you going to do this? Everything around here's abandoned,' I'd say, 'We're going to do it house by house, block by block, building by building.'" The MBD helped allocate city funds to restore apartment buildings, secure rent subsidies and rent-controlled leases, buy up abandoned parks for one dollar a pop, on and on. But their flagship project—the most visible in part because it was the most surreal—was Charlotte Gardens.

In 1983, MBD presented a plan to build eighty-nine freestanding, single-family houses along the decimated corridor of Charlotte Street. The houses were going to have yards, driveways, fences, back decks. Brooks says, "The powers that be, the planners—everybody was against it. They said it wasn't going to work because it's in the South Bronx and it would be destroyed." And yet the city went forward anyway.

The houses were built at about $110,000 each and sold for between $50,000 and $59,000, subsidized by federal funds, as well as the city and private foundations. According to CNN, 90 percent of the houses were sold to low-income Bronx residents—and in some cases, homeowners were able to pay off their mortgages in under fifteen years. Today, these properties are worth upwards of $500,000. In an unprecedented sweep, there were suddenly eighty-nine families who had the kind of capital and equity that had been made so freely available to the white middle class following World War II, but which had been, implicitly and explicitly, denied them till now.

By 1994, all of the houses had been built and sold, and today—in the middle of the South Bronx—you will find a small suburban-style neighborhood along Charlotte Street.

My father is in town and we go to the Museum of the City of New York. The first thing we see upon entering is an old photograph that's been blown up to the size of a wall—and the photo is of a wall in Harlem, flypapered with a Fight Racial and Religious Hate campaign from the Institute for American Democracy. On it, a cartoon freckled white boy is crying. "I am SO an American," he says, to which a disembodied word bubble responds, "You bet, sonny . . . no matter what your race or religion." Below the crying white boy, playing jump rope on that Harlem street, are four real-life Black girls in braids and pinafores, smiling and laughing at the camera.

It is such a bizarre juxtaposition, I almost miss the punchline. What is going on here? Does the boy feel guilty? "No," my dad has to clarify, when we scroll through the picture he snapped on his phone. "He's crying because he feels like he's been persecuted." He laughs. "It makes no sense! This is, like, Madison Avenue's best attempt to make white people think about tolerance in the 1950s."

Upstairs, there is an exhibit about activism in New York over the ages. I listen to a young tour guide gesture to the Civil Rights corner. "And you know, while all of this action around police brutality was going on, at the same time, there were things like *this*," she says, pointing to a display titled Conservative Activism, where hangs a 1960s bumper sticker with bubble letters: CELEBRATE OUR POLICE HEROES! No one, not even her, reacts to the shadowy resonance in our present—they are silent. I move on. On the top floor, I stop at Mel Rosenthal's exhibit from his book *In the South Bronx of America*: big gelatin prints of that landscape in the late seventies, collapsed buildings with blacked-out windows, hunks of concrete piled up in an alley, boulevards devoid of people, there are those. But there are also, mostly, portraits. A teenage girl striking a pose outside her building, three men playing cards, a grinning mother and daughter clasped together beside a pile of rubble.

Rosenthal would let the subjects decide which shots they liked best, and those were the ones he'd print. He was sort of known for being ambivalent about the "kind of story" he was going to be telling about the South Bronx. Was he trying to subvert people's expectations like a good liberal or was he reinforcing the master narrative of the white gaze of "the Bronx is a warzone/these poor people/save the children" kind of story? He peers at us from one frame, standing cavalierly, hands in pockets, in his childhood bedroom which appears to have been abandoned, collapsed. He'd grown up there when that block was a mostly working-class Jewish neighborhood.

Afterward my father and I take the 2 train to 174th Street and walk to Charlotte Gardens.

The houses are nearly uniform in their make, ranch and split-ranch houses, taupe and yellow and sometimes pink or green. They are pristine, really, power washed, even. They have gardens, painted fences, fruit trees, boat trailers. Today, Charlotte Gardens still looks like a new neighborhood, preserved, and the streets are lined with cars.

But, man—it's quiet, like a suburban street straight out of the eastern reaches of Queens. Boston Road and Southern Boulevard are just out of sight and earshot, but this area seems completely sealed off from the Bronx outside of it. The sidewalks are empty of people except for one guy washing his car and one old woman smoking a cigarette in a folding chair on her front lawn who smiles at us as we walk by.

We zigzag through the three blocks, silent, and then back up Charlotte Street all the way to the edge of Crotona Park, where the Bronx resumes its cacophony of traffic and prewar apartment buildings and a staggering Art Deco junior high. My father says, "It's like they took a strong existing social fabric and replaced it with a much weaker one." The shadow side of the suburban development. There is this other side to it, the American dream: debt, upward mobility, isolation.

And now the Bronx has narratives like *The Get Down*, that Netflix series from director Baz Luhrmann, which narrates a technicolor story of the rise of hip-hop, which Emily Nussbaum describes as a "mythological story of disco and the origins of hip-hop, filmed through shifting lenses of camp, blaxploitation, and kung fu." There is a young hero, who's going to bring hip-hop to the fore, a sort of mystical graffiti artist who portends Basquiat. Charlotte Street is mentioned approximately twenty times within the first half of the pilot; it is where the core group has a run-in with the Savage Warlords, and where the mystic artist leaves his tag, and where the kickback-driven councilman lays his claim. For the whole scene there is a building on fire in the background.

The Get Down is complicated. It heroizes the Bronx-in-crisis in a way that whitewashes, but it is also, perhaps, a generous and generative retelling that opens up new narratives. The narrative: The Bronx is cool, the Bronx is fun, the Bronx had and has a rich social fabric we should envy, those times were hard, but they were fun, too. The old narrative: This place is bad, this place is troubled, this place is a failure, this is a place to get out of. But what becomes tricky is the old narrative was used by civilians and government to abandon the place and the people in it; the new narrative will be used by those same civilians and government to push people out.

When I think about Charlotte Gardens, I think about the weirdness of its name—how the Judeo-Christian eschatology is that creation begins in a garden and ends in a city. But what about a suburban development called a "garden" plunked down in the middle of a city? The awkward collision of these things seems far from utopian, and yet it doesn't seem bad exactly. Just confusing. What are we supposed to want? What is the garden—a place where things grow, and blossom, fruit, stretch, wilt, die, and dissolve into a pasty brownish mash for the long cold months, only to grow up again when summer comes?

In January 2020, a month after we bought the Mutual Aid Society, I was teaching in Brooklyn and noticed that Interference Archive—a Brooklyn-based independent archive of radical history—hosting an exhibition called Building for Us. The exhibition examined the emergence of the Urban Homesteading Assistance Board in New York City in the 1970s, and all of the homesteading and cooperative sweat equity actions that had led to its existence, including but not limited to all of the groups I've addressed already. UHAB still exists, but barely. Its purpose is confused by the fact that the city that has since grown around it is a veritable monument to neoliberalism. Of course, there are still many American cities that an agency like UHAB could address today, cities who still today see levels of divestment and stratification and abandonment that far outstrip New York in the seventies, but for modern-day New York City, UHAB is more like an artifact than an action.

I ordered the pamphlet Interference Archive made for the exhibition, a thin blue tome full of reprinted photos, news articles, building plans, receipts issued to the city, organizing materials for the creation of limited equity cooperatives and the "self-help housing movement," a name that makes me cringe, considering that the housing devastation being addressed was not the fault of those doing the work, not a matter of "self-help." Vintage Images on UHAB literature show the Harlem Renigades in their matching leather vests, with letters and studs affixed to the back, toiling away at construction sites. They're beautiful images. I have this emotional experience looking at them, which I have all the time, where I am simultaneously aware that I am observing something totally miraculous and holy, and that the thing I am marveling at it is already over, already crushed, already "failed."

The accompanying pamphlet addresses the past as well as the present moment, "the recurrent public interest in exploring cooperative ownership models, particularly as a tool for addressing the current housing affordability crisis." The twenty-first-century crisis has emerged for different reasons, in a way—I guess the ouroboros of it all is that, well: I see, in the pamphlet, this twenty-three-year-old member of the Harlem Renigades quoted in the *Daily News* in 1975, while he and his friends are in the middle of restoring a twenty-three-unit building on 119th Street, from spackle to electrical. The article says, "They have operated so efficiently . . . that they will probably not need about $80,000 of their original $360,000 loan and will return the money to the city." Return the money to the city? Why, I think, for god-sake why would they ever give that money back to the city, for anything? The tone of the article feels almost threatening, like, *You're gonna give that surplus cash back, and you're gonna be happy about it.* That this community organization did something for $80,000 under budget is already unheard of in New York City municipal history, and that the consequence is that they have to return the surplus money is the brutal irony, because that money will go straight into the fund that is ultimately going to build the extractive, feudal, corporatized New York City we live in today. Once anyone knows about the movement, the movement will be co-opted for money. The city will invest in utopian rebuilding projects only so long as that will help them attract other monied interests down the line, which themselves will eventually wipe out the vitality of the neighborhoods that were used as bait. There is something then triumphant about the emergence of UHAB in the late seventies, and also immediately already failed because it was going to be used in one way or another to architect the thing the monster wanted it to.

I did not come here to tell a happy story.

utopianotes
New Day Womyn and Femme-of-Center Retreat

There is a womyn and femme-of-center retreat for New Day. Fifteen women gather at my house, the Mutual Aid Society, for a weekend, all hailing from drastically different lives, lines of descent, ancestries, and origins that have somehow conspired for us all to be together this weekend, in this way: young queer women from the Dominican Republic, or the American South by way of the Caribbean; middle-aged straight women who'd grown up in the projects of East Harlem; Black women whose grandparents were part of the Great Migration; white women from Appalachia; an eighty-seven-year-old woman from Barbados, who's called the Bronx her home for decades.

At night, we make bottomless pitchers of sangria and turn on a karaoke machine. Four women—a white woman, two Black women, and a Latina American woman—all gather around the long dining room table to play what ends up being a three-hour game of spades. Slowly, the other women at the retreat start to salsa and sway and sing around the card players, gathering in a buzzing throng on all sides of the table. "I'm singing to the Lord," Pam says, as she makes her bet and plays a queen of diamonds. The singing and the dancing ratchet up, and the game never breaks, but the singing and the dancing don't break either, and for a second it feels like we have created an alternate world, a tableau spinning sovereign in the pitch darkness of the galaxy, where this impossible group of women have gathered together to sing, and the game of cards never ceases, and we belong to each other, jubilantly, wholly, completely, in a way we will outside of that moment never be able to maintain in our daily lives, and if we pause to think it through, the moment might turn to ash as we consider all the complicity and inequality we each carry in us, but which is, drunk and dancing and laying down cards, for a flash, a kind of heaven on earth.

LIVING

Then the global COVID-19 pandemic hit. As the various shelter-in-place orders came down the pipeline, we haphazardly gathered together a veritable ark of friends, who ended up at the Mutual Aid Society for different and temporary reasons, mostly having to do with avoiding what might be several months of isolation: Robert, Jenny, Lina, and Greg. Robert was working as a freelance travel writer for Lonely Planet, and was about to take a two-month trip to South Africa, but got stranded in New York two days before his flight; Jenny had left her job in pharmaceutical compliance law, shaved her head, and had been living out of her car, road-bound, for a year; Greg was on sabbatical from his tenure-track professorship at Georgetown; and Lina was producing and reporting for *This American Life*, alone in her small one-bedroom apartment in Fort Greene, the same apartment I had convalesced from shingles in, feeling hopeless about my and Sweeney's future, exactly three years earlier.

It was our first full year in the Catskills. It snowed heavily off and on until May, well into what I had expected to be spring. The sky was high and gray. Sweeney was sober for two months, and then aggressively unsober. He worked manically to secure our self-sustaining existence as he, more than anyone I knew, intoned the end of the world as we knew it: gathering and chopping wood, building a woodshed, a toolshed, a chicken coop, a garden, from sunup to sundown, out in the still brown, still dead, still snowy fields of the land. He bristled against the household's unwillingness to accept the seriousness of the global fallout he saw on the horizon. We stayed in place. I wasn't moving around all the time, leaping from commitment to commitment. So I watched myself closely in a way I'd never had the time or wherewithal to do before, and I saw myself repeatedly reacting and adjusting to Sweeney's drinking, trying to manage or control it, maintaining a state of hyper-vigilance and self-protection I now realized was consistent with all the literature and living of codependence, that framework developed by the largest anarchist organization in the world—Alcoholics Anonymous. All the cities shut down. People started to die in massive numbers, while we—like the youths in the *Decameron*—holed up in our hideout, did our creative and intellectual work, feeling a mix of nausea and guilt and safety. We developed a sensible schema for cost-sharing things like heat and food, bought chicks and built them a brooder in the corner of my office, in a converted sunroom that looked out onto a small back porch. Sweeney and I felt more remote from each other than ever. We'd go on long blustery walks up County Road 30, trying to articulate where it was exactly we got off course, but could never agree, and so the resentment would calcify. We were road-weary strangers to each other once again. He didn't know how to relate to me—in part because he didn't know how to relate to himself, and I, as usual, was stuck in the past, trying to figure out how to fix the present. I had lost the thread.

During quarantine, Sweeney and I started doing couples therapy again, this time on Zoom, and things did start to change a little bit—even as the snow appeared fresh every morning on the struggling daffodils. Our walks, at moments, started to feel a bit like they used to, like we were expedition partners lighting out for new territory, side by side, but that territory was the saddle curve of County Road 30, back and forth, or deeper into the back end of the land. We started a small nursery of seedlings on the windowsills of each bedroom—and while every day we were free to work on whatever our hearts desired, write, read, paint, eat, watch movies, everything felt adrift and more confusing and boundaryless than ever. What was the endgame? It was everything we'd ever dreamed of, and yet it felt like purgatory at times, however good the food was—and it was good. Greg made dinner for us nearly every single night, and always at eight o'clock, and each day would orbit around that moment, drawing itself to that point with the journey of the sun across the sky. Sweeney would start a fight with someone, which would absorb the table's attention and ire for the duration of the meal, and then we'd gather around the TV to watch *Sex and the City*. It was the best possible situation we could have been in under those circumstances, but the purpose or the intent of having this house and this land at all had become murkier than ever, and meanwhile the death toll rose—thousands and thousands dying across the country every day.

Dan, my father-in-law, got COVID, was hospitalized, and ultimately survived, though we spent those two weeks sitting vigil as though he were going to die at any moment, knowing we wouldn't be able to enter the hospital if he did. After his recovery, he started to slowly deteriorate in other ways. Sweeney would make regular trips down to the Bronx to run errands for him, and sometimes we'd go together, arriving home upstate ashen-faced and exhausted, and constantly feeling like we were awaiting his death.

What does it matter to make something good, if it's available to only a few? We were repeating the same sorts of structures that we'd decried. A suburb. A closed door. A pastoral exit.

Then Breonna Taylor and George Floyd were murdered by the police, and the country rose up in protest. And because so many people didn't have jobs at that moment, people made it their job to sustain the protest against police for as long as it would take. And maybe because so many people, some reluctantly, were finally watching the system they thought just might work reveal itself as the monster it always had been right in front of their eyes, this moment of emergency didn't require that everyone protesting be on the same page, didn't require that everyone have the same impetus and analysis, only the same enemy. The issue became extremely clear: the police are an occupying force explicitly used to control and kill Black and brown people, and that is enough of a reason to stay up all night, and go to jail. So we left the compound for the city, for the protests, and stood at the front lines. We left in shifts, got arrested in shifts, came home in shifts.

There's a trick to all of this. You can't be too sure that you know where you are going, but only ever clearer about where you are, where you have already been. Late that spring, my friend the poet Rachel Levitsky sent me a PDF by the scholar Irvin J. Hunt called "Planned Failure," on Ella Baker and George Schuyler's shaping of the Young Negroes' Cooperative League in the 1930s, which was largely based on a radical assumption that the movement's greatest vitality would be found in its finitude and ability to anticipate its own eventual failure. "To imagine isn't to see a better world; it's to see the world better."

All books are written backward. Do you believe me?

Every single day, I took a long slow walk on the land. For so many months, it was mashed brown dirt, old goldenrod stalks, frozen mud. I started to name the different mini biomes of the sixty-five acres in my mind: A little clearing with five big bluestones sticking out of the ground, that I sat on in the cold mornings, Monument Valley. A creek trickling nearby, eventually bursting with buttery marsh marigolds, even when everything else was still dead, the Erotic Bog. Then, Enchanted Forest at the back of the land, which you had to pass through an aspen tunnel to enter. How colonial, though, all this naming. One day I walked with Greg to the Enchanted Forest to hunt for ramps, and when we got back there, they were everywhere, literally acres and acres of ramps undulating across the forest floor, up the hillsides. We ate ramps in every imaginable form until late May and didn't make even the tiniest dent in the population. We brought out our harvesting knives, cutting the leaves low on the fleshy, oniony stalk, but leaving the bulb. I walked every day, up and down the logging road, tiptoeing out in the meadow. Things started to transform rapidly once the weather warmed. The trees went green and leafy overnight, the hills blew up with color. I walked the road, passing trout lilies, dandelions, cinquefoil, bird's-foot trefoil, thyme, motherwort, St. John's wort, yarrow, boneset, wild mint, blue vervain, lobelia, endless iterations, the bottomless presence of creation. I read Robin Wall Kimmerer's *Braiding Sweetgrass*, a book about the ecology of this part of New York through the lens of a trained biologist and the intimate knowledge of Kimmerer's Indigenous Adirondacks ancestry. In it, she writes, "In the spring I walk across the meadow toward my medicine woods, where the plants give their gifts with unstinting generosity. It is mine not by deed, but by care," and I realize that while I had spent all of these years planning a communal life around various humans—an anthropocentric view of communality—I had not thought about plants at all, or the magnitude of what it meant to move onto a piece of land with other living organisms. The Queen of Pentacles was pulled during a tarot reading with a friend over the phone, a reading concerning my relationship with Sweeney. "Stop asking the same damn question," he said, flipping over the Four of Cups, "that's what this means." Then the Queen of Pentacles emerged. "There is something destiny-like in your relationship to this land—you're becoming the queen. Your stewardship and care of this land will give you everything you'll ever need or want, and anything your people, those you love, will ever need or want. It's like"—he pulled the Ace of Cups—"you don't just want your cup to be filled, you want it to be overflowing. Which some people might think is unreasonable, but so what." I felt pleased to hear this, and humiliated by feeling pleased, all at once. Another white lady in the woods, thinking she has some special relationship to or dominion over the natural world? I read Kimmerer's chapter on naturalization, how so many of the plants in the Catskills and the Adirondacks are colonizers themselves, brought from western Europe, some of which have taken over and choked out native plant life, though there are exceptions, like plantain. To Kimmerer, plantain models a way for invaders to become, if not indigenous to place, then considerately adaptable, naturalized in the deepest sense of the word. Plantain is accommodating and nutritive and fits into small places as a helper. "Perhaps plantain will line the homeward path." Could I ever become naturalized to this place?

At the end of *The Graduate*, Dustin Hoffman and Katharine Ross sit at the back of a municipal bus as they make their escape from her doomed wedding and her borderline mother, aka Mrs. Robinson. Ross is triumphant in her tulle wedding dress; Hoffman is sweaty and laughing. They've done it! Then they grow still, shifting on the bench seat, stop laughing, look ahead, look confused, look like they don't know where they are going at all, in a moment of open silence. Now what? The camera holds on their faces for a long time in silence, with just the grind of the bus wheels. Then "The Sound of Silence" begins. Their looks of lostness never lift. The screen goes black.

I think about this scene all the time. In part because it was how I was feeling with Sweeney, but also because it mirrors a sense I've spent a lot of time talking about in terms of failure and dissolution as hallmarks of utopianism. Changed expectations seem to be an important, if not necessary, part of utopian thought—or, as a friend of mine put it, figuring out how, at the very least, to reckon with dissipated intent, or the possibility that your intent never really counted for much at all. And when I say utopian thought, I guess, by this point, I just mean establishing modes of living that you think are alternatives to the death machine, for however long they last. Though "longevity has its place," few things should ever last very long. In an essay by Keno Evol following the conviction of Derek Chauvin for George Floyd's murder, which itself was immediately preceded by the police murder of Duante Wright, he says, "In organizing circles, one could say—and historians often do—that the history of the left is the history of failed utopias. To be a utopian thinker is to be one interested in the study of failure. The poet often has to say to the historian: There were friendships at that site of failure, at the rebellion that didn't succeed. If you look at the clusters, there was poetry you missed, music you can't seem to hear. Starlight often isn't a part of the historical record."

I think back to Irvin J. Hunt's essay "Planned Failure": What happens "when we suspend the criteria of longevity, along with its metaphors (orderliness, formalization, rationality, institutionalism, and so on)"? That's what Schuyler and Baker were mapping out in their cooperative movement, and some wisdom I've been brought to the edge of now. Maybe that's been my point the whole time, though I didn't know it and couldn't name it. "On the high seas of planned failure, we are not born in order to die, we die in order to begin."

And is that a hopeful thing or a warning? Both, I suppose. It is always both.

The months wore on. Whether I worried over outcomes or not, things just happened: Twice I reached limits around Sweeney's alcoholism. As our lives became increasingly more radical and communal, it forced interior questions that might have otherwise worked themselves out over the course of decades. My grandfather George died while I was harvesting mullein in the Enchanted Forest. My late grandmother Gale was with me in the air watching over the land, but I didn't know it yet. I thought: What is radical about living with an alcoholic patriarch? If we're going to change our world, we have to change ourselves, including the way I relate to the drinking and

to men and to marriage. I didn't know what to do. I had an ectopic preg-
nancy. The doctors blasted me full of methotrexate, a type of chemo, and I
lay in bed and walked the land alone and with the various people gathering
on it and I would say to myself in my head, as I walked, "OK, I'm just living.
I'm just living. I don't know what's going to happen. I'm just *living.*"

We brought Dan up to the Mutual Aid Society a few times, and bar-
becued on the deck and watched the sunset by the side of the pond, while I
made herbal bouillons pounded into jars of sea salt and he told stories about
his least-favorite ex-girlfriends. He'd wake in the morning howling from
the guest bedroom for Sweeney to take him to the toilet, and then he'd return to a kind of tranquility as we situated him on the dock with his morning oatmeal, banana, and cigarette. There were two fires during his visits:
a gasoline fire Sweeney started while drunk; an engine fire while Sweeney
drove Dan back to the Bronx. Things felt fraught, like they were balancing
on a knife's edge, but I couldn't put my finger on it.

Then the COVID commune began to disassemble as people returned
to their lives or started new ones, and a whole new wave of people came
to the Mutual Aid Society: Lisa, who started New Day, all those years ago;
Matthew, an old friend from The Corresponding Society days; my brother-
in-law Daniel, who started a furniture building enterprise; Bridget, Sweeney and Daniel's younger cousin, who was trying to find her way in the
world and develop her body of work as a painter; a couple, Kate and Dan,
artist-writer and philosophy scholar, respectively, whom I'd never met before but who were referred to me through Jennifer Kabat of the Adjunct
Flophouse; Jess and Julie, two clinical therapists from New Day; women
theologians from all over the world that Lisa was bringing along to stay.

The experiment was working. Without the unrelenting external pressures of the previous five years, I was surprised to observe that I was very
undisciplined and irregular in my day-to-day habits. Or at least it seemed
to me that the habits, if left to their own organic evolution, changed frequently, perhaps never becoming habits at all. When it had been just me and
Sweeney in an apartment, caring for Dan and constantly shuttling between
the Bronx and Brooklyn for work, there were perhaps obviously different
daily rituals with which I structured writing and thinking and working and

caretaking. It took a lot of time and energy to orbit around the city for work, to get Dan to appointments, commune with friends, acquire groceries. Now that I lived among a variety of people in the sticks, and all of my teaching had been moved to Zoom and I didn't have to physically be anywhere other than here, I became much more aware of how much alone time I craved, and the different ways I needed to create it, now that sociality was in surplus.

Typically I'd begin the day with a great deal of coffee, and then do morning pages outside if it was warm, or by a window indoors if it was cold. I'd either eat something hearty (eggs, veggies, toast, fruit) or kind of insane (popcorn with milk, a very sweet insubstantial pastry, a cookie). Then I'd write in a frenzied fugue state until the afternoon came in like a weather front and my mind got heavy with it. That writing time in the morning was at least 65 percent just sitting and staring, not typing or scribbling or even reading, so when I say I "wrote" for x number of hours a day, I really just mean that I showed up with the intention and hope that it would all matter in the end, even the staring.

Then I'd eat a midday meal, sometimes alone and sometimes with others, then drink a tea from an experimental apothecary I'd cobbled together from the land (and make enough for the whole house), and wouldn't be able to do intellectual or creative work again until the sun went down, so the afternoon was for teaching, doing administrative work, gathering (or hanging out with) plants in the woods, doing household chores, making calls.

In the late afternoon, I'd have a cup of coffee, sit outside, read a bit, smoke cigarettes. And, if I was working on a particular time-sensitive project, which it seemed I usually was, at sundown, I jumped back into creative work for another couple of hours.

Sundown is for revision, dropping deeper into a specific piece of writing-in-process, and pealing out new writing from a place of reseeing. I can only relate to the work in that way at night. The dark provides a silence, a muting of the world and my context or other responsibilities that allows the writing to come into sharper focus. I can hear it and myself in a way I just can't during daylight. But I found myself doing that less and less those days at the Mutual Aid Society, in part, because I had more free time than I'd ever had in my entire life, and also because I had been living with people in this more communal way, and so, increasingly as the months marched on, there emerged a group rhythm of dinner, talking, sitting by the fire. It had been so many years since I'd approached the night as a time for resting and winding down. In scarcity mode, all free or usable time had been sacred and fiercely fought for.

The experiment was working, but did I feel at home? In this new arrangement, I began to notice that the constant stress of Sweeney's drinking and increasingly reckless behavior kept me on edge. And in this new arrangement so many others found his drinking and behavior intolerable and sometimes violent, and I was faced with how much I had tolerated and enabled for years, and wondered how much my desperation for familial belonging had guided that. I'd drive to the farm stand to pick up eggs, milk, and cheese, drop my cash in the can.

When I panned out on the scene in which I was living, I saw this: pretty much every single day, everyone worked; they wrote books and dissertations; went to meetings and made Excel spreadsheets for their jobs; painted and drew; played guitar and practiced violin; built furniture and chopped wood; chatted on the dock of the pond and went on walks; made plant medicine from wildcrafting and watched *Angels in America*; and then every night we had dinner together. Sometimes we had beer and tea around the bonfire; on special occasions we had parties and turned the garage into a dance floor. Sweeney's drinking was no longer just a spectral presence in my life, but an open problem that most people around him on a daily basis were now reacting to and talking to him about. Other people, not just me, were having very direct conversations with him about how his drinking affected them and the culture of the Mutual Aid Society in general. But things didn't change.

I started to rely on people in a new way, which made questions about would-we/wouldn't-we stay together suddenly less dramatic though still devastating and unimaginable. "*We* can have kids together," Lisa shrugged to me in the kitchen during her first week, as she grabbed a box of crackers from the pantry. It was a joke, but also I suddenly felt free, like I wasn't having to hold the line or the border anymore—I could relax. It was an extraordinary shift for me. And to see the communal experiment in action,

I realized now that holding off, suspending a plan or a decision based on not knowing how, or if, the ideal will pan out—well, then nothing happens. It's true for utopian experiments and for marriages, the latter perhaps a subset of the former. Take an action and the worst-case scenario is you'll have to revise along the way.

I noticed some new things during the months that COVID became less of an immediate threat and we were able to open our doors a bit: for one, the way that the energies shifted when there were a majority of women or femme-of-center people present on-site, versus a majority of men. Basic needs were met more effortlessly, discussions happened more democratically, women actually spoke more in group settings and to one another. New questions merged: Can couples live communally? What gets to grow if the freight of life isn't put on just two people to hold, or to resolve all problems in themselves and their shared lives? And what happens to heterosexuality in a communal context, not so much as sa sexual preference but as a patriarchal social-relational structure aggressively and historically produced by capitalism's squashing of communitarianism? What about the haunted power disparities embedded in the heterosexual arrangement, despite these modern leftists' best intentions? What gets to live and breathe between men and women as comrades and collaborators that otherwise wouldn't? How does care-work shift? The questions started to be about gender, structure, and the tension between freedom, autonomy, and mutual responsibility to one another and the land, which require a constant renegotiation of what those things even mean. We drew no real conclusions. All I had were observations. And what I began to notice was that I was living in a place where the women woke up every morning and asked themselves, "What do I want to do today?" and then whatever the answer was to that question, they did. And I recognized what I was seeing was a historically remarkable event. It was, to say the least, less remarkable to me when the men did that.

I've had so many experiences where the whole of my life seems embedded in every other moment—like if I isolate a moment and read it as one would read runes or tarot cards, I could see everything, the beginning and the end. Some of those moments I can glimpse the completeness of, the arc, others not at all. Robert and I walking early in the pandemic on County

Road 30 talking about how Dan Savage reframes the end of marriage not as failure but as a success for what it was, for however long it lasted. The first night we met Pareesa, everything was already there: utopia, God, Marguerite Young, Anna. Lisa and I in the Webster Café all those years ago talking about this place, a place like this, when the idea of it all seemed utterly impossible, so remote as to be a joke. Impossible things happen all the time. If I listen closely to my own words, to what we are already doing, already saying, to what has *already* happened, I can keep building, or keep walking on that bridge that might end before I reach the other side, and history tells me it will end, but nevertheless to walk. Do not be afraid. Do not give way to evil. The beginning and the end are not so different.

I think often of an email a professor of mine once sent me during graduate school. I'd just finished reading her second book and had loved it, and I wrote her to say as much. She wrote a beautifully detailed response back, a letter I have returned to over and over again, which ends with this thought:

> I loved writing that book. Not that the life I thought I'd won turned out as it might have—one of the tricks of a life, I think. But when I listen seriously to what I had to say, I could have anticipated that. Nothing is ever done.

utopianotes
Annunciation Church

I'm in an old cathedral in Yonkers down the street from Dan's childhood home. It's a gray and rainy New Year's Eve 2020. He passed away just after Christmas. Everyone in the church is dressed in black, masked, and seated a dozen feet apart on cold pews under the long, echoey atrium. No one can talk to each other. A bagpipe player enters through the open doors playing "Amazing Grace." Sweeney is a pallbearer, in a stiff borrowed suit and muddy sneakers. I haven't seen him in a month. He doesn't look at me as he processes down the aisle. I stand in the front row with Lisa, Matthew, and Bridget as "Amazing Grace" gives way to "Danny Boy." My heart is broken. I think of a line near the end of Sweeney's dissertation on Christian grief in the Dark Ages, a quote from G. K. Chesterton's book *Orthodoxy*. "There was some one thing that was too great for God to show us when He walked upon our earth; and I have sometimes fancied that it was His mirth." I picture the face of my amused genderqueer God, the faint lines around Their Mona Lisa smile as They look down at this sorry scene. I share neither blood nor legal ties with anyone standing next to me. Instead, it feels like we are all strangers and pilgrims on a common path. The pallbearers set the coffin in the aisle next to my row with a thud. I say goodbye to Dan. I remember that nothing is ever done.

ACKNOWLEDGMENTS

How funny to attempt a book like this, a book that is in fact about attempt and about hope, and which is also a record of dashed hopes. Needless to say, none of this would have been possible without a) attempt b) hope and c) the blessings ("You can't miss 'em!"). I am especially grateful to Lisa Asedillo, Bridget Carsky, Matthew Daniel, and Cary Hooper, each of whom demonstrated new possibilities of love and care in a very dark winter of our lives, and each of whom saw to the conditions that allowed for this book to be finished when it felt like all else had been lost. A global thanks to all of the scholars of utopian experimentation whose work I am in debt to, and to everyone who has come to the Mutual Aid Society, and shown me over and over again that the revelation of this place's purpose is a collaborative and participatory process.

Thanks to Amber Stewart, Laura Henriksen, Claire Donato, Lily Herman, Lina Misitzis, Jennifer Stohlmann, Greg Afinogenov, Robert Balkovich, Anna Moschovakis, Pareesa Pourian, Alyssa Matthews, Zach Cummings, Jennifer Kabat, Kate Brock, Diana Hay, Dahlak Brathwaite, Sofi Thanhauser, Sally Howe, Dianca London Potts, Beth Loffreda, Frieda Knobloch, Jessa Crispin, Iris Cushing, Anne Elizabeth Moore, Marco Breuer, Laura Taylor, Laura Wood, Roz Foster, Emily Johnston, the angel Gabriel, Matt Peterson, David Silver, Rik Rydant, Clare Stober, Ursula Winter, Deborah Yanagisawa, and Martha Kaplan. Thanks to Doug Cunningham, Claude Copeland, and QuiShaun Hill for helping to shape my sermon that later turned into "Utopia, The Bronx." Thanks to Christopher Sweeney for the hours, days, weeks, months, years of discussion and debate, reading and editing drafts, and helping to foster my own creative and spiritual risk-taking. None of it was in vain.

Thanks to New Day Church in the Northwest Bronx and on Zoom, as well as the New Day Womyn & Femme-of-Center group. Thanks to the Millay Colony "Winter Shaker" program where I was able to develop early scratchings of this work. Thanks to the Bushel Writing Group, and to

Woodbine's Sunday dinners and lecture series. And thanks to every person and community who hosted me for visits. I am grateful to the Writing Department at Pratt Institute, which has been a continuous source of support, friendship, learning and growing almost continuously since I was nineteen years old. This project was funded in part by the generous support of the Pratt SeedGrant Initiative and the Pratt Faculty Development Fund.

Thanks to my parents and siblings, especially my mother, Erin Adair Tierney and my sister, Olivia Tierney who've been vital and unflagging accompaniments through a difficult season while I finished this book.

Thanks to the non-humans, too: Quentin the cat, the chickens, the frogs, the ancient turtle who returns to the pond every spring, the barred owl, the Eastern coyote, and all the herbaceous plants and trees that have tolerated my residence on land that is the rightful home of the Haudenosaunee.

Thanks to Mensah Demary, who, as web editor at *Catapult* magazine, supported me in the development of whatever I wanted to write about during the years they hosted me as columnist. *Catapult*'s invitation to work on serialized columns allowed me, and many other writers, to develop book-length ideas with a big audience and lots of brilliant and creative editorial support, and was the first place to publish early versions of "A Brief History of American Utopian Communities," "Odd Fellows at the Rockland Palace," and "The Beginning and the End" (formerly published as "A Visit to Charlotte Street"). Thanks to *Atlas Obscura* for publishing an earlier version of "The Big Muddy Ranch." And thanks to Caballito Negro—the flute and percussion duo Tessa Brinckman and Terry Longshore—for inviting me to contribute to their program Alone | Together, for which I wrote some of what ended up later in "Fellow Travelers on the Road to Nowhere."

Thanks to my agent Ralph Eubanks, and to the nimble, intrepid, deeply humane and visionary team at Counterpoint, especially Jack Shoemaker, Jennifer Alton, Lexi Earle, Wah-Ming Chang, and Colin Legerton.

My last thanks is to those who passed away during the writing of this book, and who made indelible marks on my life and thought during their time here on earth: my father-in-law Dan Sweeney, his mother Patricia Sweeney, my former professor the writer Brad Watson, and my grandfather George Adair.

BIBLIOGRAPHY

utopianotes: cruising

Carlisle, Belinda. *Heaven on Earth*. Virgin, 1987.

Muñoz, José Esteban. *Cruising Utopia: The Then and There of Queer Futurity*. New York: New York University Press, 2019.

Preamble

Gordon, Avery F. *The Hawthorn Archive: Letters from the Utopian Margins*. New York: Fordham University Press, 2018.

Jennings, Chris. *Paradise Now: The Story of American Utopianism*. New York: Random House, 2016.

Mariani, Mike. "The New Generation of Self-Created Utopias." *New York Times*, January 16, 2020. www.nytimes.com/2020/01/16/t-magazine /intentional-communities.html.

More, Thomas. *Utopia*. Translated by Paul Turner. London: Penguin, 2003.

Zamalin, Alex. *Black Utopia: The History of an Idea from Black Nationalism to Afrofuturism*. New York: Columbia University Press, 2019.

utopianotes: white men

Allen, Stan, et al. *Sites and Stations*: No. 7 (1996). Edited by Ostrow. Translated by Inho Choi. Brooklyn, NY: Semiotext(e).

De Botton, Alain. *The Architecture of Happiness*. London: Hamish Hamilton, 2015.

Engels, Frederick. *Socialism: Utopian and Scientific*, 3rd ed. New York: Pathfinder Books, 2008.

Pitzer, Donald E., ed. *America's Communal Utopias*. Chapel Hill: University of North Carolina Press, 2010.

Utopia, the Bronx

Caro, Robert A. *The Power Broker: Robert Moses and the Fall of New York.* London: Bodley Head, 2015.

Evans, Rachel Held. *Searching for Sunday: Loving, Leaving, and Finding the Church.* Nashville, TN: Thomas Nelson, 2015.

Federici, Silvia. *Re-enchanting the World: Feminism and the Politics of the Commons.* Oakland, CA: PM Press, 2018.

Frazier, Ian. "Utopia, The Bronx." *New Yorker,* June 26, 2006.

Harvey, David. *Rebel Cities: From the Right to the City to the Urban Revolution.* London: Verso, 2019.

Irizarry, Vivian Vázquez. *Decade of Fire.* USA, 2019. decadeoffire.com/watch.

A Brief History of American Utopianism

Cracker Box Palace. "Wayne County Animal Rescue." n.d. www.crackerboxpalace.org.

Hurley, Amanda Kolson. *Radical Suburbs: Experimental Living on the Fringes of the American City.* Cleveland, OH: Belt Publishing, 2019.

Leshko, Isa. *Allowed to Grow Old: Portraits of Elderly Animals from Farm Sanctuaries.* Chicago: University of Chicago Press, 2019.

utopianotes: North American Phalanx

Smith, Kevin. *Dogma.* 1999. USA: View Askew Productions, STKstudio, Lions Gate Films.

Fellow Travelers on the Road to Nowhere

Abdurraqib, Hanif. *They Can't Kill Us Until They Kill Us.* Columbus, OH: Two Dollar Radio, 2017.

Dillard, Annie. *The Writing Life.* London: Picador, 1990.

Hallman, J. C. *In Utopia: Six Kinds of Eden and the Search for a Better Paradise.* New York: St. Martin's Press, 2014.

Hawthorne, Nathaniel. *The Blithedale Romance.* New York: W. W. Norton, 1958.

Hurley, Amanda Kolson. *Radical Suburbs: Experimental Living on the Fringes of the American City.* Cleveland, OH: Belt Publishing, 2019.

Jennings, Chris. *Paradise Now: The Story of American Utopianism*. New York: Random House, 2016.

Lawrence, D. H. (David Herbert). *Studies in Classic American Literature*. Harlow, England: Penguin, 1971.

Lorde, Audre. *Sister Outsider: Essays and Speeches*. Berkeley, CA: Ten Speed Press, 2007.

Macdonald, A. J. "A. J. Macdonald Writings on American Utopian Communities," General Collection, Beinecke Rare Book and Manuscript Library. archives.yale.edu/repositories/11/resources/1893.

Noyes, John Humphrey. *History of American Socialisms*. Ann Arbor: University of Michigan Library, 2006.

Reece, Erik. *Utopia Drive: A Road Trip Through America's Most Radical Idea*. New York: Farrar, Straus and Giroux, 2016.

The Wolfe Tones. "Joe McDonnell." Track 13 on *A Sense of Freedom*. Triskel Records, 1983.

Young, Marguerite. *Angel in the Forest: A Fairy Tale of Two Utopias*, 2nd ed. Normal, IL: Dalkey Archive Press, 1994.

———. *Harp Song for a Radical: The Life and Times of Eugene Victor Debs*. Edited by Charles Ruas. New York: Random House, 1999.

———. 1976 interview by Charles Ruas. clocktower.org/show/marguerite-young-interview-1976.

Living

Sreenivasan, Jyotsna. *Utopias in American History*. Santa Barbara, CA: ABC-CLIO, 2008.

How to Start a Society

Duberman, Martin B. *Black Mountain: An Exploration in Community*. Evanston, IL: Northwestern University Press, 2009.

The Bruderhof

Baum, Markus. *Against the Wind: Eberhard Arnold and the Bruderhof*. Farmington, PA: Plough Publishing House, 1998.

Eggers, Ulrich. *Community for Life*. Scottdale, PA: Herald Press, 1988.

Jennings, Chris. *Paradise Now: The Story of American Utopianism.* New York: Random House, 2016.

Neima, Anna. *The Utopians: Six Attempts to Build the Perfect Society.* London: Pan Macmillan, 2021.

The Ancestors

Alfred, Taiaiake. *Wasáse: Indigenous Pathways of Action and Freedom.* Peterborough, ON, Canada: Broadview Press, 2005.

Imarisha, Walidah. "Oregon Black History Timeline." Uploaded July 19, 2013. www.youtube.com/watch?v=fo2RVOunsZ8.

Menakem, Resmaa. *My Grandmother's Hands: Racialized Trauma and the Pathway to Mending Our Hearts and Bodies.* Las Vegas, NV: Central Recovery Press, 2017.

Millner, Darrell. "Blacks in Oregon." n.d. *Oregon Encyclopedia.* www.oregonencyclopedia.org/articles/blacks_in_oregon.

Nokes, R. Gregory. *Breaking Chains: Slavery on Trial in the Oregon Territory.* Corvallis: Oregon State University, 2013.

———. *The Troubled Life of Peter Burnett: Oregon Pioneer and First Governor of California.* Corvallis: Oregon State University, 2018.

———. "Black Exclusion Laws in Oregon." n.d. *Oregon Encyclopedia.* www.oregonencyclopedia.org/articles/exclusion_laws.

The Big Muddy Ranch

Aney, Kathy. "Once a Cult Compound, Now World's Biggest Young Life Camp." *Statesman Journal,* July 22, 2015. www.statesmanjournal.com/story/news/2015/07/22/once-a-cult-compound-now-worlds-biggest-young-life-camp/30511755.

Egan, Timothy. "65,000 Acres." *Chicago Tribune,* October 28, 1995. www.chicagotribune.com/news/ct-xpm-1995-10-28-9510280123-story.html.

King, Wayne. "Red-Clad Disciples of an Indian Guru Build a Farm Community in Oregon." *The New York Times,* September 26, 1981. www.nytimes.com/1981/09/26/us/red-clad-disciples-of-an-indian-guru-build-a-farm-community-in-oregon.html.

Kopp, James J. *Eden Within Eden: Oregon's Utopian Heritage.* Corvallis: Oregon State University Press, 2009.

Way, MacLain, and Chapman Way. *Wild Wild Country.* 2018. USA: Netflix.

Shirk, Adrian. "Every Major Trope of the American West Can Be Found on One Ranch." *Atlas Obscura,* September 24, 2015. www.atlasobscura. com/articles/every-major-trope-of-the-american-west-can-be-found-on-one-ranch.

Living

Churchill, Caryl. *Light Shining in Buckinghamshire (Revised TCG Edition).* New York: Theatre Communications Group, 2018.

Federici, Silvia. *Caliban and the Witch: Women, the Body and Primitive Accumulation.* New York: Autonomedia, 2004.

Grace, Laura Jane, and Against Me! *Reinventing Axl Rose.* No Idea Records, 2002.

Graeber, David. *Fragments of an Anarchist Anthropology,* 2nd ed. Chicago: University of Chicago Press, 2004.

Lorde, Audre. *Sister Outsider: Essays and Speeches.* Berkeley, CA: Ten Speed Press, 2007.

The Team. *Five Plays by the TEAM.* London: Oberon Books, 2014.

The Simple Way

Claiborne, Shane. *The Irresistible Revolution: Living as an Ordinary Radical.* Kentwood, MI: Zondervan, 2008.

Fuller, Faith. *Briars in the Cotton Patch: The Story of Koinonia Farm.* USA: Cotton Patch Productions, 2003.

Hartman, Saidiya. *Wayward Lives, Beautiful Experiments: Intimate Histories of Riotous Black Girls, Troublesome Women, and Queer Radicals.* New York: W. W. Norton, 2020.

Marsh, Charles. *The Beloved Community: How Faith Shapes Social Justice from the Civil Rights Movement to Today.* London: Basic Books, 2006.

The Farm

Croshere, Rena Mundo, and Nadine Mundo. *American Commune*. USA: Gravitas Ventures, 2013.

Didion, Joan. *Slouching Towards Bethlehem*. Harlow, England: Penguin, 1974.

Friesen, J. *The Palgrave Companion to North American Utopias*, 4th ed. Gordonsville, VA: Palgrave Macmillan, 2016.

Gaskin, Ina May. *Spiritual Midwifery*, 4th ed. Summertown, TN: Book Publishing Company, 2002.

Gornick, Vivian. *The Romance of American Communism*. New York: Basic Books, 1978.

Halberstadt, Alex. "Out of the Woods." *New York Times Magazine*, August 6, 2015. www.nytimes.com/2015/08/09/magazine/out-of-the-woods.html.

Turner, Fred. *From Counterculture to Cyberculture: Stewart Brand, the Whole Earth Network, and the Rise of Digital Utopianism*. Chicago: University of Chicago Press, 2006.

The Flesh Failures

Addison, Virgil. 2019. "Anarchist Communes in the 1960s."

Gardner, Joyce. *Cold Mountain Farm: An Attempt at Community*. Self-published, 1970.

Fairfield, Richard. *The Modern Utopian: Alternative Communities Then and Now*. Los Angeles: Process Media, 2010.

Forman, Miloš. *Hair*. USA: CIP Filmproduktion; United Artists Pictures, 1979.

Friesen, J. *The Palgrave Companion to North American Utopias*, 4th ed. Gordonsville, VA: Palgrave Macmillan, 2016.

Guthrie, Arlo. *Alice's Restaurant*. Reprise Records, 1967.

Living

Ardolino, Emile. *Dirty Dancing*. USA: Great American Films Limited Partnership; Vestron Pictures, 1987.

Crispin, Jessa. *The Creative Tarot: A Modern Guide to an Inspired Life*. New York: Touchstone, 2016.

What's Heaven Got to Do with It?

Kushner, Tony. *Angels in America: A Gay Fantasia on National Themes*. Theatre Communications Group, 2014.

Marx, Karl, and Friedrich Engels. *The German Ideology*. Amherst, NY: Prometheus Books, 1998.

Robinson, Marilynne. *Housekeeping*. London: Faber & Faber, 2004.

Schur, Michael. *The Good Place*. USA: NBCUniversal Television Distribution, 2016.

Smith, Kevin. *Dogma*. USA: View Askew Productions, STKstudio, Lions Gate Films, 1999.

Odd Fellows at the Rockland Palace

Bentley, Gladys. "I Am a Woman Again." *Ebony*, August 1952.

Burnham, Kenneth E. *God Comes to America: Father Divine and the Peace Mission Movement*. Boston: Lambeth Press, 1979.

Koolhaas, Rem. *Delirious New York: A Retroactive Manifesto for Manhattan*. London: Thames & Hudson, 1979.

Shirk, Adrian. "Odd Fellows at the Rockland Palace." *Catapult*, December 15, 2016. catapult.co/stories/odd-fellows-at-the-rockland-palace.

Weisbrot, Robert. *Father Divine and the Struggle for Racial Equality*. Urbana: University of Illinois Press, 1983.

Divine Upstate

Feinberg, Lenny. *Father's Kingdom*. USA: Gravitas Ventures, 2017.

Jewett, Sarah Orne. *The Country of the Pointed Firs*. Mineola, NY: Dover Publications, 1994.

Mabee, Carleton. *Promised Land: Father Divine's Interracial Communities in Ulster County, New York*. Fleischmanns, NY: Purple Mountain Press, 2008.

The Catskills

Brown University. "The Catskills Institute." n.d. www.brown.edu/Research/Catskills_Institute.

Evers, Alf. *Catskills: From Wilderness to Woodstock*. New York: Overlook Press, 1984.

Foster, Brooke Lea. "Forget the Suburbs, It's Country or Bust." *New York Times*, December 14, 2018. www.nytimes.com/2018/12/14/realestate/forget-the-suburbs-its-country-or-bust.html.

Merritt, J. I. "The Catskills Cast Their Quiet Spell." *New York Times*, June 16, 1985. www.nytimes.com/1985/06/16/travel/the-catskills-cast-their-quiet-spell.html.

"Milk Not Jails." n.d. Accessed June 22, 2021. milknotjails.wordpress.com.

Silverman, Stephen M., and Raphael D. Silver. *The Catskills: Its History and How It Changed America*. New York: Alfred A. Knopf, 2015.

At Least I will Die Free

Duberman, Martin B. *Black Mountain: An Exploration in Community*. Evanston, IL: Northwestern University Press, 2009.

Katz, Vincent, ed. *Black Mountain College: Experiment in Art*. London: MIT Press, 2013.

Mingle, Kate, and Roman Mars. Episode 207: "Soul City." 99% Invisible, April 5, 2016. 99percentinvisible.org/episode/soul-city.

Mock, Brentin. "The Time Republicans Helped Build an All-Black Town Called 'Soul City.'" *Bloomberg CityLab*, November 6, 2015. www.bloomberg.com/news/articles/2015-11-06/the-true-story-of-soul-city-a-utopian-town-built-for-african-americans-with-republican-support-in-the-early-1970s.

Silver, David. 2019. "When the College Was Female" and the Lake Eden Campus Tour Addressing the BMC Farm and Work Program.

Strain, Christopher. "Soul City, North Carolina: Black Power, Utopia, and the African American Dream." *Journal of African American History* 89, no. 1 (Winter 2004): 57–74.

Gate Hill Cooperative

Richards, M. C. "To Take Stock of Our First Decade." *Landkidzink!* 5 (Winter 2003–04).

Living

Hurley, Amanda Kolson. *Radical Suburbs: Experimental Living on the Fringes of the American City.* Cleveland, OH: Belt Publishing, 2019.

Keim, Brandon. "The Salamander That Has Photosynthesis Happening Inside It." *Nautilus*, March 7, 2014. nautil.us/blog/the-salamander-that-has-photosynthesis-happening-inside-it.

Kropotkin, Petr Alekseyevich. *Mutual Aid: A Factor of Evolution.* London: Freedom Press, 1987.

Ross, Kristin. *Communal Luxury: The Political Imaginary of the Paris Commune.* London: Verso Books, 2016.

The Beginning and the End

Shirk, Adrian. "A Visit to Charlotte Street." *Catapult*, October 5, 2016. catapult.co/stories/a-visit-to-charlotte-street.

Urban Homesteading Assistance Board and Interference Archive. *Building for Us: Stories of Homesteading and Cooperative Housing.* Brooklyn, NY: Interference Archive, 2019. Exhibition.

Living

Evol, Keno. "Daunte Wright: A Billion Clusters of Rebellion and Starlight." *Mn Artists*, April 19, 2021. mnartists.walkerart.org/daunte-wright-a-billion-clusters-of-rebellion-and-starlight. Hunt, Irvin J. "Planned Failure: George Schuyler, Ella Baker, and the Young Negroes' Cooperative League." *American Quarterly* 72, no. 4 (December 2020): 853–79.

Kimmerer, Robin Wall. *Braiding Sweetgrass: Indigenous Wisdom, Scientific Knowledge and the Teachings of Plants.* Minneapolis: Milkweed Editions, 2020.

ADRIAN SHIRK is an essayist and mem-
oirist. She is the author of *And Your Daughters Shall
Prophesy*, named an NPR Best Book of 2017. Shirk
was raised in Portland, Oregon, and has since
lived in New York and Wyoming. She is a fre-
quent contributor to *Catapult*, and her essays have
appeared in *The Atlantic* and *Atlas Obscura*, among
other publications. Currently, she teaches in Pratt
Institute's BFA Creative Writing Program, and
lives at the Mutual Aid Society in the Catskill
Mountains. Find out more at adrianshirk.com.